Early Mesopotamian Law

Early Mesopotamian Law

Russ VerSteeg

CAROLINA ACADEMIC PRESS
Durham, North Carolina

For my wife, Nina, with love.

Library of Congress Cataloging-in-Publication Data
Early Mesopotamian law / Russ VerSteeg
   p.   cm.
Includes bibliographical references and index.
ISBN 0-89089-977-0
1. Law, Assyro-Babylonian. 2. Law, Sumerian. 3. Law, Ancient.
4. Law—Iraq—Sources. I. VerSteeg, Russ.

KL706.5 .E27 1999
340.5'35—dc21   99-048806

CAROLINA ACADEMIC PRESS
700 Kent Street
Durham, North Carolina 27701
Telephone (919) 489-7486
Fax (919) 493-5668
E-mail: cap@cap-press.com
www.cap-press.com

Printed in the United States of America.

Contents

Preface

Nearly a century has passed since archaeologists first discovered the now famous stela of the Laws of Hammurabi. Subsequently, other, earlier law collections from ancient Mesopotamia have also been unearthed and translated. Apparently, the people who inhabited the area in the vicinity of the Tigris and Euphrates rivers (roughly modern-day Iraq) about five thousand years ago were the first on earth to write down "laws" and to impose a semblance of order on the discipline that we today call "law". The principal goal of this book is to provide an introduction to law in ancient Mesopotamia during its formative stages—roughly 3000 b.c. (the dawn of "history") to 1600 b.c. (the sunset of the Old Babylonian period). In other words, generally speaking, this book looks at the first development of law in human history. Specifically, it surveys the famous law collections (*e.g.,* the Laws of Hammurabi, the Laws of Ur-Nammu, the Laws of Lipit-Ishtar, *etc.*), legal procedure, jurisprudence (*i.e.,* legal philosophy), and "substantive law" (*e.g.,* property, torts, and contracts).

I feel compelled to explain several things by way of my personal background. I am a lawyer and law professor, not an Assyriologist. Therefore, I do not bring to the table a first-hand knowledge of the primary sources. I do, however, have a reasonably sound background in ancient history and ancient legal systems. As an undergraduate, I majored in Latin, and I took numerous courses relating to ancient history and ancient civilizations. An Assyriologist, Dr. Ronald Sack, taught the first ancient history course that I took in college. I have always suspected that he devoted an unusually generous portion of our syllabus to the study of ancient Mesopotamia.[1] After college, I taught both Latin and Ancient History at the high school level for five years before going to law school. During the summer of 1982, I took a class on the Cultures of the Ancient Near East at my *alma mater*, the University of North Carolina at Chapel Hill, with Dr. Jack Sasson. While teach-

---

1. Our "general survey" of ancient history concluded at the end of the Third Punic War!

ing high school, I studied Middle Egyptian under Dr. Edmund Meltzer for two semesters (also at UNC-CH). Thus, before law school, I had been both a student and teacher of ancient languages and civilizations.

In law school, I studied Roman Law (an obvious choice for someone with my background), and I wrote three papers relating to ancient law and/or Latin that were eventually published.[2] Since I began teaching law, I have written four articles that relate directly to ancient law: *Law in Ancient Egyptian Fiction*,[3] *A Contract Analysis of the Trojan War*,[4] *Early Mesopotamian Commercial Law*,[5] and *The Roman Law Roots of Copyright*.[6] I have twice taught a seminar entitled "Law in the Ancient World" at New England School of Law in Boston, Massachussets.

Several years ago, I began work on a project that I intended to be a general survey of ancient law (*i.e.*, with chapters on law in ancient Mesopotamia, Egypt, Greece, and Rome). When I began doing research on Mesopotamia, I was surprised to discover that, unlike the case with both ancient Greek law and ancient Roman law, there were no general introductory texts on Mesopotamian law. I found myself reading articles, books, and doctoral dissertations that addressed specific aspects of Mesopotamian law (*e.g.*, the Laws of Hammurabi, Old Babylonian Marriage Law, Property law), but I could not find a general "survey." As a consequence, after researching ancient Mesopotamian law for a year, I realized that I had begun to accumulate so much material that it deserved to be more than just a couple of chapters in a general book about ancient law. It was then that I approached Keith Sipe at the Carolina Academic Press about the possibility of writing the present work. From the first moment that I suggested it to Keith, he has been entirely supportive. Consequently, I put aside my work on the "general ancient legal history,"[7] and devoted myself completely to working on ancient Mesopotamian law. After writing an initial draft, I en-

---

2. The paper that I wrote for my Senior Thesis was eventually published in the JOURNAL OF LEGAL HISTORY, *Law and the Security of Homeric Society*, 10 J. LEGAL HIST. 265 (1989). A paper that I wrote for my Advanced Contracts class was published in the WHITTIER LAW REVIEW, *From Status to Contract: A Contextual Analysis of Maine's Famous Dictum*, 10 WHITTIER L. REV. 669 (1989). My book, ESSENTIAL LATIN FOR LAWYERS (Carolina Academic Press 1990) began as an independent study project under the direction of my Roman Law professor, Dr. Olympiad Ioffe.

3. 24 GA. J. OF INT'L AND COMP. L. 37 (1994).

4. 40 ARIZONA L. REV. 173 (1998).

5. 30 U. TOL. L. REV. 183 (1999). The content of this article is substantially the same as chapter 11 and portions of the introduction in this book.

6. 59 MARYLAND L. REV. (forthcoming 2000).

7. I still hope to complete that project, so please stay tuned.

listed the help of three Assyriologists (two of whom are specialists in ancient Mesopotamian law) who read the manuscript and gave me very helpful feedback: my former professor, Dr. Ronald Sack at North Carolina State University; Dr. Martha T. Roth at the Oriental Institute, University of Chicago; and, Dr. Raymond Westbrook at Johns Hopkins University. I owe sincere thanks to each of them for taking the time to read the manuscript, and for making the effort to provide insight and helpful suggestions for improving the manuscript. All errors and omissions must be regarded as mine, not theirs.

Thus, although I have not been trained as an Assyriologist, I bring to the present work an abiding interest in the civilizations of the Ancient Near East, legal training, and experience teaching and writing about ancient legal systems. My aim has been to create a concise, accurate, and readable introduction to early Mesopotamian law that can be useful and informative for interested laypersons, undergraduates, graduate students, and scholars alike. In an effort to reduce the confusion caused by the multitude of variant spellings of ancient words, I have standardized most of the spellings, in quoted as well as original material.

I would be remiss if I failed to acknowledge the assistance of certain people who have helped in a number of ways. I have already mentioned the help given by Dr. Ronald Sack, Dr. Martha T. Roth, and Dr. Raymond Westbrook. They read and criticized the manuscript in an early iteration. In addition, I would like to thank the library staff at New England School of Law for their patience and perseverance in tracking down obscure articles, books, and doctoral dissertations. In particular our Reference Librarian, Barry Stearns always went out of his way to be helpful. Michael Kozuh, an assistant on the *Chicaco Assyrian Dictionary*, and Dr. Roth did a great deal of work to help standardize the spellings of Old Babylonian words and terms. I very much appreciate the advice and ideas contributed by my editor, Tim Colton, at Carolina Academic Press. Thanks are also due to my family, Nina, Whitney, and Carl, for their patience and understanding. My daughter, Whitney, helped me with the arduous task of indexing, and for that I am deeply grateful.

R.V.
London
September, 1999

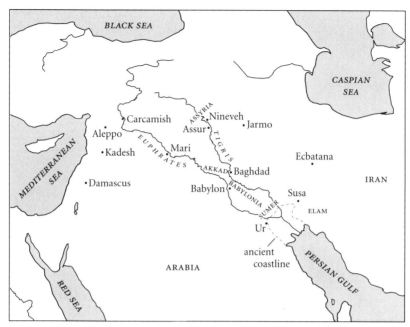

IMPORTANT SITES IN THE ANCIENT MIDDLE EAST

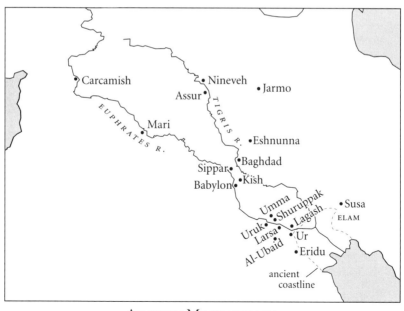

ANCIENT MESOPOTAMIA

xvii

Stela inscribed with the Laws of Hammurabi. The stela was excavated at Susa, where it was carried following an Elamite invasion in the 12th century B.C. Hirmer Fotoarchiv 614.6146.

Bronze head, probably of Sargon the Great. Hirmer Fotoarchiv 624.3116.

Fragments of a stela of Ur-Nammu depicting a libation offering. University of Pennsylvania Museum, Philadelphia (Neg. # S4-140070).

Mesopotamian legal document with its clay envelope. The document was written, then sealed in a clay envelope. A summary of the document was then written on the envelope. Photo NBC 1906 courtesy of the Yale Babylonian Collection.

An archaic cuneiform tablet from Ur. This document is from the beginning of the third millennium B.C., and records deliveries of barley and grain to a temple. British Museum 128897.

Cuneiform contract and envelope. British Museum 33238 + A.

Kassite Kudurru, boundary stone. British Museum 90841.

Babylonian boundary stone (c. 1400 B.C.). British Museum 90858.

Old Babylonian cylinder seal. British Museum 132153.

Register of fields from the Ur III period. British Museum 110116.

Part I

Overview,
Justice, Organization
and Procedure

CHAPTER 1

Introduction

§ 1.1 Scope & General Approach

At the outset it is important to clarify the general approach and scope of this book. First, it is not intended to be a "history" of Mesopotamian law. The goal is not to provide a chronological excursus. Instead this work synthesizes law in ancient Mesopotamia from its beginnings (roughly 3000 B.C.) to about 1600 B.C. Second, this book explains Mesopotamian law using modern legal categories as points of reference.

There are good reasons for limiting the period of time under consideration to before 1600 B.C. First, we have ample material from which to draw. There are numerous law collections (or "codes") as well as other legal documents that have survived. Assyriologists refer to the period around 1600 B.C. (about 150 years after Hammurabi) as the end of the "First Dynasty of Babylon," and generally consider this one of the "landmarks of ancient history."[1] It represents a significant break in Mesopotamian civilization, for it was in 1595 B.C. that the Hittite king, Mursilis I, sacked both Mari and Babylon. After his departure, a Kassite invasion hobbled much of Mesopotamia.[2]

---

1. H.W.F. Saggs, The Greatness That Was Babylon 74 (1962) [hereinafter "Saggs, Babylon"].

2. Walter Sommerfeld, *The Kassites of Ancient Mesopotamia: Origins, Politics, and Culture, in* 2 Civilizations of the Ancient Near East 917, 918 (Jack M. Sasson ed., 1995); Saggs, Babylon 74. *See also* Georges Roux, Ancient Iraq 84 (2d ed. 1979) ("The Hittite raid on Babylon (1595 B.C.) and the long period of semi-anarchy that followed the Kassite domination put an end to the political supremacy of the south.") [hereinafter "Roux, Ancient Iraq"]; G.R. Driver & John C. Miles, The Babylonian Laws 4 (Vol. I: Legal Commentary 1952) [hereinafter "Driver & Miles, Babylonian Laws"], and Raymond Westbrook, Old Babylonian Marriage Law 1 (1988) (remarking that the end of the Old Babylonian period is easy to identify with the "presence of a foreign ruling class—the Kassites."); Nels Bailkey, *Early Mesopotamian Constitutional Development*, 72 American Hist. Rev. 1211, 1212 (1967).

Saggs summarizes this complete disruption as follows: "With the Hittite sack of Babylon and the [K]assite invasion the political achievements of Hammurabi had been finally brought to an end."[3] Some Assyriologists refer to the period after Hammurabi as a "Dark Age" that exhibited characteristics of feudalism.[4] After Hammurabi, there is a paucity of legal documents relating to private legal affairs, such as the sale of real estate, the making of wills, hiring of persons for services, and the documenting of marriage settlements.[5] This lack of legal documentation may suggest a "decline in private initiative" and "an economic world grown different."[6]

§ 1.2 Synthetic Approach

Despite the obvious drawbacks and weaknesses inherent in making broad-sweeping generalizations about Mesopotamian law—generalizations that literally span millennia— there is some validity in taking a synthetic approach to the study of Mesopotamian law. Assyriologists note that there was a great deal of consistency in the Mesopotamian cultural institutions across the centuries.[7] Saggs makes this very point, concluding: "Despite development, decay, and changes in many details, especially as a result of successive waves of Semitic immigrants, Sumerian institutions were so well adapted to their *milieu* that in many aspects of life they remained as

---

3. SAGGS, BABYLON 76.
4. A. LEO OPPENHEIM, ANCIENT MESOPOTAMIA: PORTRAIT OF A DEAD CIVILIZATION 159 (revised Ed., completed by Erica Reiner, 1977) [hereinafter "OPPENHEIM, ANCIENT MESOPOTAMIA"]. *See* Robert C. Ellickson and Charles DiA. Thorland, *Ancient Land Law: Mesopotamia, Egypt, Israel,* 71 CHICAGO-KENT L. REV. 321, 331 (1995) ("In the sixteenth century B.C. . . . all of Mesopotamia entered into something of a dark age after successive foreign invasions) [hereinafter "Ellickson & Thorland, *Ancient Land Law*"]. *But see* WALTER SOMMERFELD, *The Kassites of Ancient Mesopotamia in* 2 CIVILIZATIONS OF THE ANCIENT NEAR EAST *supra* ch. 1 note 2 at 917, 923–25 (questioning the feudalistic nature of Mesopotamian society under the Kassites).
5. OPPENHEIM, ANCIENT MESOPOTAMIA 159.
6. *Id.*
7. *Id.* at 35. *See also id.* at 49–50; ROUX, ANCIENT IRAQ 21 (remarking that Mesopotamian culture "grew, blossomed in the dawning light of history and lasted for nearly three thousand years, remaining remarkably uniform throughout, though repeatedly shaken by political convulsions and repeatedly rejuvenated by foreign blood and influence."); and J.J. Finkelstein, *Ammisaduqa's Edict and the Babylonian "Law Codes,"* 15 J. CUNEIFORM STUD. 91 (1961) [hereinafter "Finkelstein, *Ammisaduqa's Edict*"] (mentioning the "homogeneous civilization of Southern Mesopotamia from ca. 2000 to 1700 B.C.").

long as Babylonian civilization survived."[8] Westbrook characterizes the Mesopotamians as having had "a common legal tradition which persisted...with no radical change...[that was] particularly noticeable in the academic tradition of the law codes."[9] Thus, Westbrook concludes: "We may be confident therefore that throughout the gamut of sources from Old Sumerian to Neo-Babylonian, we are dealing with essentially the same underlying laws...."[10] Similarly, Ellickson and Thorland remark: "Although published by rulers of distinct regimes in different centuries, these codes share numerous themes and provisions. These similarities suggest enduring commonalities in the customary law of Babylonia."[11]

There are also sound reasons for organizing the information around modern legal categories rather than presenting the material in ancient Mesopotamian groupings. The Mesopotamians tended to group their laws according to subject matter. For example, laws relating to oxen were grouped together, laws relating to boats were grouped together, laws relating to slaves were grouped together, and so on.[12] In contemporary law, on

---

8. SAGGS, BABYLON 157. Driver & Miles state the same regarding the commonality of legal principles found in the Sumerian and Akkadian laws: "the principles underlying them all are in a general sense the same." DRIVER & MILES, BABYLONIAN LAWS 11 (footnote omitted).

9. Raymond Westbrook, *Slave and Master in Ancient Near Eastern Law*, 70 CHICAGO-KENT L. REV. 1631, 1634 (1995) [hereinafter "Westbrook, *Slave and Master*"].

10. *Id.* at 1634.

11. Ellickson & Thorland, *Ancient Land Law*, 71 CHICAGO-KENT LAW REV. 321, 331 (Footnote omitted).

12. *See* Jean Bottéro, *The "Code" of Hammurabi* (Ch. 10 in MESOPOTAMIA: WRITING, REASONING, AND THE GODS, translated by Zainab Bahrani and Marc Van De Mieroop, U. Chicago Press (1982)) 157 [hereinafter "BOTTÉRO, WRITING, REASONING, AND THE GODS" ("According to our logic, such an order of subject matters, and the distribution of 'articles' inside these divisions, is not always easy to justify: they evidently presuppose a way of viewing and evaluating things quite removed from our own..., and we do not always have the means to penetrate this approach."); *Id.* ("We certainly do not understand the reasons for the plan that controls their placement. That is, however, due more to our ignorance, both of the mentality of the times and of the bias by which they associated one thing with another, than to any whims of the compiler in strewing them around randomly."); B.L. Eichler, *Literary Structure In The Laws Of Eshnunna*, in LANGUAGE, LITERATURE, AND HISTORY: PHILOLOGICAL AND HISTORICAL STUDIES PRESENTED TO ERICA REINER, Vol. 67, *American Oriental Series* (1987)(Francesca Rochberg-Halton ed.) 72 (hereinafter "Eichler, *Literary Structure*"); and Norman Yoffee, *Context and Authority in Mesopotamian Law* 101, (ch. 5 in POLITICAL ANTHROPOLOGY (1988)) (hereinafter "Yoffee, *Context and Authority*") (Remarking that, regarding Hammurabi's Laws, "[t]he arrangement of the rules is by groups

the other hand, we tend to group our laws by conceptual or theoretical principles of law rather than concrete subject matter. For example, we cluster laws appertaining to contracts, negligence, or agency. Thus, in terms of the legal principles applicable, it would not really matter to us whether any given contract involved the sale of an ox, a slave, or a cart. What matters to modern law is that it is a sale of a good. Apparently, the ancient Mesopotamians did not even have the legal terminology necessary to express the concept of a "legal principle" or even "law" in the modern sense.[13]

Thus, although an ancient Mesopotamian would not have classified his laws using modern categories (or anything analogous to them[14]), this book, nevertheless, uses modern categories to present and explain ancient Mesopotamian laws.[15] Given our modern, shared legal vocabulary, a student or an educated layreader today is likely to appreciate the nexus of principles relating to contract or criminal law more readily than the connection between laws relating to oxen. Others have taken a similar approach. For example, in his article, "Capital Punishment and Its Alternatives in Ancient Near Eastern Law,"[16] Edwin Good analyzes Mesopotamian law using modern legal categories rather than ancient groupings.[17] In his book, *The Greatness That Was Babylon*, Saggs uses a similar approach to explain Mesopotamian literature.[18] This, of course, does not mean that this approach to studying ancient Mesopotamian civilization is perfect.[19]

---

dealing with the same general topic.) (citation omitted); and, Finkelstein, *Ammisaduqa's Edict*, 15 J. CUNEIFORM STUD. 91, 97 (1961)("these law collections were not logically organized, and the cases chosen for inclusion are often random.").

13. BOTTÉRO, WRITING, REASONING, AND THE GODS 178.

14. SAMUEL GREENGUS, *Legal and Social Institutions of Ancient Mesopotamia*, in 1 CIVILIZATIONS OF THE ANCIENT NEAR EAST 469, 473 (Jack M. Sasson ed., 1995).

15. Driver & Miles thought that it was beneficial to preserve the original order of Hammurabi's Laws. DRIVER & MILES, BABYLONIAN LAWS 50.

16. Edwin M. Good, *Capital Punishment and Its Alternatives in Ancient Near Eastern Law*, 19 STAN. L. REV. 947–977 (1967) [hereinafter "Good, *Capital Punishment*"].

17. *Id.* at 950 ("The categories are derived from my own analysis and do not represent any ancient scheme.").

18. SAGGS, BABYLON 390.

19. *See e.g.*, OPPENHEIM, ANCIENT MESOPOTAMIA 27 ("It is necessary, but extremely difficult, to free oneself from one's own ingrained concepts in attempting to organize data pertaining to another civilization."). *See also Id.* at 28 ("All extant data that can be easily and, for the most part, uncritically collected are projected, in complete disregard for chronological, regional, and contextual differences, upon one level in time and one dimension in space within a framework that reflects nothing but the cultural background of the scholar at work. When one thus 'synchronizes' and 'consolidates' an array of data, one can achieve rather easily what the undemanding reader and the layman would term reasonable coverage."); and, BERNARD S. JACKSON, ESSAYS IN JEWISH AND COMPARATIVE LEGAL HISTORY, (ch. 1 "Sources and Problems") 1–15

Clearly, we lose some sense of the true nature of Mesopotamian thought by forcing their laws into our own categories. We are certain to fail to appreciate a degree of subtlety and nuance. But on balance, the advantages to this approach seem to outweigh the disadvantages.

§ 1.3 A Word of Caution Regarding "Sources For Mesopotamian Law"

It is important to acknowledge the tenuous nature of any conclusions that we may attempt to draw from the sparse evidence that we possess about Mesopotamian civilization. Oppenheim aptly characterizes the problem as follows:

> The cuneiform texts have given us a strangely distorted picture of more than two thousand years of Mesopotamian civilization. This picture is composed of abundant but very spotty detailed information and of rough and incomplete outlines of major political and cultural developments. All this theoretical framework, moreover, is torn to shreds again and again by immense gaps in time and space. It requires much patient work on the part of the philologist to hold these shreds together by a crisscrossing web of connections based on the slimmest textual evidence. He has to link minutiae to minutiae, analyze and correlate highly recalcitrant material, in order to gauge developments and to trace these trends through the ever-recurring blackouts of information.[20]

We have discovered only a limited number of genres or "types" of writing from ancient Mesopotamia.[21] Fortunately for us, a significant percentage of the written texts that we do possess relate in some way to law. To judge by excavated texts, writing was most commonly used for bureaucratic records. In terms of sheer volume, the law collections are also one of the most significant types of writing from ancient Mesopotamia.[22]

(1975) [hereinafter "JACKSON, ESSAYS"] (Discussing the problems associated with attempting to piece together a coherent presentation for ancient law in the near east).

20. OPPENHEIM, ANCIENT MESOPOTAMIA 11. *See also Id.* at 27; MARTHA T. ROTH, *Gender and Law: A Case Study From Ancient Mesopotamia*, in GENDER AND LAW IN THE HEBREW BIBLE AND THE ANCIENT NEAR EAST 173, 175 (Victor H. Matthews, Bernard M. Levinson and Tikva Frymer-Kensky eds., 1997) (Commenting on "the usual constraints of the accidents of preservation, recovery, and publication.").

21. Regarding the "invention" of writing in Mesopotamia, *see generally* ROUX, ANCIENT IRAQ 80–82.

22. OPPENHEIM, ANCIENT MESOPOTAMIA 230 (Oppenheim says that there are only a limited number of "types" of writing in Ancient Mesopotamia. The most fre-

In general, our sources for Mesopotamian law—from Sumerian to Neo-Babylonian—include a number of law collections (or "codes"), *mīšarum* edicts[23] (written advice given by the king regarding specific legal topics),[24] and private and public legal documents such as letters, contracts, wills, adoption documents, loans, boundary markers, administrative texts, and international agreements.[25] With these materials, scholars are able to appreciate some "period and local differences in legal practices."[26] Oppenheim describes the non-"code" legal documents as "an impressive bulk of cuneiform tablets that contain records of the day-to-day activities of the inhabitants of Mesopotamia, from kings down to shepherds. In time span and geographical distribution, in bulk and in topical variety, they quite often surpass the traditional texts."[27]

---

quently-occurring, he says, is writing that functions as "recording for administrative purposes" and the second most frequently occurring type of writing is "for the codification of laws.").

23. SAMUEL GREENGUS, *Legal and Social Institutions of Ancient Mesopotamia, in* 1 CIVILIZATIONS OF THE ANCIENT NEAR EAST, *supra* ch. 1 note 14 at 469, 471; DOMINIQUE CHARPIN, *The History of Ancient Mesopotamia: An Overview, in* 2 CIVILIZATIONS OF THE ANCIENT NEAR EAST 807, 817 (Jack M. Sasson ed., 1995). *See also infra* § 3.3.

24. *See generally* Sophie Lafont, *The Ancient Near Eastern Laws: Continuity and Pluralism* in THEORY AND METHOD IN BIBLICAL AND CUNEIFORM LAW 91, 97–100 (Bernard M. Levinson ed., 1994) [hereinafter "Lafont, *Continuity and Pluralism*"] ("These texts might be called rescripts, in the Roman sense of the word: they are answers given by the king to practical questions asked by jurists or individuals." (*Id.* at 97)). According to Lafont, "The only oriental example known at the moment for this legislative application is a letter, kept in four copies and sent by Samsu-iluna to the judges of Sippar." *Id.* "The main significance of this text is to show how a legal rule is built up: the king's response to the consultation which is addressed to him acquires normative weight." *Id.* at 100.

25. OPPENHEIM, ANCIENT MESOPOTAMIA 55–56. Oppenheim portrays the day-to-day legal documents of ancient Mesopotamia as follows: "[C]lay tablets record private legal transactions, such as sales, rentals, and loans as well as marriage contracts, adoptions, wills, and so on. There exist also, a number of international agreements scattered through a period of one millennium." *Id.* at 24. *Also see Id.* at 25; DRIVER & MILES, BABYLONIAN LAWS 56; WESTBROOK, OLD BABYLONIAN MARRIAGE LAW 2 ("thousands of private legal documents"); Westbrook, *Slave and Master*, 70 CHICAGO-KENT L. REV. 1631, 1633 (1995) ("The documents are mostly legal transactions such as sale, hire, redemption, etc., with a much smaller number of litigation records and miscellaneous records such as letters."); Yoffee, *Context and Authority* 98 (Yoffee describes these documents as "thousands of contracts and letters" in which "[p]rincipal actors' specific arrangements, oaths and statements that the contract will not be renounced, witnesses, and calendrical dates are all regularly detailed. The texts deal with marriages, divorces, adoptions, sales, rentals of movable and immovable property, and many other activities.").

26. *Id.* at 11, 13, 24.

27. OPPENHEIM, ANCIENT MESOPOTAMIA 23, 25–26. For further discussion re-

Luckily, many traditional texts changed very little over the course of time. This may also have been true of the law collections. Thus, once "frozen," a text was likely to reflect law and society from an early time; not the age of scribal copying, but rather the age of original composition and standardization.[28] This makes the law collections especially useful tools for studying Mesopotamian law.

As a general rule, the law collections are relatively easy to understand; and most of the "law" described in this book is based on the "law" as it is presented in these law collections.[29] The records and documents used on a daily basis, however, pose significant problems. Oppenheim explains that philological ambiguities pose one of the principal reasons why the day-to-day administrative documents and letters are difficult to interpret. According to Oppenheim, "their diction is terse, abbreviated, and full of mysterious technical terms. It is a delicate and difficult task to establish the meanings of terms that, in the course of time, often underwent subtle changes and to reconstruct their institutional and economic background."[30]

---

garding other legal and commercial documents in Sumerian and Akkadian, *see* DRIVER & MILES, BABYLONIAN LAWS 6.

28. OPPENHEIM, ANCIENT MESOPOTAMIA 18.

29. Scholars in the field of Mesopotamian law have previously — and quite unashamedly — focused their work on the law collections as well. *See e.g.,* WESTBROOK, OLD BABYLONIAN MARRIAGE LAW 3 ("Our starting point must be the assumption that CH [*i.e.,* Codex Hammurabi] provides us with what is claimed for it in its epilogue: a work of reference for discovery of the contemporary law." (footnote omitted)); *Id.* at 4 ("even the most idealized paragraphs...did not arise *ex nihilo*, but undoubtedly represented existing schools of thought. In this sense, therefore, the whole of CH is a valid source of OB law."); Yoffee, *Context and Authority* 97 (1988). *Also see* Ellickson & Thorland, *Ancient Land Law*, 71 CHICAGO-KENT L. REV. 321, 331 (1995) (Characterizing "the law codes" as "a primary source of legal information.").

30. OPPENHEIM, ANCIENT MESOPOTAMIA 25, 48. In his Epilogue, Oppenheim, himself, admitted that he was unable to make much use of these sources for his own discussion of law. He apologized for using "the textbooks" for his presentation of Mesopotamian law instead of "the fountainhead of primary information offered by the tablets which report actual legal practices." He says that the legal practices tablets have "protean variability" that has forced him "to turn toward" the textbook material "as an expedient refuge from the superabundance of detailed information." *Id.* at 332–333. *Also see* SAGGS, BABYLON 55 ("[T]he documents are written in very condensed phraseology and are full of technical words upon which the exact sense turns but which scholars at present understand only very approximately.").

§ 1.4 Formulaic Patterns in Mesopotamian Legal Documents

There is one final introductory note probably worth mentioning about Mesopotamian legal documents in general. As is true with most legal systems, the ancient Mesopotamians required certain formulaic patterns in order for many documents to obtain legal significance or validity.[31] As a general rule, it is clear that the ancient Mesopotamians respected the rule of law.[32] It is equally clear that the Mesopotamians prized formulaic structure in their legal documents. We have an ancient text, called *ana ittišu*, that recites standard legal phrases and formulae. Apparently, scribes used this text and others like it to memorize the forms and phrases necessary to compose standard contracts, wills, deeds, and the like.[33] Generally speaking, all legal documents — whether a record of sale, lease, marriage, or adoption — were written in the same characteristic pattern. First the object was identified (*i.e.*, the thing being sold or leased, or the person being married or adopted). Then the document recited the persons involved (*i.e.*, the seller and buyer, lessor and lessee, etc.). Next followed the financial details, including the amount of money to be exchanged and the timing for the ex-

---

31. SAMUEL GREENGUS, *Legal and Social Institutions of Ancient Mesopotamia, in* 1 CIVILIZATIONS OF THE ANCIENT NEAR EAST *supra* ch. 1 note 14 at 469, 475 ("Legal transactions often involved the recitation of ritualized formulas...."). *See* Johannes M. Renger, *Institutional, Communal, and Individual Ownership or Possession of Arable Land in Ancient Mesopotamia from the End of the Fourth to the End of the First Millennium B.C.*, 71 CHICAGO-KENT L. REV. 269, 291–92 (1995) ("As perhaps everywhere, Mesopotamian legal documents...employ a specific formulary — the actual form of it depending on the nature of the transaction to be recorded and particular stipulations deemed essential by the parties to a transaction.) [hereinafter "Renger, *Ownership or Possession of Arable Land in Ancient Mesopotamia*"].

32. SAGGS, BABYLON 196. *Also see* OPPENHEIM, ANCIENT MESOPOTAMIA 103 and ROUX, ANCIENT IRAQ 102.

33. *See* SAMUEL GREENGUS, *Legal and Social Institutions of Ancient Mesopotamia, in* 1 CIVILIZATIONS OF THE ANCIENT NEAR EAST, *supra* ch. 1 note 14 at 469, 472; OPPENHEIM, ANCIENT MESOPOTAMIA 248. *Also see* the *Sumerian Laws Handbook of Forms* dating from about 1700 B.C., translated in MARTHA T. ROTH, LAW COLLECTIONS FROM MESOPOTAMIA AND ASIA MINOR 46–54 (1995) [hereinafter "ROTH, LAW COLLECTIONS"] ("This late Old Babylonian prism is a Sumerian compendium of contracts and contractual clauses, legal provisions comparable to those found in the law collections, and isolated phrases such as might be found in Old Babylonian contracts." *Id.* at 46). *See also* DRIVER & MILES, BABYLONIAN LAWS 25–26, 127; Martha Roth, *The Law Collection of King Hammurabi: Toward an Understanding of Codification and Text*, Strasbourg Codification Conference 20 (1997) [hereinafter, "Roth, *The Law Collection of King Hammurabi*"].

change. If there were any additional agreements peculiar to the transaction, they were appended last.[34] In some instances, specific words and phrases had to be used in prescribed arrangement. Even the size and shape of the clay tablet on which some documents were written had to conform to pre-set standards.[35]

Regarding formulaic patterns, it is also interesting to note the similarities shared by Mesopotamian legal documents and Mesopotamian divination texts. The Mesopotamians employed divination with animals in many types of important decision-making,[36] but not for law. Animals were routinely observed for prognostication when an army was poised to engage in battle, prior to religious processions, and before festivals.[37] The structure of Mesopotamian divination texts and the structural pattern of the Mesopotamian laws in the law collections (codes) are basically analogous. Each begins with a protasis ("if" clause) and concludes with an apodasis ("then" clause).[38] The protasis establishes the conduct or circumstance that, in the case of divination texts, holds the meaning that needs interpretation, and, in the case of laws, requires an application of law. The apodasis, then, articulates the prognostication and the legal result respectively.[39]

---

34. OPPENHEIM, ANCIENT MESOPOTAMIA 280–81.

35. *Id.* at 276.

36. *See* JEAN BOTTÉRO, *Akkadian Literature: An Overview, in* 4 CIVILIZATIONS OF THE ANCIENT NEAR EAST 2293, 2299 (Jack M. Sasson ed., 1995). Roth, *The Law Collection of King Hammurabi* 6–7 ("F.R. Kraus and J. Bottéro have led the way in demonstrating that literary principles of extrapolation and expansion, principles that also operate in the omen, lexical, and other scientific-list-literatures, account for a great deal of the development of the internal sequence of law provisions." (footnotes omitted)).

37. OPPENHEIM, ANCIENT MESOPOTAMIA 218–19.

38. *See* WESTBROOK, OLD BABYLONIAN MARRIAGE LAW 3 ("This accounts for the style of the rules, which are cast into the casuistic form—a conditional clause beginning with «if» (protasis) followed by the main clause (apodosis)—in the manner of omens...."); JACK M. SASSON, *King Hammurabi of Babylon, in* 2 CIVILIZATIONS OF THE ANCIENT NEAR EAST 901, 908 (Jack M. Sasson ed., 1995); Eichler, *Literary Structure* 71 ("The basic literary unit of the law collections is the legal case. Its formulation is basically casuistic—with the protasis setting forth the legal situation and the apodasis stating the legal prescription."). *See also* Yoffee, *Context and Authority* 99, 101; Raymond Westbrook, *Biblical and Cuneiform Law Codes,* 92 REVUE BIBLIQUE 248, 249 (1985) [hereinafter "Westbrook, *Biblical and Cuneiform Law Codes*"] ("They are predominantly formulated in casuistic style (albeit in varying degrees), that is to say, a particular set of circumstances is given, followed by the legal ruling appropriate to that case (footnote omitted)"); and, BOTTÉRO, WRITING, REASONING, AND THE GODS 158 (describing this structure in the Laws of Hammurabi).

39. OPPENHEIM, ANCIENT MESOPOTAMIA 210–212 ("Each entry in these collections consists of a protasis that states the case, in exactly the same way as does a section of a law code, and of an apodosis that contains the prognostication." (*Id.* at

§ 1.5 Summary

This book examines early Mesopotamian law during the period from its beginnings in approximately 3000 B.C. to about 1600 B.C. Law is considered using modern legal categories as points of reference, rather than ancient groupings even though there are drawbacks to this approach. We admit that to some degree this study is inherently deficient because our textual sources are so tenuous. One interesting characteristic of Mesopotamian law that one should bear in mind is its use of formulaic patterns in legal documents.

211–12)). For more on the relationship between the genres of omen texts and law collections, *see* Westbrook, *Biblical and Cuneiform Law Codes* 252–264.

CHAPTER 2

The Law Collections ("Codes")

§ 2.1 Overview

Without doubt, the great law collections (codes) are among the most important sources for any study of Mesopotamian law. Today most scholars refer to these as "collections" not as "codes" because the word "code" suggests a comprehensive treatment of law—something that the Mesopotamian collections clearly are not.[1] Oppenheim posits two purposes for Mesopotamian codification. First, the people wished to supersede oral tradition and practices. Second, they wished to have their laws synchronized with "changed social, economic, or political conditions."[2] To a certain degree, the codifications expressed a king's interest in the welfare of his citizens and his desire to change their lives for the better.[3] Most Mesopotamian legal scholars have concluded, however, that it is unlikely that these collec-

---

1. SAMUEL GREENGUS, *Legal and Social Institutions of Ancient Mesopotamia, in* 1 CIVILIZATIONS OF THE ANCIENT NEAR EAST, *supra* ch. 1 note 14, at 469, 471 ("These ancient law collections are often referred to as 'codes,' but the modern term can be misleading. The collections are not 'codes' in the modern, comprehensive sense of that term because they convey only a part of all of the operative laws at that time."). According to Driver & Miles, the convention of referring to these legal documents as "codes" goes back to the early translator named Scheil. DRIVER & MILES, BABYLONIAN LAWS 45, n. 1. *See also* Roth, *The Law Collection of King Hammurabi* 2 ("Although Schiel, who edited and published the editio princeps of the text on the stela excavated in 1902, labeled the text as a 'code de lois,' subsequent scholars have had trouble with the label 'code.'" (footnote omitted)).
2. OPPENHEIM, ANCIENT MESOPOTAMIA 231.
3. Commentators are fond of referring to this purpose as "the royal *apologia*": "its primary purpose was to lay before the public, posterity, future kings, and, above all, the gods evidence of the king's execution of his divinely ordained mandate: to have been 'the Faithful Shepherd'...." Westbrook, *Biblical and Cuneiform Law Codes* 249. *See also* SAMUEL GREENGUS, *Legal and Social Institutions of Ancient Mesopotamia, in* 1 CIVILIZATIONS OF THE ANCIENT NEAR EAST, *supra* ch. 1 note 14, at 469, 472 ("a means of publicly conveying the king's commitment to justice.").

tions ever received practical application in daily life.[4] There are many theories about the nature of the collections. Most scholars agree that they were not meant to be exhaustive statutes like the Justinian Code or the Napoleonic Code.[5] Edwin Good summarizes the debate as follows:

> Scholars of the ancient Near Eastern cultures have debated the question whether any of these codes actually represents legislation which was intended to be enforced. Some scholars hold that most or all of the codes are simply compilations of precedents brought together to guide judges in what had been done before in similar cases but not necessarily to bind them. Others hold that the codes are statements of the ideal, describing in legal terms what the desired society would be, utopian in the strict sense of the term.[6]

---

4. *See e.g.,* Lafont, *Continuity and Pluralism* 94; OPPENHEIM, ANCIENT MESOPOTAMIA 231–232.

5. *See e.g.,* DRIVER & MILES, BABYLONIAN LAWS 45–48, 324; Raymond Westbrook, *Slave and Master,* 70 CHICAGO-KENT L. REV. 1631, 1633 (1995) ("[T]hese documents are not legislation in the modern sense, but rather academic treatises on law expressed in casuistic form (citing the work of F.R. Kraus (1960) and J. Bottéro (1982)); Raymond Westbrook, *Cuneiform Law Codes and the Origins of Legislation,* 79 ZEITSCHRIFT FÜR ASSYRIOLOGIE UND VORDERASIATISCHE ARCHÄOLOGIE 201, 222 (1989) ("they were not normative legislation."); Lafont, *Continuity and Pluralism* 101 ("Oriental codes do not aim at exhaustiveness; they rather clarify debated points or regulate topics thought to be interesting by their promulgators. By nature, written oriental law is lacunary: it is only designed to complete a mostly oral tradition."); Yoffee, *Context and Authority* 108; Westbrook, *Biblical and Cuneiform Law Codes,* 92 REVUE BIBLIQUE 248–251 (1985); BOTTÉRO, WRITING, REASONING, AND THE GODS 161 ("By all accounts the document should not be considered more than a type of anthology at best. It is certainly not a code in the true sense of the word — even if, for the sake of convenience and by convention I have no difficulty in preserving this almost century-old designation, being careful, however, to place it in quotation marks."); and Finkelstein, *Ammisaduqa's Edict,* 15 J. CUNEIFORM STUD. 91, 103 (1961) ("It is probably well to stress first of all that the *purpose* of the lower Mesopotamian 'law codes' was decidedly *not* legislative, if indeed it is not altogether anachronistic to speak of 'legislation' in the ancient Mesopotamian context.").

6. Good, *Capital Punishment,* 19 STAN. L. REV. 947, 949 (1967) (footnotes omitted). For more on the question regarding the purpose and nature of the Mesopotamian law collections ("codes"), *see* Eichler, *Literary Structure,* 71 n. 1 (citing especially the work of F.R. Kraus and JJ. Finkelstein); Westbrook, *Biblical and Cuneiform Law Codes,* 92 REVIEW BIBLIQUE 248, 254 (1985) ("We suggest that the compiling of lists of legal decisions served... [as] ...a reference work for consultation by judges when deciding difficult cases.") and *Id.* at 257–58 ("To summarize: in our view the Ancient Near Eastern law codes derive from a tradition of compiling series of legal precedents in the same manner as omens, medical prognoses and other scientific treatises. The purpose of these series to act was as reference works for the royal judges in deciding difficult cases. Probably this began as an oral tradition and only gradually became a systematic written corpus (footnote omitted).").

J.J. Finkelstein emphatically rejects the possibility that the law collections were statutes and argues that they represent a more macroscopic purpose than mere legislation:

> These "law codes" with their stylized prologues and epilogues of purely "historical" and religious import must be viewed in the first instance as royal apologia and testaments. Their primary importance was to lay before the public, posterity, future kings, and, above all, the gods, evidence of the king's execution of his divinely ordained mandate: to have been "the Faithful Shepherd"....[7]

The debate about the purpose of the law collections has often focused on the most extensive collection of laws—the Laws of Hammurabi. In short, the questions most often asked are these: Were these laws statutes intended to be applied to given situations? Were they statements of abstract principles? Were they summaries of actual decisions? Or were they something else? According to Westbrook, "it has long been recognized that Codex Hammurabi is neither a comprehensive digest of the contemporary law, nor even a statute—whether reforming or codifying—in the modern sense."[8] Saggs addresses this issue in his book, *The Greatness That Was Babylon*:

> [T]he 'Code' of Hammurabi does not constitute a complete system of law. Hammurabi in his prologue and epilogue makes no claim to having codified the whole of the existing law, and many matters which must at times have needed legal decisions are not included. For instance, there is no reference to parricide, cattle-lifting, or kidnapping a person other than a freeman's son. It therefore has to be concluded that Hammurabi was simply dealing with matters which needed amendment, adoption of one of a number of alternatives found in different cities, or simply recapitulation of regulations liable to fall into desuetude. It has been pointed out that 'there is not a single case in the thousands of legal documents and reports which have been preserved in which reference is made to the wording of the text of the Laws', and this is clear evidence that whatever the laws were, they were not statute law to be given a verbal interpretation but rather incorporated principles to be observed, or which actually had been observed, in particular cases.[9]

The epilogue of Hammurabi's Laws is potentially helpful in understanding what these collections represent. In the epilogue, he refers to his "laws"

---

7. Finkelstein, *Ammisaduqa's Edict*, 15 J. Cuneiform Stud. 91, 103 (1961).
8. Westbrook, Old Babylonian Marriage Law 2 (footnote omitted).
9. Saggs, Babylon 211. *See also* Yoffee, *Context and Authority* 102–103; and, Bottéro, Writing, Reasoning, and the Gods 158.

as "just decisions."[10] The phrase "just decisions" suggests that, perhaps, these laws are summaries of actual cases that were decided under Hammurabi's authority.[11] In one letter from Hammurabi to a local official, Hammurabi instructs his underling to rely on precedent and apply written ordinances to resolve a case brought before him.[12] Interestingly, records of court cases that were tried over a thousand years after Hammurabi's death reveal that the Mesopotamians were still, at that time, applying principles found in Hammurabi's Laws.[13]

Although modern scholars have concluded that it is unlikely that Hammurabi's Laws were ever used as precedent for an actual case in ancient Babylon,[14] Hammurabi's epilogue suggests that that may have been his intention: "Let any wronged man who has a lawsuit come before the statue of me, the king of justice, and let him have my inscribed stela read aloud to him, thus may he hear my precious pronouncements and let my stela reveal

10. Samuel Greengus, *Legal and Social Institutions of Ancient Mesopotamia, in* 1 Civilizations of the Ancient Near East, *supra* ch. 1 note 14, at 469, 472; Roth, Law Collections 133. *See also* Bottéro, Writing, Reasoning, and the Gods 164. *See also* Driver & Miles, Babylonian Laws 48 ("On the face of them, the Laws are a collection of decisions on the facts of a number of isolated cases. * * * * The sections are somewhat like the headnotes to a reported case, and the whole may in some respects be compared with a Digest of Case-law or a collection of records.").
11. Roth, Law Collections 133. *See also* Martha T. Roth, *Mesopotamian Legal Traditions and Laws of Hammurabi*, 71 Chicago-Kent L. Rev. 13, 20 (1995); Westbrook, Old Babylonian Marriage Law 2 ("Hammu-rabi himself states in the epilogue that the preceding rules are «the just judgments that Hammu-rabi, the powerful king, established»."(footnote omitted)); Westbrook, *Biblical and Cuneiform Law Codes*, 92 Revue Biblique 248, 251 (1985) (citing the work of F.R. Kraus); and, Saggs, Babylon 199.
12. Saggs, Babylon 199. *See also* Driver & Miles, Babylonian Laws 19. *But see* Lafont, *Continuity and Pluralism* 97–100 (citing several specific examples where a king's written advice to judges contradicts doctrine enunciated in Hammurabi's Laws).
13. Saggs, Babylon 211.
14. Driver & Miles, Babylonian Laws 53 ("There is not a single case in the thousands of legal documents and reports which have been preserved in which reference is made to the wording of the text of the Laws; indeed, neither judges nor private persons in their documents seem to have regarded it as verbally binding on them."); Westbrook, *Biblical and Cuneiform Law Codes*, 92 Revue Biblique 248 (1985) (citing the work of B. Landsberger: "Codex Hammurabi is never cited as authority in judgments, nor does it state that judges must in [the] future decide according to these laws. Since Landsberger's article two cases have been found which appear to refer to the text of a *narûm*, but they are too obscure to resolve the question of practical application. (footnotes omitted)."). *See also* Oppenheim, Ancient Mesopotamia 154 ("Observation of the law code of Hammurabi gives us a unique opportunity to study the gap between facts and aspirations."); *Id.* at 158; Bottéro, Writing, Reasoning, and the Gods 163; and Roth, *The Law Collection of King Hammurabi* 12–14.

the lawsuit for him; may he examine his case, may he calm his (troubled) heart...."[15] Hammurabi also implores future rulers to follow his decisions: "May any king who will appear in the land in the future, at any time, observe the pronouncements of justice that I inscribed upon my stela. May he not alter the judgments that I rendered and the verdicts that I gave...."[16] But Hammurabi also says something in his epilogue that makes it sound as though his Laws reflect nutshell versions of cases that he actually decided: "[M]ay that stela reveal...the traditions, the proper conduct, [and] the judgments of the land that I rendered...."[17] In addition, Hammurabi implies that one of his goals is to influence future decision-making. He expresses his desire that judges in the future will use his Laws to render judgments and verdicts, and to "eradicate the wicked and the evil from this land" and to "enhance the well-being of...[the] people."[18]

Opinions continue to differ and we may never completely resolve the question of the nature of the Mesopotamian law collections. Nevertheless, given their prominence, it seems wise to treat them as valid sources for studying the law of ancient Mesopotamia. At the very least they are formal "prescriptions and prohibitions with their penalties reflecting actual custom and usage."[19]

Saggs notes that, when considered alongside one another, the ancient Mesopotamian law collections share certain similarities, but each also bears its own unique characteristics: "All these collections...exhibit both common matter and their own peculiarities, and it has become clear that there was in the ancient Near East a large body of common or generally recognized law. Some of this was incorporated in various local collections of laws, with modifications to suit local circumstances...."[20]

---

15. ROTH, LAW COLLECTIONS 134. *See* Raymond Westbrook, *Cuneiform Law Codes and the Origins of Legislation*, 79 ZEITSCHRIFT FÜR ASSYRIOLOGIE UND VORDERASIATISCHE ARCHÄOLOGIE 201, 202 (1989) ("[C]ertain remarks in the epilogue to CH are taken to show that the text of the code was intended to be cited in court." (footnote omitted)). For an interesting discussion of this statement in the epilogue, *see* Roth, *The Law Collection of King Hammurabi* 10–12. Roth interprets the "wronged man" as someone "who has already lost a case — not one who is about to enter into a lawsuit." *Id.* at 11.
16. ROTH, LAW COLLECTIONS 135.
17. *Id.*
18. *Id.*
19. Good, *Capital Punishment*, 19 STAN. L. REV. 947, 950 (1967) (footnote omitted). *See also* Yoffee, *Context and Authority* 98 (Describing the "codes" "as a set of abstract rules designed to regulate jural behavior.") (citations omitted).
20. SAGGS, BABYLON 197.

Of course, the most famous and extensive law collection is that attributed to the Babylonian king, Hammurabi (1792–1750 B.C.).[21] But there are about a half-dozen additional, extant law collections that predate Hammurabi. Of these the three most significant (or "major") collections are, in chronological order: 1) The Laws of Ur-Nammu (c. 2100 B.C.); 2) The Laws of Lipit-Ishtar (c. 1930 B.C); and 3) the Laws of Eshnunna (c. 1770 B.C.).[22] In addition to the collections, the "Reforms of Urukagina" (who is now ordinarily referred to as "Uru-inimgina") represent the earliest written legal text from Mesopotamia of appreciable length and breadth. And even though Urukagina's (Uru-inimgina's) Reforms cannot be classified as a "collection," it is necessary at least to mention this text due to its primacy in chronology.

§ 2.2 Urukagina's (Uru-Inimgina's) Reforms

Among the earliest writings that purport to have had legal significance in Mesopotamia are Urukagina's (Uru-inimgina's) "Reforms." Urukagina (Uru-inimgina) was the ruler of Lagash around 2400 B.C.[23] I.M. Diakonoff proposes the following outline of provisions for the Reforms:

---

21. SAMUEL GREENGUS, *Legal and Social Institutions of Ancient Mesopotamia, in* 1 CIVILIZATIONS OF THE ANCIENT NEAR EAST, *supra* ch. 1 note 14, at 469, 471; Roth, *The Law Collection of King Hammurabi* 2 ("[T]he Hammurabi document is the longest, includes the largest number of provisions concerning the largest number of legal situations, received the widest circulation in antiquity in its own contemporary moment and in the centuries to follow, and demonstrates the most sophisticated internal organization.").

22. SAMUEL GREENGUS, *Legal and Social Institutions of Ancient Mesopotamia, in* 2 CIVILIZATIONS OF THE ANCIENT NEAR EAST, *supra* ch. 1 note 14, at 469, 471. In addition to these, in her book *Law Collections from Mesopotamia and Asia Minor* (1995) (*see supra* ch. 1, n. 33), Martha Roth translates several other law collections that predate Hammurabi (and a few that are either contemporaneous or subsequent), which are not as extensive or complete as the laws of Ur-Nammu, Lipit-Ishtar, and Eshnunna: 1) the Laws of X (c. 2050–1800 B.C.)(origin unknown — perhaps belonging to Ur-Nammu's Laws); 2) Laws about Rented Oxen (c. 1800 B.C.); 3) Sumerian Laws Exercise Tablet (c. 1800 B.C.); and, 4) Sumerian Laws Handbook of Forms (c. 1700 B.C.). Unless otherwise noted, all translations from ancient Mesopotamian law collections in this book are from ROTH, LAW COLLECTIONS. For convenience, I cite them by the name of the relevant collection (e.g., HAMMURABI ¶ ___, UR-NAMMU ¶ ___, LIPIT-ISHTAR ¶ ___, etc.).

23. DOMINIQUE CHARPIN, *The History of Ancient Mesopotamia: An Overview, in* 2 CIVILIZATIONS OF THE ANCIENT NEAR EAST, *supra* ch. 1 note 23, at 807, 808, 809 (Charpin, like most modern scholars, refers to Urukagina as "Uru-inimgina").

> [F]irst comes the abolition of certain exactions from the temple
> personnel and the priests…and the restoration of divine property
> rights to the temple estates…, then the abolition of law court du-
> ties…, introduction of new rates of rations and payments to priests,
> etc., which also were in the nature of a duty levied from the popula-
> tion…, abolition of compulsory services (?) of…the temple arti-
> sans…, protection of possession-rights of [a subgroup of the popu-
> lation]…, and a summary of criminal laws.[24]

Apparently the main purpose of his Reforms was to decrease taxes and lend
assistance to the poor.[25] Obviously, his inscription, which lists his changes,
does not really rise to the level of organization and complexity necessary to
call it a "code" or "collection" on par with the later collections.

§ 2.3 Ur-Nammu

[A] Introduction

The oldest of the ancient Mesopotamian law collections is that ascribed
to king Ur-Nammu (2112–2095 B.C.) (who founded the Third Dynasty of
Ur (Ur III), uniting Sumer and Akkad in about 2100 B.C.) or his son Shulgi
(2094–2047 B.C.) [26] This collection contains a prologue plus about forty
laws. In the prologue, Ur-Nammu claims to have received his authority

---

24. I.M. Diakonoff, *Some Remarks on the "Reforms" of Urukagina*, 52 REVUE
D'ASSYRIOLOGIE ET D'ARCHÉOLOGIE ORIENTALE 1, 13 (1958).

25. SAGGS, BABYLON 47; ROUX, ANCIENT IRAQ 133. *See* Yoffee, *Context and Authority* 99 ("Most of the 'reforms' are intended to end specific royal taxes on, and the con-
fiscation of, temple property."). *See also* I.M. Diakonoff, *Some Remarks on the "Reforms" of Urukagina*, 52 REVUE D'ASSYRIOLOGIE ET D'ARCHÉOLOGIE ORIENTALE 1, 12
(1958). Curiously, Urukagina's Reforms provide what may be the only prohibition on
polyandry in the ancient Near East. According to Edwin Good, Urukagina "says that
women used to take two husbands, but if they do it now, they are stoned." Good, *Capital Punishment*, 19 STAN. L. REV. 947, 961 (1967) (footnote omitted). For more on the
issue of polyandry, *see* JERROLD COOPER, SUMERIAN AND AKKADIAN ROYAL HYMNS, 1
American Oriental Society Translation Series 70 ff. n. 8 (1986) [hereinafter "COOPER,
ROYAL HYMNS"]. *See also infra* § 5.2.

26. *See generally* DOMINIQUE CHARPIN, *The History of Ancient Mesopotamia: An
Overview, in* 2 CIVILIZATIONS OF THE ANCIENT NEAR EAST, *supra* ch. 1 note 23, at
807, 811–812; S.N. Kramer, *Ur-Nammu Law Code*, 23 ORIENTALIA 40–51 (1954).
ROUX, ANCIENT IRAQ 154–55, 161. *See also* Yoffee, *Context and Authority* 99; and BOT-
TÉRO, WRITING, REASONING, AND THE GODS 159.

from the gods.[27] He takes credit for having "established justice in the land" and freedom for Akkadians and foreigners, and "for those conducting foreign maritime trade."[28] He declares that he has standardized weights and measures—an immensely important step for an efficient economy—and that he has regulated riverboat traffic on the Tigris and Euphrates. Boldly he asserts: "I eliminated enmity, violence, and cries for justice in the land."[29] For the modern reader, it may seem strange that there is no clear division between laws which we would characterize as criminal (*i.e.,* laws dealing with conduct for which the state prosecutes and imposes a physical punishment or monetary fine; for example murder and tax evasion) *versus* laws which we would characterize as civil (*i.e.,* laws dealing with conduct for which individuals must seek redress by means of money damages or equitable remedies such as specific performance or an injunction; for example personal injury caused by another's negligence or breach of contract).[30]

One striking feature of this most ancient of law collections is its apparent civility.[31] Imprisonment is a penalty for only one offense—detaining another. The death penalty[32] is imposed in only four instances: homicide; rape; adultery; and "lawless" behavior.[33]

---

27. According to Kramer, "The prologue may be divided in accordance with its contents into three sections which are respectively theological, historical, and ethical in character." S.N. Kramer, *Ur-Nammu Law Code*, 23 Orientalia 40, 41 (1954).

28. Roth, Law Collections 15.

29. *Id. See* S.N. Kramer, *Ur-Nammu Law Code*, 23 Orientalia 40, 41 (1954).

30. Samuel Greengus, *Legal and Social Institutions of Ancient Mesopotamia*, in 1 Civilizations of the Ancient Near East. *supra* ch. 1 note 14, at 469, 473.

31. Roux, Ancient Iraq 155 (Roux remarks: "[I]t appears that at least some crimes (such as physical injury) were not punished by death or mutilation, as later in the Code of Hammurabi or the Hebraic law, but the offender was obliged to pay compensation in silver, the weight of which varied according to the gravity of the crime. This, of course, is the sign of a society far more polished and civilized than is usually imagined."). *But see* Finkelstein, *Ammisaduqa's Edict*, 15 J. Cuneiform Stud. 91, 98 (1961) (suggesting that pecuniary satisfaction is actually a more "barbaric" remedy than physical punishment).

32. The imposition of capital punishment is significant in the Mesopotamian law collections. Good has argued that "those crimes for which the offender is put to death represent the most blatant rejection of the common values." Good, *Capital Punishment*, 19 Stan. L. Rev. 947 (1967).

33. Obviously this is a difficult concept. The Sumerian word that translates as "lawless" occurs more in the law collections than in any other place in Mesopotamian literature. It may have connotations relating to treason or piracy.

[B] Outline of the Provisions

Thematically speaking, the laws are, for the most part, grouped into small clusters. Occasionally a single law appears to have no theoretical connection to the law that either precedes or follows it.[34] Below is a thumbnail sketch of the topics as they appear in Ur-Nammu's Laws.[35]

- The collection begins with two laws that are very serious: laws that impose the death sentence either for homicide or for acting "lawlessly"[36] (¶¶ 1,2).
- A single law imposes a penalty of fine plus imprisonment for detaining another against his will (¶ 3).

The next dozen laws appear to involve family matters in some loose fashion (sex, divorce, and marriage) (¶¶ 4–16).

- Two laws dealing with slave-marriages and slave manumission (¶¶ 4,5).
- Two laws imposing the death penalty (one for rape, the other for a woman who commits adultery) (¶¶ 6,7).
- A single law (perhaps thematically related to the two immediately before it since they concern sex) imposing a fine on a man who "deflowers the virgin slave woman of a man") (¶ 8).
- Three laws together pertaining to divorce settlements and the status of widows (¶¶ 9–11).
- Two sections that are procedural.[37] Both impose fines (or damage payments) on someone who unsuccessfully brings charges against another. The charges in one law deal with sexual promiscuity, and may in the other as well. (¶¶ 13,14).
- One law giving money damages to a young man when the father of his betrothed breaches his promise (¶ 15).

---

34. According to Driver & Miles, the Laws of Ur-Nammu are "merely a hotch-potch of miscellaneous laws such as no legislator can possibly have promulgated in their present form." DRIVER & MILES, BABYLONIAN LAWS 15.

35. Driver & Miles suggest categories for Ur-Nammu's Laws. DRIVER & MILES, BABYLONIAN LAWS 12–13.

36. The precise meaning of "lawlessly" is unclear. It may have a connotation of lying in wait and then attacking. It may have something to do with piracy. It may relate in some way to being treasonous. We only know that whatever it was it must have been serious to have warranted the death penalty, since the death penalty was reserved for only three other crimes in Ur-Nammu's Laws (rape, adultery, homicide).

37. ¶ 12 is too fragmentary to categorize.

- A fragmentary law providing that a person must pay another two shekels for some unknown reason (¶ 16).
- One law states that someone who returns a runaway slave is entitled to receive a fixed reward (¶ 17).
- The next seven laws establish fixed damage payments for various injuries; some are bodily injuries (*e.g.*, 40 shekels for cutting off someone's nose) and some are injuries to property (some kind of injury to a slave) (¶¶ 18–24).[38]
- A pair of laws penalize a slave woman who acts impudently. One punishes "a slave woman [who] curse[d] someone acting with the authority of her mistress" by "scour[ing] her mouth with one [litre] of salt." (¶¶ 25,26).
- A couple of laws impose penalties for perjury and also for refusing to take a witness's oath in a law case (¶¶ 28,29).[39]
- The last three legible laws in the collection deal with damage to fields (flooding) or failure to cultivate as promised (¶¶ 30–32).[40]

[C] Values Promoted and Interests Protected

When considering legal history, one useful inquiry that often explains a people's jurisprudence better than a mere recitation of their laws is to ask what values the laws promote and what interests they protect. Therefore, in addition to simply identifying the subject-matter categories and making a few generalizations about them, it is instructive (at least to some extent) to examine the more prominent values and interests discernable in the Mesopotamian law collections. Thus, we will consider these questions here in connection with the Laws of Ur-Nammu, and then again below when reviewing the Laws of Lipit-Ishtar, Eshnunna, and Hammurabi.

Ur-Nammu's Laws promote several values and protect a number of interests of the citizenry as a whole. Although, it is clear that the Laws are primarily directed at protecting the interests of the upper class citizens. Laws relating to slaves indicate a sharp difference in treatment for them. Overall, the Laws protect the interests of the family structure, the integrity of an individual's own body and personal freedom, his property, and his authority.

Ur-Nammu's Laws reflect a deep concern for the family. At least one quarter of the provisions deal with family law matters such as marriage, di-

---

38. ¶ 23 is too fragmentary to categorize.
39. ¶ 27 is too fragmentary to categorize.
40. ¶¶ 33–37 are too fragmentary to categorize.

vorce, and fidelity. The Laws protect the reasonable expectations of persons in positions of relative weakness. For example, a man who divorces his "first-ranking wife" must pay her 60 shekels of silver as a settlement.[41] A man must pay 30 shekels of silver to a widow whom he divorces.[42] If a father gives away his daughter to a friend of the man to whom he had originally promised his daughter (*i.e.*, a friend of the "promised" son-in-law— essentially breaking a marriage contract), the breaching father-in-law must pay double the amount of the property value that the promised son-in-law originally brought with him ("twofold (the value of) the prestations [which he (the ["promised"] son-in-law) brought (when he entered the house)])."[43] Thus, the divorcee and the jilted son-in-law, who occupy weaker social positions (*i.e.*, have less power) than the husband and father-in law, gain a certain measure of security through the Laws.

Many laws secure the personal integrity of an individual's body. About half a dozen provisions provide specific damage awards for personal injury. For example, one law requires that someone who cuts off another's nose must pay 40 shekels of silver.

One law defends an individual's freedom of movement — the liberty to go about as one pleases. That law imposes both a 15-shekel fine and imprisonment on a person who detains another. This may be an early version of our modern notion of false imprisonment.Several laws safeguard property rights. One law imposes a 5-shekel penalty on a man who "deflowers" someone else's virgin slave. Another law provides that a slave owner must pay a certain sum as a reward for the return of a runaway slave. There is also a specific rule stating that if one property owner floods another's field, he must pay compensation to the injured landowner based on the amount of acreage damaged by the water.

A slave owner's authority was considered inviolate. One law provides that a female slave will have her mouth scoured with a litre of salt if she curses someone who acts with her mistress's authority.[44] This law is interesting for another reason. Unlike many of the laws designed to remedy damage to a person, his property, or his economic interests, this law is aimed at a purely intangible loss — an affront to the owner's authority.

At least four of the laws appear to promote procedural efficiency. Two laws impose a financial penalty on persons who unsuccessfully accuse oth-

---

41. UR-NAMMU ¶ 9.
42. UR-NAMMU ¶ 10.
43. UR-NAMMU ¶ 15.
44. UR-NAMMU ¶ 25.

ers of wrongdoing. In one case a man must pay 20 shekels of silver for accusing another's wife of promiscuity, if "the divine River Ordeal clears her."[45] In the other provision of this type, the penalty for the unsuccessful litigant is only 3 shekels, but the text is unclear about the nature of the alleged wrongdoing. Nevertheless, the imposition of financial penalties on unsuccessful prosecutors probably served as a deterrent for those who might otherwise have been inclined to bring unsubstantiated accusations. Since the divine River Ordeal may have been something like a roll of the dice,[46] litigants may have been disinclined to subject themselves to the risk of financial penalties unless they were very certain of the truth of their accusations. Another law that apparently fosters procedural efficiency provides that if a witness refuses to take an oath, he must pay the amount that is disputed in the case. Clearly, this law would encourage witnesses to take the oath and testify, thereby helping the judicial process to run more smoothly.[47] Another law helped advance procedural efficiency by imposing a fine of 15 shekels on a witness who committed perjury.

§ 2.4 Lipit-Ishtar

[A] Introduction

The ruler Ishme-Dagan (1953–1935 B.C.) enjoys a reputation as one who "set law in the land."[48] Although he may have sponsored a law collection of some sort, we have no primary source as evidence of it. His successor, Lipit-Ishtar, however, championed a law collection, and we do possess at least parts of it.[49] Lipit-Ishtar was the fifth king of the First Dynasty of the city Isin. He ruled for about ten years (1934–1924 B.C.).[50] In addition to nearly fifty laws, Lipit-Ishtar's law collection has also both a prologue and epilogue.[51] But unlike Hammurabi's Laws some 200 years later, one must

---

45. UR-NAMMU ¶ 14.

46. *See infra* § 4.3.

47. *See infra* § 4.3 regarding oaths.

48. SAGGS, BABYLON 63.

49. *Id. See also Id.* at 200. *See* WESTBROOK, OLD BABYLONIAN MARRIAGE LAW 1 (Westbrook characterizes Lipit-Ishtar's Laws as "the last great work of law in Sumerian").

50. DOMINIQUE CHARPIN, *The History of Ancient Mesopotamia, in* 2 CIVILIZATIONS OF THE ANCIENT NEAR EAST, *supra* ch. 1 note 23, at 807, 814; ROUX, ANCIENT IRAQ 172. *See also* Yoffee, *Context and Authority* 99.

51. *See generally* DRIVER & MILES, BABYLONIAN LAWS 15–17.

strain to find any cohesiveness in these laws.[52] There tend to be short groups; sometimes only two or three laws relate to one another.[53]

[B] Outline of the Provisions

Briefly stated, the following is a capsule summary of the topics in Lipit-Ishtar's Laws (in the order in which they appear in the collection).

- The first law establishes the amount of money charged for renting an ox for two years (¶ a).
- The next two laws deal with a daughter's inheritance upon her father's death (¶¶ b,c).
- Three laws follow dealing with the liability of a man who strikes another man's pregnant daughter (¶¶ d,e,f).[54]
- Two laws are about a boat renter's liability for loss of the rented boat (¶¶ 4,5).[55]
- Five laws involve orchards and agricultural property rights (leasing, trespass, conversion, maintenance) (¶¶ 7–11).[56]
- There is a group of three laws concerning slaves and the penalties for harboring another's slave (¶¶ 12–14).
- Two laws are about the special status of a *miqtu*-person ("A member of a social or economic class of persons, possibly under royal patronage."[57]) (¶¶ 15,16).
- One procedural law provides that a person who unsuccessfully brings a false or unsubstantiated claim against another must "bear the penalty of the matter for which he made the accusation." (¶ 17).
- The next law is about gaining property rights by paying taxes on real estate (¶ 18).[58]

---

52. Good characterizes this collection's structure as "chaotic, hardly justifying the term 'code' for that collection." Good, *Capital Punishment*, 19 Stan. L. Rev. 947, 950 n.16 (1967).

53. Roux summarizes Lipit-Ishtar's Laws by saying: "[T]hese laws deal mostly with succession, real estates, hire contracts and the condition of privately owned slaves...." Roux, Ancient Iraq 172. Westbrook notes that "internal evidence" suggests that Lipit-Ishtar's Laws "served as a model; at least for some of the paragraphs of Codex Hammu-rabi." Westbrook, Old Babylonian Marriage Law 2.

54. ¶ g is too fragmentary to categorize.

55. ¶ 6 has something to do with a gift, but it is too fragmentary to categorize.

56. ¶ 7a is too fragmentary to categorize.

57. Roth, Law Collections 271.

58. The next law in the sequence (¶ 19) *may* have dealt with the same topic but it is too fragmentary to tell for sure.

- Next come four laws that concern adults who are not the biological parents of children, but who have some type of relationship with a child (*e.g.*, raising the child, caring for the child, training the child as an apprentice) (¶¶ 20,20a,20b,20c).[59]
- Then there is the biggest group in the collection: twelve laws that deal with marriage and the status of wives and children (¶¶ 21–32).[60]
- One law imposes a fine on someone who unsuccessfully accuses a man's daughter of sexual promiscuity (¶ 33).
- The collection concludes with four provisions dealing with an ox renter's liability for damage to rented oxen (¶¶ 34–37).[61]

[C] Values Promoted and Interests Protected

In terms of policy, Lipit-Ishtar's Laws promote a variety of interests. Perhaps the predominant interest that they protect is an owner's right to property. The Laws of Lipit-Ishtar preserve the rights of an owner in situations where he has bailed his property, rented his property, and had his property damaged or taken by others. These individual property rights are applicable to things as diverse as boats, oxen, orchards, and slaves.

Several laws guard the rights of children. An unmarried daughter was entitled to inherit. Children by a second wife were given a measure of financial security. Children of a slave woman were considered free if their mother's master was their father. Children of a prostitute were considered free and could inherit from their father.

More than one law penalized someone who unsuccessfully accused another. One such law imposed the same penalty on the accuser that the accused would have borne had he been found guilty of the wrong. These laws promoted procedural efficiency by acting as a deterrent to those who might have otherwise brought weak claims.

One interesting point about Lipit-Ishtar's Laws deserves special mention. In generalizing about laws from the ancient Near East, we often assume that the laws were primitive, almost barbaric. Thus, there is a conventional misconception that the death penalty was common. In truth it was not. This is especially noticeable in Lipit-Ishtar's laws, where the death

---

59. ¶ 20a is so fragmentary that we cannot ascertain its meaning, but it is not too fragmentary to categorize.

60. Technically speaking, ¶ 23b is too fragmentary to categorize, but in all likelihood it relates in some way to the other laws in this group.

61. Technically speaking, ¶ 38 is too fragmentary to categorize, but in all likelihood it relates in some way to the other laws in this group.

penalty was only imposed for one offense (striking and killing the pregnant daughter of a man).

§ 2.5 Eshnunna

[A] Introduction

The Laws of Eshnunna come from about 1800 B.C, a time just before the Laws of Hammurabi.[62] They are "the earliest laws in Akkadian" and are inscribed "on two clay tablets found in 1947 at Tell Harmal, a suburb of Baghdad."[63] The laws are attributed to a king of Eshnunna (a city about 120 kilometers north-northeast of Babylon) named Dadusha.[64] It seems somewhat unfair that the three other prominent law collections from Mesopotamia are known by the names of the kings to whom they are ascribed (*i.e.*, Ur-Nammu, Lipit-Ishtar, and Hammurabi), but that the Laws of Eshnunna are known by a city name rather than the king's name. Tradition partly accounts for this, but some scholars also speculate that the Laws are not in fact Dadusha's.[65] In any event, Dadusha was a contemporary of Hammuarabi's, and Hammurabi ultimately overthrew Dadusha.

Although the Eshnunna Laws are similar in certain respects to those in Hammurabi's collection,[66] it is doubtful that either borrowed directly from the other. "Scholars conclude, from a detailed study, that there is no clear evidence of this [*i.e.* direct borrowing] and postulate that the basic material of both was ultimately derived from an older common source."[67] For years, historians have used both the Laws of Eshnunna and the Laws of Hammurabi to gain insight into the stratification of Babylonian society. Al-

---

62. SAMUEL GREENGUS, *Legal and Social Institutions of Ancient Mesopotamia, in* 1 CIVILIZATIONS OF THE ANCIENT NEAR EAST, *supra* ch. 1 note 14, at 469, 471; JACK M. SASSON, *King Hammurabi of Babylon, in* 2 CIVILIZATIONS OF THE ANCIENT NEAR EAST, *supra* ch. 1 note 38, at 901, 904.

63. SAGGS, BABYLON 203. *See also* ROUX, ANCIENT IRAQ 175–76; DRIVER & MILES, BABYLONIAN LAWS 7.

64. *See* WESTBROOK, OLD BABYLONIAN MARRIAGE LAW 4 ("Codex Eshnunna is a near contemporary of Codex Hammu-rabi, being generally dated to the reign of Dadusha...."). *See also* ROUX, ANCIENT IRAQ 126, 175; BOTTÉRO, WRITING, REASONING, AND THE GODS 159; and, Yoffee, *Context and Authority* 100.

65. *See* DRIVER & MILES, BABYLONIAN LAWS 6.

66. *See Id.* at 9.

67. SAGGS, BABYLON 206; WESTBROOK, OLD BABYLONIAN MARRIAGE LAW 3 ("Both codes therefore appear to be drawing from a common academic legal tradition, a set of standard examples going back to much earlier law-codes." (footnote omitted)).

though most of the laws in the Eshnunna collection deal with the upper class (*awīlum*), some laws also refer to the commoner-class (*muškēnum*), slaves of free persons (*wardum* and *amtum*) and of the palace (*ekallum*), and a few other categories of persons as well.[68]

These laws have neither prologue nor epilogue. As was the case with Lipit-Ishtar's Laws, it is difficult to perceive an overall, macroscopic organization or plan to the Laws of Eshnunna. We can, however, discern some groups.[69] But even in the groups, a law here or there is included that to modern eyes relates only tangentially to the rest of the laws in the group.[70] Nevertheless, certain groups of laws suggest that the Laws of Eshnunna may have functioned as "a legal textbook, featuring 'socratic' methodology, designed for the teaching of Mesopotamian legal thought and the appreciation of the complexities of legal situations."[71]

[B] Outline of the Provisions

The following is a capsule summary of the groups in the Laws of Eshnunna.[72]

- The first group deals largely with financial matters (except for two laws—sandwiched in the midst of laws about agricultural laborers (¶¶ 12,13) dealing with trespass in fields and houses): prices for commodities; rentals of wagons, oxen, and goats; fees and contracts for agricultural workers; wages for fullers; and a few laws pertaining to merchants and credit for young sons (¶¶ 1–11, 14–16).
- The next group consists of two laws concerning marriage gifts. In short, these laws relate to ownership of marriage gifts when the bride or groom dies either shortly before or shortly after the marriage (¶¶ 17,18).
- The next four laws are about loans, credit, and interest (¶¶ -18A-21).

---

68. Samuel Greengus, *Legal and Social Institutions of Ancient Mesopotamia, in* 1 Civilizations of the Ancient Near East, *supra* ch. 1 note 14, at 469, 475–77.

69. For one scholar's attempt at identifying groups in this collection, *see* Eichler, *Literary Structure* 73, 81–84.

70. Driver & Miles remark that "the order is wholly unscientific" and the arrangement of subject categories as characterized by a "chaotic lack of order." Driver & Miles, Babylonian Laws 10.

71. Eichler, *Literary Structure* 81.

72. For another categorization of these laws, *see* Driver & Miles, Babylonian Laws 7.

- Three provisions impose penalties on a person who takes either a slave or wife as a "debt-hostage," falsely claiming to be a creditor of the owner/husband (¶¶ 22–24).
- Six laws relate to marriage (¶¶ 25–30).
- One law then imposes a fine on someone who "deflowers" another's slave woman (¶ 31).
- A group of four laws concerns the support and care of children (¶¶ 32–35).
- Two laws deal with bailment and a bailee's liability (¶¶ 36,37).
- Four laws are about business of one sort or another (partnership, real estate sales, slave sales, and sales of beer by a "woman inkeeper") (¶¶ 38–41).
- The next seven sections establish damage amounts due for various personal injuries (biting off a nose or an ear; cutting off a finger; breaking a hand, a foot, a collarbone) (¶¶ 42–47A).
- Three laws in a row deal with unrelated subjects: one about procedure and jurisdiction (¶ 48); one about being caught in possession of a stolen slave (¶ 49); and one about abuse of authority by military or municipal officials) (¶ 50).
- Two laws concern slaves as property (¶¶ 51,52).
- Six provisions establish monetary damages when animals cause injuries (oxen and dogs) (¶¶ 53–57).
- The last three sections in the collection relate to houses—but that is the only thing that they share in common. One imposes liability on the owner of a wall that collapses (¶ 58), one is about expelling a man from his house if he has children by a first marriage and then divorces and remarries (¶ 59), and the third makes a guard liable if the house he is guarding is burgled (¶ 60).

[C] Values Promoted and Interests Protected

Most of the Laws of Eshnunna protect the interests of the well-to-do—the upper class people who have financial resources to begin with. For example, the laws that fix commodity prices protect the interests of buyers and sellers, since fixed prices help to avoid irregularities and unexpected surprise in the marketplace. The same can be said for the laws that establish wages or rental prices for oxen, donkeys, wagons, boats, drivers, harvesters, and fullers. In a similar way, laws setting interest rates protect commercial borrowers and the credit system in general. Other provisions operate to protect domestic businesses at the expense of foreigners.

A number of sections protect an owner's property interest. Examples include laws that provide compensation for an owner of property when it is damaged or stolen (*e.g.*, property that is bailed, agricultural fields, oxen, and slaves).

In addition to these individual interests, the Laws also helped promote a number of societal values and public policies, such as family unity, caring for children, marriage (consent of a daughter's parents, a marriage contract,[73] and a marriage feast[74] were all required), participation in the military (wives and property were protected during soldiers' absence), individual bodily integrity, freedom from abuse by officials, and public safety (*e.g.*, laws encouraging animal owners to control them, laws requiring homeowners to maintain their property).

Thus, on the whole, one can conclude that the Laws of Eshnunna protected the economic interests of the upper class, although many provisions promoted institutions that we today would consider beneficial to society in general: the family, marriage, children, public safety, and public welfare.

§ 2.6 The Laws of Hammurabi

[A] Introduction

Hammurabi, king of Babylon, inherited what was actually a relatively modest kingdom from his father (Sin-Muballit), and over the course of more than forty years (1792–1750 B.C.) gradually conquered and annexed his neighboring cities in southern Mesopotamia.[75] He probably promulgated his collection of laws in the final years of his reign.[76] The collection

---

73. *See infra* § 6.2 [A].

74. The term translated as "marriage feast" is *kirrum*. According to Westbrook, "[t]he exact meaning of *kirrum* is a matter of dispute, but appears to be a formality involving the drinking of beer which, inter alia, attended various types of contract." WESTBROOK, OLD BABYLONIAN MARRIAGE LAW 30 (footnote omitted).

75. JACK M. SASSON, *King Hammurabi of Babylon, in* 2 CIVILIZATIONS OF THE ANCIENT NEAR EAST, *supra* ch. 1 note 38 at 901, 905–907. *See generally* ROUX, ANCIENT IRAQ 184–189.

76. JACK M. SASSON, *King Hammurabi of Babylon, in* 2 CIVILIZATIONS OF THE ANCIENT NEAR EAST, *supra* ch. 1 note 38, at 901, 907 ("[I]nternal evidence makes it unlikely that the copy we have now was consecrated before his thirty-ninth year of reign."). Finkelstein, *Ammisaduqa's Edict*, 15 J. CUNEIFORM STUD. 91, 101 (1961) ("[I]t is generally recognized that the laws of Hammurabi—at least in the form in which they have been preserved—could not have been compiled except in the last years of his reign, after he had accomplished all of the conquests enumerated in his prologue."). *See also* DRIVER & MILES, BABYLONIAN LAWS 34.

has 275–300 provisions (the traditional number is 282[77]) arranged according to subject (*e.g.,* procedure, family, inheritance, commerce, personal injury, *etc.*[78]). French archaeologists discovered the most famous and most complete copy of Hammurabi's Laws during a December 1901–January 1902 excavation at Susa, the ancient Elamite capital.[79] The Laws are carved on a cone-shaped black diorite stela that stands over seven feet tall.[80] This principal copy is now in the Louvre in Paris.[81] Other less-complete copies and fragments also have been found.[82] It is likely that Hammurabi's Laws existed on at least three stelae in antiquity.[83] Apparently the Elamites carried three back to Susa when they sacked Babylon in the twelfth century B.C.[84] At the top of the stela is an artistic representation of what many be-

---

77. *See* BOTTÉRO, WRITING, REASONING, AND THE GODS 158.

78. The Louvre stele itself does not indicate any lines or divisions that separate the subject categories. But other copies of the text do divide the laws by lines or spaces to create "sections." DRIVER & MILES, BABYLONIAN LAWS 42.

79. DRIVER & MILES, BABYLONIAN LAWS 28. *See also* BOTTÉRO, WRITING, REASONING, AND THE GODS, 157; Martha T. Roth, *Mesopotamian Legal Traditions and the Laws of Hammurabi*, 71 CHICAGO-KENT L. REV. 13, 21, 23–24 (1995) ("[T]he stela did not leave the Elamite workroom for almost another two thousand years, until A.D. 1901, when the French Archaeological Mission, under the direction of Jacques de Morgan, working in the Acropole in Susa, found it along with other Babylonian trophies brought there in antiquity.").

80. JACK M. SASSON, *King Hammurabi of Babylon, in* 2 CIVILIZATIONS OF THE ANCIENT NEAR EAST, *supra* ch. 1 note 38, at 901, 908; ROUX, ANCIENT IRAQ 191. *See also* Yoffee, *Context and Authority* 100–101; Roth, *The Law Collection of King Hammurabi* (describing the stela as "a physically imposing monument: a 2.25-meter tall black basalt stela...."). Driver & Miles say that the structure is 2.25 meters high, and 1.65 meters circumference at the top and 1.90 meters at the base. DRIVER & MILES, BABYLONIAN LAWS 28.

81. DRIVER & MILES, BABYLONIAN LAWS 29; BOTTÉRO, WRITING, REASONING, AND THE GODS 160; Martha T. Roth, *Mesopotamian Legal Traditions and the Laws of Hammurabi*, 71 CHICAGO-KENT L. REV. 13, 24 (1995).

82. SAMUEL GREENGUS, *Legal and Social Institutions of Ancient Mesopotamia, in* 1 CIVILIZATIONS OF THE ANCIENT NEAR EAST, *supra* ch. 1 note 14 at 469, 471; DRIVER & MILES, BABYLONIAN LAWS 30; Martha T. Roth, *Mesopotamian Legal Traditions and the Laws of Hammurabi*, 71 CHICAGO-KENT L. REV. 13, 20 (1995) ("Well over fifty manuscripts are known to me, coming originally from the ancient centers in Susa, Babylon, Nineveh, Assur, Borsippa, Nippur, Sippar, Ur, Larsa, and more.").

83. Martha T. Roth, *Mesopotamian Legal Traditions and Laws of Hammurabi*, 71 CHICAGO-KENT L. REV. 13, 19 (1995) ("The imposing stela with which we are so familiar today is the sole surviving complete example of what was probably a set of at least three duplicate stelae, erected in the temple squares or other public gathering places of Mesopotamian cities under Hammurabi's rule.").

84. *Id.* at 21 ("[I]t was taken to Susa, perhaps by Shutruk-Nahhunte I, a Middle Elamite ruler, or by his son and successor Kutir-Nahhunte, as booty only in the twelfth century B.C., six hundred years after it was first erected (probably in Sippar) by Hammurabi." (footnote omitted)). OPPENHEIM, ANCIENT MESOPOTAMIA 287 ("At least three such stelae were in existence, as fragments excavated in Susa show. The ste-

lieve is Shamash, the god of justice, seated, delivering or dictating the laws to Hammurabi.[85] The laws themselves are arranged in columns of vertical writing that encircle the stela.[86] In addition to the laws, there is also a prologue and an epilogue (both written in poetic form).[87] The prologue recounts many of Hammurabi's accomplishments and enunciates his desire to establish justice.[88] The epilogue articulates Hammurabi's purpose and pronounces curses on anyone who would disobey or deface the stela. Driver and Miles note that the laws themselves mostly relate to incidents and offenses "likely to occur in a farming or agricultural community...."[89] Furthermore, Driver and Miles counsel the modern reader: "Though ancient, the laws are not primitive; they are based on sound common sense and good logic...."[90]

[B] Outline of the Provisions

Saggs notes that Hammurabi's Laws have "a much more ordered arrangement" than any other collection of laws from ancient Mesopotamia.[91] A brief description of the kinds of laws in Hammurabi's

---

lae were brought to Susa as spoils by victorious Elamite raiders.") (footnote omitted). *See also* Roux, ANCIENT IRAQ 191; Yoffee, *Context and Authority* 101; and, BOTTÉRO, WRITING, REASONING, AND THE GODS 157.

85. Martha T. Roth, *Mesopotamian Legal Traditions and the Laws of Hammurabi*, 71 CHICAGO-KENT L. REV. 13, 22 (1995) ("On the top, covering almost one-third of the 2.25 meter monolith, is an imposing illustration of the sun-god Shamash, god of justice, seated on his throne, and standing before him the king, Hammurabi."); Roth, *The Law Collection of King Hammurabi* 1. Jean Bottéro suggests that the god in question is Marduk, not Shamash. BOTTÉRO, WRITING, REASONING, AND THE GODS 157.

86. *See* DRIVER & MILES, BABYLONIAN LAWS 28.

87. DRIVER & MILES, BABYLONIAN LAWS 36, 37, 40.

88. *See infra* § 3.4. *See also generally* DRIVER & MILES, BABYLONIAN LAWS 36–37; and, Yoffee, *Context and Authority* 101 ("The prologue consists essentially of a hymn to [the] glory of Hammurabi, announcing his divine election to kingship and praising his piety.") (citation omitted).

89. DRIVER & MILES, BABYLONIAN LAWS 46.

90. *Id.* at 57.

91. SAGGS, BABYLON 206. Roth says that the Laws of Hammurabi "demonstrate[] the most sophisticated internal organization" of the Mesopotamian law collections. Roth, *The Law Collection of King Hammurabi* 2. *Also see* Martha T. Roth, *Mesopotamian Legal Traditions and the Laws of Hammurabi*, 71 CHICAGO-KENT L. REV. 13, 21 (1995) ("Although Hammurabi's court scribes and scribal schools did not originate the genre of the law collection, they did refine it to a more sophisticated and comprehensive level than it had achieved in the previous centuries. The Laws of Hammurabi then became something of the model for other later collections (none of which attained the sophistication of Hammurabi's), and certainly a staple of the scribal training curriculum for centuries to come."). For an enlightening comparison

collection—a macroscopic look at the groups—is probably a helpful place to begin when considering this famous collection of laws.[92] For convenience, it is possible to identify 11 groups of laws in the collection: 1) Procedure (¶¶ 1–5); 2) Property (¶¶ 6–25); 3) Military (¶¶ 26–41); 4) Land & Agriculture (¶¶ 42–65); 5) Miscellaneous Gap Provisions (29 sections, gap ¶¶ a–cc); 6) Principal & Agent (¶¶ 100–112); 7) Debts & Bailment (¶¶ 113–126); 8) Family Law (¶¶ 127–195); 9) Personal Injury (¶¶ 196–214); 10) Professional Wages and Liability (¶¶ 215–277); and 11) Sale of Slaves (¶¶ 278–282).[93] Like most ancient Mesopotamian law collections, the groups reflect attention to subject matter, not to legal theory.[94]

[1]   Procedure (¶¶ 1–5)[95]

The first five laws are procedural. The first four provisions appear especially linked by a common theme—they punish witnesses and litigants who make false or unsubstantiated statements. It is here that we first encounter the shocking severity of Hammurabi's Laws. The first three laws carry the death penalty (for false or unsubstantiated accusation of homicide, false or unsubstantiated accusation of practicing witchcraft, and false or unsubstantiated accusation of any other capital offense). Fully 10% of all of Hammurabi's Laws involve a death sentence.[96] Later in the Laws, we see punishments such as amputation of limbs and the gouging of eyes. In truth, however, one must remember that Hammuarabi was first and foremost an aggressive military leader, and conquest in the ancient world was brutal. One can imagine that Hammuarabi would logically take the same stern, no-

---

between the structure of the Laws of Eshnunna with the Laws of Hammurabi, *see* Eichler, *Literary Structure* 83. For more on the order and arrangement of Hammurabi's Laws, *see* DRIVER & MILES, BABYLONIAN LAWS 49.

92. *See generally* ROUX, ANCIENT IRAQ 192–194.

93. This is roughly the same categorization as described by Driver & Miles and Jean Bottéro. *See* DRIVER & MILES, BABYLONIAN LAWS 43–45; and, BOTTÉRO, WRITING, REASONING, AND THE GODS 159.

94. As regards the order of the groups, Driver & Miles state that "the connexion of thought in the order given to the varied subject-matter is not always apparent to the modern mind, a connected thread (though sometimes the connexion is purely verbal) runs through the whole work...." DRIVER & MILES, BABYLONIAN LAWS 48. *See also Id.* at 51 ("Internally, the laws occasionally follow a chronological order. For example, marriage laws begin with betrothal laws, then move to marriage itself, then laws about adultery, and then provisions dealing with divorce. Thus, the laws reflect the chronology of a marital relations.").

95. Driver & Miles remark on the relative paucity of provisions relating to "the law of procedure or of the judicature." DRIVER & MILES, BABYLONIAN LAWS 47.

96. *See supra* ch. 2 note 32, and generally Good, *Capital Punishment*, 19 STAN. L. REV. 947–977 (1967). *See also infra* § 8.9 regarding punishments generally.

nonsense approach to dispute resolution. He incorporated a certain degree of militaristic, swift decision-making and forceful punishment into his Laws. This does not mean that his Laws are heartless, however. In fact, we will find many that have a humanistic tone and many that are intended to protect the interests of the poor and disadvantaged. After the first four, the next law—which also deals with procedure—tells us that a judge who reverses his decision is punished by being permanently removed from the bench and, in addition, that he must pay 12 times the amount involved in the case.

[2] Property (¶¶ 6–25)

All of these laws relate in some fashion to property. This group includes laws dealing with contracts, slaves, children, purchase and sale, and theft.

[3] Military (¶¶ 26–41)

It is not surprising that Hammurabi, who rose to prominence in Mesopotamia at the head of an army, should issue special laws governing the military. These laws consider the public interest as well, since they tend to encourage military service. There are laws that protect a soldier's property (including his wife) while he is away on campaign. There are also laws that prohibit and punish abuse of power by military officers. It was common in ancient cultures for kings and generals to reward their soldiers by giving them land.[97] Several provisions in Hammurabi's Laws prohibit soldiers from selling or in any way transferring land that had been given to them as military payment. Perhaps these laws were designed to encourage soldiers to settle down and raise a family after their military life was done.

[4] Land & Agriculture (¶¶ 42–65)

Laws relating to agriculture were vital, since, as Johannes Renger observes, "Mesopotamian society and its economy are based on agriculture with integrated animal husbandry."[98] Driver and Miles characterize these laws as relating "to the rights and duties of certain tenants of crown-lands and to the rules governing their tenure."[99] They also note that many of these laws concern farmers,[100] their debts,[101] and "offences in connexion

---

97. This was especially true later in ancient Rome.

98. Renger, *Ownership or Possession of Arable Land in Ancient Mesopotamia*, 71 CHICAGO-KENT L. REV. 269 (1995).

99. DRIVER & MILES, BABYLONIAN LAWS 111.

100. *Id.* at 127 (specifically noting ¶¶ 42–48).

101. *Id.* (specifically noting ¶¶ 49–52).

with irrigation."[102] Included among these laws are laws protecting the yield of an owner's fields and orchards. Renters are held liable for failing to produce crops, and several sections deal with gardeners who care for an owner's land.

[5] Miscellaneous GAP Provisions (29 Sections, GAP ¶¶ a–cc)

In the twelfth century b.c., the Elamites stole the famous copy of Hammurabi's Laws that is now in the Louvre.[103] They carted it from Babylon to Susa, their capital. It seems that they erased certain sections—the sections that represent the gap between ¶ 65 and ¶ 100—and intended to write some things of their own in that space.[104] For one reason or another they never got around to it, and, so, the result is a gap in the text that probably originally included 5–7 columns and perhaps 30–40 provisions. Using other tablets and fragments, scholars have been able to fill in much of the missing material.[105]

It is difficult to perceive any one common bond that relates the gap provisions to one another. Many of them deal with financial relationships and financial arrangements. Some involve payment for goods and services. Others cover a wide range of topics, including landlord-tenant relations, debtor-creditor issues, fixed interest rates, businesses, and partnerships.

[6] Principal-Agent; Women Inkeepers (¶¶ 100–112)

These laws mostly articulate the rights and responsibilities of merchants who act as agents. Some laws deal with merchants who are dispatched to sell goods and others relate to merchants who travel afield with their principal's money for investment. Several laws detail an agent's liability to his principal. There are also a few laws that govern various types of conduct of women inkeepers (e.g., methods of accepting payment, harboring criminals).

[7] Debts & Bailment (¶¶ 113–126)

The laws relating to debts address issues such as self-help for repayment and the taking of family members of a debtor as "debt-hostages." The laws regarding bailment are chiefly about the particulars necessary for a valid

---

102. *Id.* (specifically noting ¶¶ 53–56).

103. *See supra* § 2.6 [A].

104. BOTTÉRO, WRITING, REASONING, AND THE GODS 157 ("The last seven columns were later erased by Šutruk-Naḫḫunte, the Elamite king who transported this heavy stele as war booty to Susa around the year 1200."). *See also* DRIVER & MILES, BABYLONIAN LAWS 28–29.

105. DRIVER & MILES, BABYLONIAN LAWS 30–34. Roth identifies and translates 29 provisions in the gap. ROTH, LAW COLLECTIONS 94–99.

bailment contract and the liability of a bailee for loss of or damage to the bailor's goods.

[8] Family Law (¶¶ 127–195)

This series of laws is the longest group in Hammurabi's Laws. It is possible to identify subdivisions of this category. Laws 127–153 deal with marriage, marital property, and divorce settlements. Laws 154–158 prohibit incest. Laws 159–164 cover the legal expectations, property transfers, and gifts between brides, grooms, and their families. Laws 165–175 relate to inheritance from mothers and fathers, and include provisions about gifts to children. Then there are three laws (¶¶ 175, 176a, and 176b) that seem not to fit well into this general category. They are about slave owners and people who marry slaves. Number 177 appears virtually to stand alone. It deals with the interests of widows and children. Sections 178–184 are special laws governing specific classes of priestesses and the manner in which they were permitted to inherit property.[106] Numbers 185–193 pertain to adoption, in particular, the rights of adopters and adoptees. There are also a couple of related laws about apprentices and other child caregivers. Number 194 is unique. If a child died while in the care of a wetnurse, that wetnurse was required to obtain permission from the deceased child's father prior to serving as a wetnurse for someone else.[107] And, lastly, ¶ 195 provides that the punishment for a child who strikes his father is to have his hand cut off.

[9] Personal Injury (¶¶ 196–214)

This group of laws is typical of many Mesopotamian law collection provisions. In some respects, these are the hallmark laws with which most students of Western Civilization are familiar. In cases where the victim is a member of the upper class (*awīlum*) many of these laws are retributive (*lex talionis*). In other words, the punishment for causing personal injury is often the infliction of the same personal injury to the wrongdoer (*e.g.*, breaking a bone, blinding an eye, knocking out a tooth). But in other in-

---

106. DRIVER & MILES, BABYLONIAN LAWS 245 ("A number of sections, from § 127 to § 184, deal with questions affecting the marriage relation, such as the constitution of marriage, the property rights of married women, the marriage of certain classes of priestesses, succession, adultery and other sexual offences, and divorce.").

107. Failure to obtain permission resulted in the woman's breast being amputated as punishment.

stances, for example, when the wrongdoer is a member of the upper class (*awīlum*) and the victim is a commoner (*muškēnum*), the wrongdoer merely pays money as a form of restitution.

[10] Professional Wages and Liability (¶¶ 215–277)

Generally speaking, these laws establish both fixed wages for various professions and services and also the liability that attached to the particular services. Among the professions and services governed by these sections are doctors, veterinarians, and barbers. Barbers, for example, are not allowed to cut the hair of a slave in a way that would leave the slave looking like a free person. Punishment for cutting a slave's hair in this manner is death (unless the barber was defrauded into believing that the slave's owner had given permission). There are a number of provisions about builders. Some deal with fees and some deal with a builder's liability for injuries or deaths caused by a building's collapse. In addition, this group contains laws about boatmen, the liability of boat renters, and renting oxen.

Some of the laws about oxen are especially interesting. For example, laws 250–252 limit the liability of an ox owner whose ox gores someone to death. Aside from the predictable disparity between the liability involved when the victim is a member of the upper class as opposed to a slave, it is revealing to note that the owner of the goring ox pays only money damages. The owner is not himself gored to death as punishment, nor is the ox itself destroyed. Obviously, oxen were extremely important to the economy in ancient Babylonian society. This limit on liability for ox owners reminds us of the limited liability that was afforded in the modern era to the developers of railroads in the nineteenth century and automobiles in the twentieth century. Lawmakers often limit liability for injuries caused by instrumentalities that people consider beneficial to society as a whole. In short, such limited liability rules help to shape the progress of civilization by reducing legal risk.

This group concludes with laws associated with agricultural workers, renters, ox-drivers, shepherds, craftsmen, goat and donkey rental, cattle and wagon rental, boat rental, and the theft of plows.

[11] Sale of Slaves (¶¶ 278–282)

This last group deals mainly with special rules about buying slaves. For example, one provision extends an implied warranty to slave purchasers: it allows a buyer to revoke acceptance of a slave who is stricken with epilepsy within one month of purchase.

[C] Specific Legal Principles

When one reads Hammurabi's Laws for the first time, it is striking to notice how contemporary many of the provisions seem. It may be helpful here briefly to summarize—according to modern legal categories—some of the more salient features of the laws and legal principles found in Hammurabi's Laws.

[1] Contracts

- It is very important—although not absolutely necessary—to have witnesses and written proof of transactions for contracts. This includes bailment and marriage contracts.
- Several provisions occasionally acknowledge that "acts of god" and force majeure operate to relieve a party of liability. This is basically the same as recognizing failure of a presupposed condition or impossibility in modern contract law.
- Several provisions grant expectation damages for breach of contract. Some laws also give punitive damages in a number of contract contexts.

[2] Sales

- The Laws contain some recognition of the concept of a bona fide purchaser for value, but these laws use presumptions different from the modern Uniform Commercial Code.
- The Laws impose a one year warranty for boat repair.

[3] Social Insurance

- The Laws provide social insurance for property theft, social insurance for life, and social insurance for prisoners of war.

[4] Property

- Property given to soldiers by the king is inalienable.
- Some provisions in the Laws show that the ancient Mesopotamians recognized the principle of a life-estate.
- The Laws envision the use of dowry and bridewealth as antecedent to marriage.

[5] Women

- As a general rule, women can inherit and own property.
- On occasion women have some choice in marriage decisions.

[6] Torts

- The Laws use compensation as the remedy for negligence in property damage suits when the damage was foreseeable or actually foreseen.
- There is some recognition of either comparative negligence or assumption of risk (injury in a "brawl").
- The Laws establish the presumption that an upstream boat is liable for damages in a collision with a downstream boat.
- The ox-goring provisions limit liability in a manner that is similar to the modern judicial response to new technology and important industry (*e.g.*, railroads and automobiles).
- The Laws distinguish between injuries that occur through negligence *vs.* unforeseeable "acts of god."
- The Laws impose damages for theft (conversion) at five times the value of the property taken.

[7] Debts

- The Laws sanction debt slavery.
- The maximum that a family member can serve as a debt-slave is three years.
- The Laws permit a creditor to attach either goods or people ("debt-hostages") to satisfy a debt.

[8] Business Law

- The Laws recognize corporate entities such as partnerships.
- Under the Laws' provisions, all partners share profits equally (pro-rata).
- The Laws carefully delineate the duties of agents in principal-agent relationships.

[9] Procedure

- Hammurabi's Laws make clear the importance of having eyewitnesses for legal proceedings. Oaths are used to establish truth. The River Ordeal is used to make decisions for certain serious crimes.
- If an accuser fails to prove his allegations, several laws impose on the accuser the same punishment that the charge itself carries.
- Many laws use the Lex Talionis; retribution in kind as the means of punishment.

[10] Inheritance

- The Laws impose a number of rules for intestate succession (*i.e.*, inheritance in the absence of a will).
- Under Hammurabi's Laws, bastard children whom a father has acknowledged during his lifetime inherit equally along with legitimate children.
- The Laws allow parents to disinherit children for cause (*i.e.*, on the second offense).
- As a general rule, the Laws consider children free and capable of inheriting (*i.e.*, not slave) if one parent is slave but the other is free.

[D] Values Promoted and Interests Protected

The procedural laws promoted truth as a value. This was accomplished by punishing false witness and unsubstantiated accusation. These laws also promoted efficiency, because they discouraged the bringing of lawsuits in cases where an accuser had a weak case.

Many of the laws pertaining to property promoted an individual's interest in protecting his property. Many of Hammurabi's Laws were designed to protect the property interests of the palace as well as personal property of individuals such as slaves, oxen, and other chattels. In addition, there are many provisions that protected a property owner's interest in his land and fields. To be sure, economic interests are protected whenever property rights are protected.

It is useful to recall that certain types of contracts were considered invalid without witnesses or without observing other formalities for the agreement. These laws apparently protected the interests of both buyers and sellers.

A number of laws protected the interests of children. There was, for example, a law criminalizing kidnapping, and another law penalized a builder if a house that he built collapsed and injured the owner's son. Other laws protected the interests of children in a variety of ways, including prohibiting incest and protecting a child's property rights in inheritance.

In addition to the general laws that protected the interests of property owners, there were laws that protected the interests of slave owners. Some laws even protected the health and wellbeing of slaves. Many laws safeguarded a slave owner's pure interest in physically retaining his slaves. Some laws rewarded the return of a lost slave, while others punished those who failed to return slaves.

As was true in the Laws of Eshnunna, Hammurabi's Laws promoted an interest in public safety and welfare by creating laws that protected those who engaged in military service. But also in the midst of the military laws, we see provisions that protected individual privacy and freedom by punishing military officers who abused their power.

Quite a number of laws had the effect of protecting the interests of wealthy land owners, such as laws that punished tenants for failing to produce crops and laws that punished defaulting debtors and their families.

But the Laws are not completely one-sided in favor of the wealthy. Some laws protected debtors, too. For example, debtors were, under some circumstances, permitted to pay debts with goods, not just silver, and creditors were legally required to accept these alternative forms of payment. In addition, there were laws that held creditors to their contracts, and other provisions punished creditors who tried to defraud their debtors. Some laws were intended to keep debtors out of debt-slavery, and one law put a ceiling on the number of years that a family member could be held as a "debt-hostage."

Roth notes that Hammurabi's Laws go a long way to protect "the oppressed and downtrodden — politically, legally, and economically."[108] According to Roth, in the final analysis:

> [W]e find that an overwhelming number of law provisions protect the downtrodden and powerless in Babylonian society who are largely dependent on the whims and good-will of the empowered: the falsely accused, the soldier away on a tour of duty, the depositor, the unwary victim of poorly trained physicians, boat builders, and construction workers, the small-time renter of oxen and agricultural tools, and especially women and children whose property rights (in marriage, adoption, and inheritance) are most easily usurped by the adult free males.[109]

The marriage laws show a strong desire to preserve families and to promote fidelity and the institution of marriage itself. These and other laws also demonstrate an interest in protecting some of the rights of women. This is particularly true in the laws dealing with marriage settlements. Men who divorced their wives without an appropriate reason were legally required to pay a certain amount of money. Several of these laws helped to preserve a wife's interest in marital property and encouraged her husband to treat her fairly.[110] A woman may also have been entitled to divorce her husband.

---

108. Roth, *The Law Collection of King Hammurabi* 11.
109. *Id.* at 11–12.
110. Of course it is possible to be cynical. Presumably, laws that protect the interests of women arguably protect the economic interests of their husbands as well.

CHAPTER 3

Justice & Jurisprudence: The Role of Law

§ 3.1 Introduction

In his book *Writing, Reasoning, and the Gods*, Jean Bottéro summarizes the essence of law in ancient Mesopotamia as follows:

> Mesopotamian law was essentially an unwritten law. Unwritten does not mean nonexistent or unknown, but potential: because it was constantly presented to the people in the form of positive or prohibitive customs, transmitted together with education, or even in the form of traditional solutions to particular problems.[1]

Bottéro also explains the Babylonian concept of justice.[2] His explanation is lucid, and it would be difficult to improve upon it by paraphrasing. Thus, I take the liberty of quoting Bottéro's discussion at length:

> The Babylonians used especially two words that we can associate more or less with the word "justice": *kittu* and *mêsaru*, which they often combined: *kittu mêsaru*, and always in this order, as if the second complimented and enclosed the first. *Kittu* by its basic meaning (*kânu: to establish firmly*) evokes something firm, immobile, and is best understood as that which derives its solidity from its conformity to the law (abstracting from the law's presentation, written or unwritten). We translate it best by *honesty* or by *justice* in the narrow sense, depending on the context. *Mêsaru*, derived from *esêru* (*to go straight, in the right way; to be in order*) contains a more dynamic element; one can understand it, depending on the context, as a state or as an activity. As a state it reflects the *good order* of each thing in

---

1. Bottéro, Writing, Reasoning, and the Gods 181.
2. *Id.* at 182.

its place and according to its ways, in other words, its nature and its role (its "destiny" one would have said in Mesopotamia). As a type of activity or of conduct it renders or attributes to each being and to each man that which comes to him by nature or by his place in society: again his "destiny" — *justice* in short.[3]

§ 3.2 Mythological Foundations of Jurisprudence

The Akkadian word for "justice" literally means "the straight thing."[4] The most ancient Mesopotamians considered justice to have been a gift from the gods.[5] According to Sumerian myth, the god Enki got drunk and, in his over-generous, inebriated state, began lavishing gifts upon Innin, the goddess of Erech. Among the gifts that Enki bestowed were justice, truth, and falsehood. Thus, the Sumerians received the foundations of law — justice, truth, and falsehood — from Enki when he was drunk.[6] Ancient Mesopotamians believed that the gods punished wrongdoing by inflicting illness or misery. Consequently, the gods might punish someone for commercial fraud, real estate fraud, trespass, adultery, battery, or homicide.[7]

Justice and goodness were related concepts in Mesopotamian mythology.[8] Several deities were identified with justice. Shamash, who was the principal god of justice, was also the deity who represented the sun.[9] He was the son of Sin and Nin-Gal.[10] The goddess Nintura was associated with justice.[11] The goddess Ishtar was also linked with justice.[12] Sargon of Agade claimed that the god Enlil acted as a judge when Sargon fought against Lugalzagesi.[13]

To the Mesopotamians it was logical that Shamash, the sun god, should also serve as the main god of justice. The sun god shone his light every-

---

3. *Id.*
4. SAGGS, BABYLON 197.
5. *Id.* at 222.
6. *Id.* at 36.
7. *Id.* at 319–320.
8. *Id.* at 327 (One prayer to the goddess Ishtar says: "At your right is Justice, at your left Goodness....").
9. SAMUEL GREENGUS, *Legal and Social Institutions of Ancient Mesopotamia, in* 1 CIVILIZATIONS OF THE ANCIENT NEAR EAST, *supra* ch. 1 note 14 at 469, 471; SAGGS, BABYLON 331. *See* Martha T. Roth, *Mesopotamian Legal Traditions and the Laws of Hammurabi,* 71 CHICAGO-KENT L. REV. 13, 17 (1995).
10. ROUX, ANCIENT IRAQ 92. SAGGS, BABYLON 332, 336.
11. ROUX, ANCIENT IRAQ 93. SAGGS, BABYLON 328 (A hymn to Nintura says "Your neck is Marduk, judge of heaven and earth....").
12. SAGGS, BABYLON 333.
13. *Id.* at 48–49.

where and thus could see all.[14] No one could hide a secret from Shamash. He alone had the capacity to discover all truth—the essence of justice. His iconographic symbols were the rod and ring, which signified straightness (right) and completeness (justice).[15] Although Assyriologists differ in opinion on this point, the majority believe that it is Shamash who appears at the top of Hammurabi's stela, giving him the rod and ring, the symbols of justice.[16]

In mythology Shamash typically serves as a judge and arbiter.[17] He was the judge of heaven and earth, and, was therefore, the principal figure responsible for protecting those who were poor or those who had been wronged. Anu, "the overpowering personality of the sky,"[18] acts in Mesopotamian mythology as arbitrator of disputes.[19] Sin and Gira (the son of Anu) also appear in myth as judges.[20] The gods were responsible both for creating justice as well as administering it. Thus, through their gods, the ancient Mesopotamians perceived an inseparable link to justice.

§ 3.3 Misharum

An ancient Mesopotamian institution which helps to provide a more complete understanding of their concept of justice is the *misharum* (*mīšarum*).[21] *Misharum* is the Akkadian word that denotes "the quality of 'equity' in human society, that which is achieved by the king's attempt to bring human affairs into balance with *kittum*, 'natural law.'"[22] Generally

---

14. Roux, Ancient Iraq 93.
15. Saggs, Babylon 332.
16. *Id.* at 339. At least two other gods in Mesopotamian myth—Ashur and Enlil—also occasionally appear with the rod and ring. *See Id.* at 343 ("Ashur was represented in art bearing, like Shamash and Enlil, the rod and ring....").
17. Oppenheim, Ancient Mesopotamia 195–96.
18. Roux, Ancient Iraq 94.
19. *Id.*
20. Saggs, Babylon 305 (Saggs relates an incantation to the god Gira: "Flaring Gira, son of Anu, the hero, you are the fiercest among your brothers. You who judge cases like the gods Sin and Shamash, judge my case, make a decision concerning me.").
21. Samuel Greengus, *Legal and Social Institutions of Ancient Mesopotamia, in* 1 Civilizations of the Ancient Near East, *supra* ch. 1 note 14 at 469, 471. *See* Driver & Miles, Babylonian Laws 21–22; Nels Bailkey, *Early Mesopotamian Constitutional Development,* 72 American Hist. Rev. 1211, 1232–1233 (1967).
22. Yoffee, *Context and Authority* 106. *See also* Ellickson & Thorland, *Ancient Land Law,* 71 Chicago-Kent L. Rev. 321, 401–402 (1995); Driver & Miles, Babylonian Laws 23 (definition of *kittum* as "justice").

speaking the *misharum* was an institution unique to the Old Babylonian period. At the beginning of a king's reign,[23] he pronounced his *misharum*—an edict—which ordinarily comprised various temporary economic reforms intended to alleviate financial hardships created by the previous rulers.[24] Ellickson and Thorland remark that "[a] typical edict of this sort canceled specific debts and tax claims, and ordered the release of debt slaves."[25] It is likely that the king then followed up his *misharum* with a more formal, official text.[26] Unlike the law collections, the *misharum* "appears to address itself exclusively to the business at hand."[27] These were "not legal rules in the technical sense...."[28]

> The arrangement of the edict, its style and formulation bear little resemblance to the "codes." The various situations that come within the purview of the reform are not stated as hypothetical cases... with appropriate rulings reserved for the apodosis, but consist for the most part of directives, for specific measures to be taken for specific situations which clearly are understood to exist.[29]

Kings routinely copied or borrowed from previous *misharums,* so that they were not "reinventing the wheel" each time.[30] One such edict, the edict of

---

23. Finkelstein, *Ammisaduqa's Edict*, 15 J. Cuneiform Stud. 91, 102 (1961) ("In the first full-year of his reign a king proclaimed a *mīšarum*."); Raymond Westbrook, *Social Justice in the Ancient Near East, in* Social Justice in the Ancient World 149, 158 (K.D. Irani and Morris Silver eds., 1995) ("It is clear that, traditionally, a king would be expected to declare a release in the first year of his reign, as part of the pomp and circumstance surrounding his accession to the throne. The copious evidence of the Old Babylonian period, however, reveals that a king in the course of his reign might issue one or more further decrees."); Ellickson & Thorland, *Ancient Land Law*, 71 Chicago-Kent L. Rev. 321, 402 (1995) ("The frequency of ancient debt-relief edicts is uncertain. It is thought that a Mesopotamian king typically would declare a *misharum* at the outset of his reign, and thereafter perhaps at intervals of seven or more years." (footnote omitted)).

24. *See* Raymond Westbrook, *Slave and Master*, 70 Chicago-Kent Law Rev. 1631, 1633 (1995) ("Kings occasionally decreed the cancellation of existing debts and related transactions. These are genuine examples of legislation, if somewhat narrow in scope."); Raymond Westbrook, *Social Justice in the Ancient Near East, in* Social Justice in the Ancient World 149, 154–55 (1995); Sophie Lafont, *Continuity and Pluralism* 93–94; and Finkelstein, *Ammisaduqa's Edict*, 15 J. Cuneiform Stud. 91, 93 (1961) ("the proclamation of a *mīšarum* reform...seems to have become one of the expected formal acts of a new king....").

25. Ellickson & Thorland, *Ancient Land Law*, 71 Chicago-Kent L. Rev. 321, 401 (1995).

26. Finkelstein, *Ammisaduqa's Edict*, 15 J. Cuneiform Stud. 91, 102 (1961).

27. *Id.* at 92.

28. Lafont, *Continuity and Pluralism* 96.

29. Finkelstein, *Ammisaduqa's Edict*, 15 J. Cuneiform Stud. 91, 92 (1961).

30. Lafont, *Continuity and Pluralism* 97.

Ammisaduqa, addresses such diverse topics as: debtor-creditor law;[31] administration of palace-owned property;[32] crop division between tenant and landowner;[33] tax computations;[34] the law of distraint ("debt-hostages");[35] laws relating to the *sabītum* (woman inkeeper);[36] and contracts to buy and sell slaves.[37]

Finkelstein summarizes the *misharums* (and remarks on their temporary nature) as follows:

> The *mīšarum*-act, in the strict sense then, consisted of a series of measures designed to restore "equilibrium" in the economic life of the society, which, once presumed to have created the necessary effect of a *tabula rasa* for certain types of financial or economic obligations, ceases to have any force.[38]

Finkelstein remarks that the *misharums* had only a narrow and limited purpose: "A *mīšarum*-act is mainly characterized by measures designed to remit—at the time of promulgation only—certain types of obligation and indebtedness."[39] Westbrook identifies three types of provisions that are ordinarily found in the *misharum*: 1) "Adjustments to royal administrative machinery. Offices are created or abolished, malpractices of officials are forbidden and their future repetition punished, and the administration of the state institutions is regulated."[40] 2) "Fixing of tariffs for certain activities such as interest on loans and the price of goods and services."[41] 3) "Debt release decrees."[42]

---

31. Finkelstein, *Ammisaduqa's Edict*, 15 J. CUNEIFORM STUD. 91, 94 (1961).
32. *Id.* at 95.
33. *Id.*
34. *Id.* at 96.
35. *Id.* at 97.
36. *Id.* at 99.
37. *Id. See also* RAYMOND WESTBROOK, *Social Justice in the Ancient Near East, in* SOCIAL JUSTICE IN THE ANCIENT WORLD 149, 155 (1995) (Westbrook comments: "The most complete text of a debt release decree is the Edict of King Ammisaduqa of Babylon, the great-great-grandson of Hammurabi....The twenty-two paragraphs preserved reveal a complex set of provisions designed to focus the effects of the decree on its intended beneficiaries while limiting disruption of normal commerce.").
38. Finkelstein, *Ammisaduqa's Edict*, 15 J. CUNEIFORM STUD. 91, 100 (1961).
39. *Id.* at 101.
40. Raymond Westbrook, *Cuneiform Law Codes and the Origins of Legislation*, 79 ZEITSCHRIFT FÜR ASSYRIOLOGIE UND VORDERASIATISCHE ARCHÄOLOGIE 201, 216 (1989).
41. *Id.* at 217.
42. *Id.*

§ 3.4 Jurisprudence in the Law Collections

Obviously, the written law collections are useful in helping us understand Mesopotamian law. As regards justice and jurisprudence, the prologues and epilogues provide considerable insight into what the ancient Mesopotamians perceived the role of the laws to be—their legal philosophy.[43] Arguably, these prologues and epilogues consolidate the principal elements of justice in ancient Mesopotamia; in them we see goals and aspirations manifest. Prologues and epilogues commonly state that the promulgating ruler established justice. It is *how* they articulate their conceptions of what justice is that is telling. Kings tout the accomplishments that they say have helped them to achieve justice. Using the prologues and epilogues from the collections as a basis for analysis, taken as a whole, we may postulate that there are at least eight predominant elements that defined "justice" for the ancient Mesopotamians. According to the law collections, justice is a combination of the following ingredients: 1) freedom (especially for the weak and poor, freedom from oppression by the strong and rich);[44] 2) public safety; 3) economic prosperity;[45] 4) peace; 5) order; 6) family security (ensuring that family members cared for one another); 7) truth;[46] and, 8) the existence of a dispute resolution process.

---

43. Bottéro, Writing, Reasoning, and the Gods 183 ("the terms *mêsaru*... and the corresponding verb *esêru*...appear most often in the prologue and the epilogue [of Hammurabi's Laws].")*. See also* Yoffee, *Context and Authority* 106–108; and, Saggs, Babylon 196 ("Many third millennium kings laid claim to having promoted the cause of law and justice, and there is no good reason to doubt that they were active in such matters.").

44. *See* Raymond Westbrook, *Social Justice in the Ancient Near East, in* Social Justice in the Ancient World 149 (1995) ("Social justice was conceived...as protecting the weaker strata of society from being unfairly deprived of their due: the legal status, property rights, and economic condition to which their position on the hierarchical ladder entitled them.") *See also* Saggs, Babylon 171–172, 372.

45. Saggs interprets "justice" in the Mesopotamian law collections to mean "primarily, economic justice...." According to Saggs, "The 'justice' referred to meant, primarily, economic justice, and there is clear evidence that for the king to 'set forth justice in the land' involved some kind of moratorium or general remission of debts." Saggs, Babylon 198.

46. Edwin Good emphasizes the role of truth in Mesopotamian jurisprudence:

> I would argue that integrity was considered a prime virtue in Babylonia. Falsity was severely punished, whether it be false accusation, false testimony, false taking of oaths, the falsification of relationships such as marriage, or the falsification of the quality of work, such as the builder. In all of these cases, the punishment is based on a person's alleging or implying what he knows not to be true.

Good, *Capital Punishment*, 19 Stan. L. Rev. 947, 975 (1967).

One does not have to search far to find these elements. For example, in Ur-Nammu's prologue, he boasts that he "established freedom for the Akkadians and foreigners(?) in the lands of Sumer and Akkad, for those conducting maritime trade...."[47] It seems remarkable that an ancient ruler would strive to attain freedom for both citizens and foreigners. It is also noteworthy that Ur-Nammu singles out commerce (*i.e.,* to promote economic prosperity) as an element of society that he wished to protect.[48]

In his prologue, Lipit-Ishtar proclaims that he wished "to establish justice in the land, to eliminate cries for justice, to eradicate enmity and armed violence (*i.e.,* to foster peace, safety, and order), to bring well-being to the lands of Sumer and Akkad."[49] He states emphatically: "I established justice in the lands of Sumer and Akkad."[50] He is proud that he "liberated" people who were "subjugated" (freedom) and "restored order."[51] Family security was a central concern to Lipit-Ishtar: "I made the father support his children, I made the child support his father. I made the father stand by his children, I made the child stand by his father."[52] In Lipit-Ishtar's epilogue, he mentions specifically that he imposed a system of legal procedure: "I made the lands of Sumer and Akkad hold fair judicial procedure" (dispute resolution process).[53] He also asserts that he "made right and truth shine forth...."[54]

The prologue of Hammurabi's Laws contains multiple references to the elements of justice. Early in the prologue, Hammurabi relates his central purposes: "to make justice prevail in the land, to abolish the wicked and the evil, to prevent the strong from oppressing the weak, to rise like the sun-god Shamash over all humankind...."[55] Here we clearly see freedom as a central element of Hammurabi's justice. At the close of the prologue, Hammurabi underscores the purpose of his laws, saying that Marduk "commanded" him "to provide just ways for the people of the land (in order to attain) appropriate behavior" and "truth and justice."[56] He declares that he "has directed the land along the course of truth and the correct way of

---

47. Roth, Law Collections 15. *See also* Saggs, Babylon 199.
48. *See* Saggs, Babylon 56.
49. Roth, Law Collections 25.
50. *Id.*
51. *Id.*
52. *Id.*
53. *Id.* at 33.
54. *Id.*
55. *Id.* at 76–77.
56. *Id.* at 80–81.

life."[57] He says that he has made people safe. Hammurabi refers to himself as a "shepherd who brings peace, whose scepter is just."[58] He emphasizes that he has protected the powerless and prevented the strong from wronging the weak.[59] In particular, he remarks that he has "provide[d] just ways for the waif and the widow."[60] He tells us that he is "the king of justice" and that he has intended "to provide just ways for the wronged."[61] He invokes the god of justice, Shamash: "By the command of Shamash, the great judge of heaven and earth, may justice prevail in the land."[62]

---

57. *Id.* at 133. *See* SAGGS, BABYLON 199.
58. ROTH, LAW COLLECTIONS 133. *See* SAGGS, BABYLON 371.
59. ROTH, LAW COLLECTIONS 133.
60. *Id.*
61. *Id.* at 134.
62. *Id.*

CHAPTER 4

Legal Organization & Personnel, & Legal Procedure

§ 4.1 Organization & Personnel

[A] The Role of the "Assembly" as an Early Court

One of the most important functions of any government is the administration of a legal system.[1] Most decision-making (even legal decision-making) in the early stages of a civilization rests with either a monarch,[2] a council of elders,[3] or a completely democratic "town meeting" involving all citizens. Some Sumerologists theorize that the earliest Sumerians governed themselves by means of a "general assembly of all citizens — probably including women as well as men — who came together to decide upon action when some emergency threatened."[4]

Assuming "that the organization of the gods must be a reflection of the organization of a human society within the memory of the time at which that society crystallized,"[5] the Sumerian myths suggest that, at some early

---

1. Norman Yoffee, *Context and Authority* 95 ("[O]ne of the most important attributes thought to be possessed by an emergent state, indeed, a characteristic considered by some as defining the state…[is] its putative 'monopoly on law.'" (citations omitted)).

2. *See* Roux, Ancient Iraq 130–31.

3. Samuel Greengus, *Legal and Social Institutions of Ancient Mesopotamia, in* 1 Civilizations of the Ancient Near East, *supra* ch. 1 note 14 at 469, 473; Ellickson & Thorland, *Ancient Land Law*, 71 Chicago-Kent L. Rev. 321, 357 (1995).

4. Saggs, Babylon 37. *See also* Samuel Greengus, *Legal and Social Institutions of Ancient Mesopotamia, in* 1 Civilizations of the Ancient Near East, *supra* ch. 1 note 14 at 469, 473.

5. Saggs, Babylon 160; Roux, Ancient Iraq 92 (According to Roux, "The divine society was conceived as a relic of the human society of Sumer and organized accordingly.").

stage of development, a general assembly of all adult men made important decisions.[6] But as early as the Early Dynastic period (c. 2900–2350 B.C.), Sumerian mythology provides an example of an individual (a king)—not the democratic assembly—making legal decisions. The myth of the warrior-god, Nintura, depicts the king functioning as a judge, "redresser of wrongs."[7] In addition to the mythological tradition, there is inscriptional evidence suggesting that an early king of Kish named Me-Silim served as an arbitrator, "settling the terms of peace and setting up a boundary stone between the territories of the two cities...."[8]

The citizen Assembly in early Mesopotamia probably "functioned like a tribal gathering, reaching agreement by consensus under the guidance of the more influential, richer, and older members."[9] Most Assyriologists believe that the Assembly was the original "court" or judicial body in Mesopotamia.[10] According to Saggs: "In Babylonia, although at some periods and places the king or his official alone might settle a case, this was exceptional, and generally speaking the Assembly retained a concern in cases involving private individuals down to the end of the New Babylonian period."[11] It is also likely that the early Mesopotamian Assembly made legal decisions, even in cases involving murder or robbery outside of the city limits (at least within close proximity).[12] According to Driver and Miles, "In ancient times assembly and court were not clearly distinguished and an assembly often exercised the functions of a court."[13] In the Old Babylonian period (c. 2000–1600 B.C.), the judicial Assembly was probably comprised of all adult male citizens.[14]

It is possible that the Assembly met in a place called the *rebitu*, which was just inside the city next to the gate.[15] We also know that a building

---

6. SAGGS, BABYLON 160.
7. *Id.* at 39.
8. *Id.* at 45.
9. OPPENHEIM, ANCIENT MESOPOTAMIA 112.
10. SAMUEL GREENGUS, *Legal and Social Institutions of Ancient Mesopotamia, in* 1 CIVILIZATIONS OF THE ANCIENT NEAR EAST, *supra* ch. 1 note 14 at 469, 473.
11. SAGGS, BABYLON 216.
12. OPPENHEIM, ANCIENT MESOPOTAMIA 112.
13. DRIVER & MILES, BABYLONIAN LAWS 242 n. 8, 493 (citing both contemporary Old Babylonian documents as well as Hammurabi's Laws ¶¶ 126, 142, 251).
14. SAGGS, BABYLON 216.
15. OPPENHEIM, ANCIENT MESOPOTAMIA 128 ("The elaborate gateways had yet another function as the town's 'civic centers.' Here, probably on a place (*rebitu*) next to the gate inside the city, the assembly met and made decisions and the mayor administered the town or, at least, that quarter to which the gate led."); Ellickson & Thorland, *Ancient Land Law*, 71 CHICAGO-KENT L. REV. 321, 365 (1995) ("The area just within the city gate appears often to have been a key public space." (footnote omitted)).

called the *ekallum* served as the royal palace and administrative governor's residence in most large cities. It was in the *ekallum* that "the king or governor heard the cases brought before him, and it served in some respects as a police-court."[16] Otherwise, we really do not know where the judges held their courts. Paragraph 5 of Hammurabi's Laws mentions the assembly, but contemporary documents indicate that courts convened primarily in local temples, like the temple of Shamash, although other locations are also mentioned.[17]

It was during the Old Babylonian period that several different types of courts appear to have emerged, but our information is too sparse to clearly distinguish them.[18] The Old Babylonian term *bâbtum* (technically "city quarter") is occasionally used in contemporary documents to refer to a court or group of judges ("judges in a court of law").[19] "The persons acting as jurors or judges of fact would be members of the ward selected partly for their mature wisdom and partly for their special knowledge of the facts of the case before them."[20]

[B] Judges & "Courts"

According to myth, after he died, Gilgamesh became "divine judge" for the dead.[21] Historical sources mention judges at least as early as the time of Sargon of Akkad (c. 2300 B.C.).[22] We know that there were professional judges of some sort at the time of the Old Babylonian period[23] because we have at least one reference to a "chief justice."[24] It is very likely that the king

---

16. DRIVER & MILES, BABYLONIAN LAWS 492 (footnote omitted).

17. SAMUEL GREENGUS, *Legal and Social Institutions of Ancient Mesopotamia, in* 1 CIVILIZATIONS OF THE ANCIENT NEAR EAST, *supra* ch. 1 note 14 at 469, 473 ("The judges often held hearings and proceedings in the city temples."). DRIVER & MILES, BABYLONIAN LAWS 492.

18. DRIVER & MILES, BABYLONIAN LAWS 491.

19. *Id.* at 243–244.

20. *Id.* at 242. *See also Id.* at 244.

21. OPPENHEIM, ANCIENT MESOPOTAMIA 258. *See also* WILLIAM L. MORAN, *The Gilgamesh Epic: A Masterpiece from Ancient Mesopotamia, in* 4 CIVILIZATIONS OF THE ANCIENT NEAR EAST 2327, 2335 (Jack M. Sasson ed., 1995).

22. SAGGS, BABYLON 217. ROUX, ANCIENT IRAQ 148. (Roux gives Sargon's dates as 2334–2279 B.C.).

23. DRIVER & MILES, BABYLONIAN LAWS 490 ("The judge . . . appears to have been a member of a profession. . . .").

24. *See* Ronald A Veenker, *An Old Babylonian Legal Procedure for Appeal: Evidence from the tuppi lā ragāmim,* HEBREW UNION COLLEGE ANNUAL 5, n. 19 (1974) [hereinafter Veenker, *Procedure for Appeal*] ("*Hazannum* (elsewhere 'chief magistrate') is rarely attested in OB sources, occurring only in witness lists."). For another reference

appointed most judges, but on occasion the elders of a community must have functioned as judges as well.[25] A town's mayor may also have had a hand in judging along with the elders.[26] The fifth of Hammurabi's Laws refers to a judge as maintaining a "judgeship in the assembly" and as "sit[ting] in judgment with the [other] judges."[27] According to Driver and Miles, the Old Babylonian judges "almost invariably...sat in threes or fours"[28] and judges ordinarily heard cases as part of a college or bench.[29] Greengus states that they "presided in groups from three to six persons."[30]

Other evidence shows that scribes learned legal phrases in school in order to serve as scribes for judges, and that the judges themselves probably were chosen from these same scribal students.[31] It is likely, therefore, that ancient Mesopotamian judges were a specialized group that sat with the Assembly and gave advice and assistance regarding the technical aspects of law and legal procedure.[32] Later, the judges probably conducted legal proceedings on their own, while the Assembly merely observed.[33]

Hammurabi himself generally preferred to delegate judicial decision-making "to his local governors or to a court of law."[34] The only direct reference to a king rendering legal decisions in Hammurabi's Laws is in ¶ 129, where the king pardons an adultress's paramour in cases where the husband pardoned his wife.[35] Records from actual trials for adultery corroborate that the king could play a significant role in determining punishments

---

to a "chief justice" during the Old Babylonian period, see OPPENHEIM, ANCIENT MESOPOTAMIA 227.

25. SAMUEL GREENGUS, *Legal and Social Institutions of Ancient Mesopotamia, in* 1 CIVILIZATIONS OF THE ANCIENT NEAR EAST, *supra* ch. 1 note 14 at 469, 473 ("The persons who served as judges...were leading members of the community who knew its standards of justice; their judgment would therefore be respected and accepted by the litigating parties."). DRIVER & MILES, BABYLONIAN LAWS 492–493.

26. DRIVER & MILES, BABYLONIAN LAWS 492–493.

27. HAMMURABI ¶ 5.

28. DRIVER & MILES, BABYLONIAN LAWS 76–77.

29. *Id.* at 491 ("The judges, since they are almost always mentioned in the plural number, seem normally to have sat as a college or bench...."). *See also* SAGGS, BABYLON at 217.

30. SAMUEL GREENGUS, *Legal and Social Institutions of Ancient Mesopotamia, in* 1 CIVILIZATIONS OF THE ANCIENT NEAR EAST, *supra* ch. 1 note 14 at 469, 473.

31. *Id.* at 472; Eichler, *Literary Structure* 82.

32. SAGGS, BABYLON 217.

33. *Id.* at 218.

34. JACK. M. SASSON, *King Hammurabi of Babylon, in* 2 CIVILIZATIONS OF THE ANCIENT NEAR EAST, *supra* ch. 1 note 38, at 901, 908; DRIVER & MILES, BABYLONIAN LAWS 490.

35. *See* WESTBROOK, OLD BABYLONIAN MARRIAGE LAW 35, 75. *See also infra* § 8.4 [B].

for adultery.[36] In addition to special cases where the king himself acted as the court, it is possible that, on occasion, Old Babylonian kings "gave a decision on the point of law and remitted the case for a decision on questions of fact to the local judges or authorities."[37] Furthermore, an Old Babylonian king could remand a case completely by sending it back to the local judges.[38]

[C] Jurisdiction of Judges and Royal Jurisdiction

In the Laws of Eshnunna, judges had jurisdiction to decide cases where the amount in controversy was 20 to 60 shekels. Only the king had jurisdiction to hear capital cases.[39] In Hammurabi's Laws, a judge was not permitted to reverse his decision once judgment was rendered, a verdict given, or his sealed opinion was deposited. The penalty for doing so was to pay twelve times the amount involved in the case, and he was removed from the bench as well.[40] Presumably, this law, at least in part, was intended to curb judicial bribery.[41] Otherwise, the great law collections, like Hammurabi's "tell us next to nothing about procedure before a court or of the execution of a judgement."[42]

The traditional view is that, in the Old Babylonian period, the state began assuming more control over judicial procedure, and cases were tried "under secular authority" rather than "in temple grounds."[43] Another theory suggests that, instead of a transition from religious to secular, there was

---

36. WESTBROOK, OLD BABYLONIAN MARRIAGE LAW 75.

37. *Id.* at 2.

38. JACK. M. SASSON, *King Hammurabi of Babylon, in* 2 CIVILIZATIONS OF THE ANCIENT NEAR EAST, *supra* ch. 1 note 38, at 901, 908; WESTBROOK, OLD BABYLONIAN MARRIAGE LAW 2.

39. ESHNUNNA ¶48. *See* Good, *Capital Punishment,* 19 STAN. L. REV. 947, 972 (1967).

40. HAMMURABI ¶5. *See* DRIVER & MILES, BABYLONIAN LAWS 68–79. According to Driver & Miles, the interpretation of this provision is especially difficult, and "depends so much on the meaning of certain technical expressions." *Id.* at 68 (footnote omitted).

41. *Id.* at 69.

42. *Id.* at 220.

43. Yoffee, *Context and Authority* 104–105. *See* Ronald A. Veenker, The Old Babylonian Judiciary and Legal Procedure (unpublished Ph.D dissertation, Hebrew Union College-Jewish Institute of Religion (Cincinnati, OH 1967)) 10 [hereinafter, Veenker, Legal Procedure].("Most scholars have believed that the administration of justice was controlled by the temple, at least prior to the rule of Hammurabi. * * * [B]y the time of Hammurabi, the administration of justice was under state control." (footnote omitted)).

instead "a separation of responsibility between the civil and religious authorities."[44] Veenker points out that prior to Hammurabi there were state judges — like the "royal judge" — who appear to have been more involved with adjudication than temple judges.[45] Thus, it is perhaps more likely that the state was involved in adjudication early on, but became more controlling during the Old Babylonian period.[46] In fact, by the Old Babylonian period, Veenker concludes that "one might well question the very existence of a temple authority...."[47]

In his essay, "Legal and Social Institutions of Ancient Mesopotamia," Greengus formulates the following picture of Mesopotamian court jurisdiction:

> Local courts handled most claims dealing with movable property; this included conflicts over boundaries, sale, inheritance, and cases involving burglary or theft of property. Disputes between merchants were often handled by the *karum*, or "port authority." Situations involving loss of life or offenses meriting capital punishment would, however, be handled by royal judges and officials. These situations included homicide, treason, and adultery when the parties were caught in the act. The royal judges did not function as a court of higher appeal except when the royal court — often the king himself — was called upon to hear complaints of malfeasance on the part of officials and to order redress or restitution.[48]

As a general rule, it seems that local judges had authority to try cases involving kinship relations or cases in which the litigants were "not members of public organizations."[49] In cases involving more serious disputes, such as adultery, the state — or more specifically, the king — had jurisdiction. Yoffee summarizes Old Babylonian jurisdiction by stating: "[S]ome disputes, because of their very nature, were properly resolved under community auspices, but other disputes could not be resolved by such local authorities. In

---

44. Veenker, Legal Procedure 11 (citing the work of Cuq).

45. *Id.* at 19 ("Therefore, with regard to persons actively engaged in adjudication, if any trend is indicated, it would seem to be in favor of a state or secular jurisdiction.").

46. *Id.* at 20 ("As far as we can tell, state authority is always present and we assume it to be in control in the OB period.").

47. *Id.* at 29.

48. Samuel Greengus, *Legal and Social Institutions of Ancient Mesopotamia, in* 1 Civilizations of the Ancient Near East, *supra* ch. 1 note 14, at 469, 473.

49. Yoffee, *Context and Authority* 105.

some cases the only legitimate triadic authority that overarched the disputants would, in fact, be the state."[50]

§ 4.2 Lawsuits: Trial Procedure

The Sumerian word for lawsuit is *dīnum*.[51] We have a cuneiform record of a murder trial that took place around 1800 B.C. In it we get a vague sense of the procedure followed. The complaint was first made before the king of Isin. The king, in turn, ordered that the complaintants take up their case with the Assembly of Nippur. The Assembly then listened to the arguments, announced its verdict, and delivered the defendants over for execution.[52] We know that Hammurabi and subsequent rulers issued ordinances that established procedures for conducting lawsuits. Procedures varied, depending on the types of issues involved (*e.g.*, contracts, personal injury, homicide, etc.).[53] Although following specific procedures was important to a degree, according to Driver and Miles, "there is no record of a case in which a man was deprived of justice by a technicality or by an error made by him in procedure."[54]

There exists an interesting group of Sumerian literary texts, called disputation texts, which may shed some additional light on Mesopotamian judicial procedure. In these literary texts, two inanimate, poetic litigants argue their cases to divine judges. Each attempts to convince the tribunal that he is more useful to mankind than his opponent. For example, we have texts involving Winter against Summer, Silver against Bronze, and an Axe against a Plow. The disputants plead their cases in stylized language and form.[55] It is possible that these disputants mirror the kind of argumentation used by ancient litigants in a Sumerian trial.[56]

Some scholars have described the ancient Mesopotamian litigation procedure as a contract. According to this model, the litigants agree, as if by a contractual arrangement, to abide by the decision of the court. Thus, the "judges and court officers serv[e] as witnesses" and "[t]he decisions then

---

50. *Id.* at 106.
51. Veenker, Legal Procedure 7.
52. SAGGS, BABYLON 217 (Saggs translates the account of the case).
53. *Id.* at 199.
54. DRIVER & MILES, BABYLONIAN LAWS 53.
55. In some respects, these speeches are similar to the *controversiae* of Roman schoolboys. *See* GEORGE KENNEDY, THE ART OF RHETORIC IN THE ROMAN WORLD 314–322 (1972).
56. *See* OPPENHEIM, ANCIENT MESOPOTAMIA 275.

function as contracts in succeeding stages of a complicated litigious process."[57]

In many cases we know that parties were not permitted any opportunity to appeal decisions to a higher authority.[58] The clay tablets that record legal decisions frequently state that the parties shall not be allowed to re-open a case.[59] In fact, ordinarily at the conclusion of a lawsuit, the prevailing party received a document that recorded the judge's decision or verdict.[60] This document stated that it was a "'tablet of no complaining,' or less literally, 'document of no (further) contest.'"[61] The phrase used was *tuppi lā ragāmim*. Thus, the *tuppi lā ragāmim* served an evidentiary function, showing that the case was essentially *res judicata*—and the losing party could not initiate any further legal proceedings regarding the same matter.[62] But several court documents indicate that, under certain conditions, a party could bring a second suit, even if he lost in an initial trial.[63] A second trial was possible if new evidence was discovered[64] or if some material mistake had been made in the first trial.[65] The texts of "second trials" show that the party who lost in the first litigation in most cases lost in the second as well, and that he usually had to pay an additional fine.[66] Thus, Veenker summarizes the prospects for "appeal" in Old Babylonian law as follows:

> Although one cannot call the third stage [*i.e.,* the "second trial"] "appeal" in the manner of modern jurisprudence, it is, nevertheless,

---

57. Yoffee, *Context and Authority* 98 (citation omitted).

58. Veenker, *Procedure for Appeal* 6–7 (citing the views of commentators). *See also* SAMUEL GREENGUS, *Legal and Social Institutions of Ancient Mesopotamia, in* 1 CIVILIZATIONS OF THE ANCIENT NEAR EAST, *supra* ch. 1 note 14, at 469, 473.

59. Veenker, *Procedure for Appeal* 6. *See also* SAGGS, BABYLON 220 ("The tablet dealing with a case often specifically stipulates that the case shall not be reopened."). *See also* SAMUEL GREENGUS, *Legal and Social Institutions of Ancient Mesopotamia, in* 1 CIVILIZATIONS OF THE ANCIENT NEAR EAST, *supra* ch. 1 note 14, at 469, 474.

60. Veenker, *Procedure for Appeal* 4.

61. *Id.* at 1–15.

62. DRIVER & MILES, BABYLONIAN LAWS 74 ("It was the general practice for an unsuccessful plaintiff to swear that he would not again make the same claim, and a sworn statement to this effect was added at the end of most records."). Driver & Miles analogize this to our modern principle of *res judicata*, and remark: "The Babylonians seem to have had no such rule but to have obtained this effect by requiring a sworn promise not to sue again on the same issue...." DRIVER & MILES, BABYLONIAN LAWS 74. For more regarding the *tuppi lā ragāmim, see Id.* at 75.

63. Veenker, *Procedure for Appeal* 6–15.

64. *Id.* at 12.

65. *Id.* at 7.

66. *Id.* at 6–15.

a legitimate and distinct litigation, i.e., the plaintiff at this stage can win his case. So we see that judicial decisions could be altered and that the directives "he shall not raise further claim" were not irrevocable or absolute. Rather, one can unde[r]stand these directives to have meant, "If he raises further claim, he does so at his own risk."[67]

§ 4.3 Evidence

In ancient Mesopotamia, as in many modern trials, evidence could be a life and death matter. For example, in Hammurabi's Laws, a father-in-law received capital punishment (he was bound and cast into the water) if he had sexual relations with his-daughter-in-law *after his son had had sexual relations with her.*[68] But he merely paid 30 shekels as punishment for nearly the same offense if his son had *not* yet had sex with her.[69] Thus, in order to avoid capital punishment, a father-in-law who was accused of having had sex with his daughter-in-law would have to prove either that he had not had sex with her at all, or if he had, he would have to prove that he had done so *before* his son had had sex with her. One can imagine the tremendous obstacles to proving the chronological sequence of events in such a case!

The Mesopotamians understood the importance of concrete evidence. There is a law in Lipit-Ishtar's collection that states: "If a man rescues a child from a well, he shall [take his] feet [and seal a tablet with the size of his feet (for identification).]"[70] Texts that record lawsuits often relate that the parties introduced a number of written documents (*e.g.*, contracts) and witnesses to provide evidence at trial.[71] Some laws had the effect of discouraging lawsuits in cases where a plaintiff's evidence was weak. For example, in Lipit-Ishtar's collection one law states: "If a man, without grounds(?), accuses another man of a matter of which he has no knowledge, and that man

---

67. *Id.* at 14 (footnote omitted). *See also* Veenker, Legal Procedure 60–70.

68. Hammurabi ¶ 155. *See* Good, *Capital Punishment*, 19 Stan. L. Rev. 947, 960 (1967).

69. Hammurabi ¶ 156. *See* Westbrook, Old Babylonian Marriage Law 37; Driver & Miles, Babylonian Laws 319 (Driver & Miles express the opinion that the father, considered an adulterer, paid the money to the girl—not to her father and not to her husband).

70. Lipit-Ishtar ¶ 20.

71. Veenker, *Procedure for Appeal* 3–7. Veenker refers to such items as "first stage" procedure in Old Babylonian civil law. *Id.* at 3. *See esp. Id.* at 6, n. 23. Driver & Miles refer to Hammurabi ¶¶ 9–10 as examples of laws where witnesses were required for proof, but not oaths. Driver & Miles, Babylonian Laws 198.

does not prove it, he shall bear the penalty of the matter for which he made the accusation."[72]

In the Old Babylonian period, "the admission of verbal evidence was accompanied by the oath."[73] There were a number of circumstances in which the taking of an oath regarding a matter was considered conclusive evidence of the oath-taker's truthfulness.[74] In addition to the instances where the law collections required the use of oaths, it was also possible for the Assembly or the judges to require a party or a witness to take an oath, if the evidence was otherwise contradictory.[75] And there were, in fact, cases where a party lost his case because he refused to take an oath.[76] Through the Old Babylonian period, it was the temple that was responsible for administering oaths and conducting the Divine River Ordeal (see below) in conjunction with legal controversies.[77] The temple had the sacred objects necessary for administering oaths. Veenker summarizes this process as follows:

---

72. LIPIT-ISHTAR ¶ 17.

73. Veenker, Legal Procedure 45. *See also Id.* at 53–58 (Discussing, explaining, and distinguishing "promissory oaths" and "assertory oaths."). *See also* SAMUEL GREENGUS, *Legal and Social Institutions of Ancient Mesopotamia, in* 1 CIVILIZATIONS OF THE ANCIENT NEAR EAST, *supra* ch. 1 note 14, at 469, 473–74.

74. *See e.g.,* HAMMURABI ¶ 103 (A trading merchant was absolved from liability if he swore an oath that enemy forces made him abandon his goods); HAMMURABI ¶ 20 (If a captured slave escaped from the finder's custody, the finder was not held responsible if he swore "an oath by the god to the owner"); HAMMURABI ¶ 131 (If a husband accused his wife of adultery (but she had not been caught in the act), the wife could swear an oath to her innocence, and then, she could "return to her house"); ESHNUNNA ¶ 37 (When a bailee lost bailed goods "without evidence that the house ha[d] been broken into," the bailee had to replace the bailor's goods. But he did not have to replace bailed goods if he swore an oath that they were stolen, so long as some of his property also had been stolen along with the bailed goods.); HAMMURABI ¶ 206 (When an *awilu* injured another *awilu* in a brawl, if the person causing the damage swore an oath stating that he did not strike the other man "intentionally," he only had to pay the victim's medical expenses (but no punitive damages).). Driver & Miles cite five provisions in Hammurabi's Laws as illustrations where oaths were used as a means of proof (¶¶ 23, 120, 240, 266, 281). DRIVER & MILES, BABYLONIAN LAWS 198.

75. SAGGS, BABYLON 218 ("In actual court procedure, where there was a clash of evidence between the parties involved or between witnesses, the Assembly or the judges might order any of those concerned to take an oath at a temple.").

76. *Id.* at 219 ("Records of cases are known in which one party recoiled from the oath." Saggs translates an example involving aggravated theft). *See* DRIVER & MILES, BABYLONIAN LAWS 468 ("The oath...is always accepted as final, since the taking of a false oath is inconceivable and to refuse the oath is tantamount to admitting one's guilt or the invalidity of one's case." (footnote omitted)).

77. SAMUEL GREENGUS, *Legal and Social Institutions of Ancient Mesopotamia, in* 1 CIVILIZATIONS OF THE ANCIENT NEAR EAST, *supra* ch. 1 note 14, at 469, 473; OPPENHEIM, ANCIENT MESOPOTAMIA 187.

In cases where the court has convened in the temple, the witness appears to exonerate himself there, before (in most cases) a divine emblem; in the language of the documents he is "given for the divine oath." However, when the court has convened outside the temple, a point is made of "giving" the witness *to the temple* for the administering of the oath. It may be that the prime importance of the temple in the administration of justice was the fact that it contained the emblems whereby the witness might give deposition.[78]

Another type of evidence occasionally used in the Mesopotamian laws is the Divine River Ordeal. Saggs describes the Mesopotamian use of the Divine River Ordeal in litigation:

> When there was a clash of evidence, and neither side admitted guilt by refusing the oath by the life of the gods, the decision would then be handed over to the gods themselves. This was given, as in many other cultures, by the Ordeal. In Babylonia the Ordeal was by the river, and the rule — opposite to that found in mediaeval England — was that the guilty person sank and the innocent was saved.[79]

§ 4.4 Witnesses & Perjury

Strict penalties for perjury encouraged witnesses to tell the truth while testifying in lawsuits. As a general rule, it appears that witnesses and litigants who were found guilty of perjury were punished by imposing the penalty that would have been given the accused if *he* had been found guilty of the transgression.[80] In Hammurabi's Laws, if a witness was found guilty of perjury, he was required to pay the monetary penalty involved in the case.[81] Similarly, both the first and third provisions in Hammurabi's Laws

---

78. Veenker, Legal Procedure 22.

79. Saggs, Babylon 219 (quoting Hammurabi's provision concerning witchcraft — Hammurabi ¶ 2). *See* Tikva Simone Frymer-Kensky, The Judicial Ordeal in the Ancient Near East (unpublished Ph.D. dissertation, Yale University (New Haven, CT. 1977)) (this two-volume dissertation is a comprehensive analysis). *See also* Samuel Greengus, *Legal and Social Institutions of Ancient Mesopotamia, in* 1 Civilizations of the Ancient Near East, *supra* ch. 1 note 14, at 469, 473. Saggs, Babylon 302; Driver & Miles, Babylonian Laws 63. For more about the River Ordeal, *see Id.* at 63–65.

80. Good, *Capital Punishment*, 19 Stan. L. Rev. 947, 968 n. 100 (1967) (citing I. A. Falkenstein, Die Neusumerischen Gerichtsurkunden 130–31 (1956)).

81. Hammurabi ¶ 4.

impose capital punishment for false statements in capital cases.[82] Capital punishment was also the penalty for perjury—or at least unsubstantiated claims—in cases involving lost property.[83] The Laws of Lipit-Ishtar appear to have employed the same general principal.[84]

§ 4.5 Enforcement of Judgments

One recurring problem with many ancient judicial systems is that there was no means of enforcing judicial decisions. We are accustomed to expecting physical enforcement in modern law through government agencies like sheriffs, deputies, police, and marshals. Driver and Miles point out that a lack of "teeth" was certainly problematic during the Old Babylonian period:

> How far, if at all, the decisions of a court were enforced by public authority is not known; there was no police, no public prosecutor, and no public executioner. The duty of the judge was to find the facts of the case before him and to declare what was the law applicable, but he seems to have had no power to execute his judgement.[85]

Scholars suggest that in order to enforce judgments, the aggrieved party had to physically bring the perpetrator before the judges.[86] As a last resort, presumably, the winning party to a lawsuit would have been allowed to seize the loser's property or even the loser himself as a means of self-help "enforcement."[87] But this brand of self-help enforcement would have produced essentially the same results as the physical (*i.e.* violent) solutions that must have been in place prior to orderly judicial settlements, and thus could not have been preferred. By the Old Babylonian period, it seems likely that the decisions of judges were binding on the parties; they were not merely proposals for settlement that the parties could accept or reject.[88]

---

82. *See infra* § 8.7. *See also* Good, *Capital Punishment*, 19 STAN. L. REV. 947, 968 (1967).

83. HAMMURABI ¶¶ 11, 13. *See* Good, *Capital Punishment*, 19 STAN. L. REV. 947, 968 (1967). *See also* DRIVER & MILES, BABYLONIAN LAWS 81, 95–105.

84. LIPIT-ISHTAR ¶ 17. *See* Good, *Capital Punishment*, 19 STAN. L. REV. 947, 968 (1967).

85. DRIVER & MILES, BABYLONIAN LAWS 493.

86. *Id.* at 494 (citing HAMMURABI ¶ 127 as an illustration).

87. DRIVER & MILES, BABYLONIAN LAWS 494.

88. Veenker, *Procedure for Appeal* 4, n. 14 (citing authorities on this debate).

Substantive Law

CHAPTER 5

Personal Status

§ 5.1 Citizenship & Status in General

In his book, *Ancient Iraq*, Roux summarizes status in ancient Sumer as follows:

> [I]n Presargonic times the Sumerian society was divided into three main layers: at the bottom slaves,[1] usually recruited among prisoners of war or kidnapped in foreign countries but never very numerous; then those peasants and workers who served the temple or the palace, were maintained by them and possessed no land; and then the large group of landowners or 'freemen', which covers the whole range from artisans to members of the royal family. And above all these, of course, the ruler of the city-state....[2]

The status of the king was completely unique. According to Oppenheim: "From the point of view of Mesopotamian civilization, there was only one institution in the modern sense of the word: kingship."[3] The king was the only one capable of protecting the underprivileged. He established legal procedure. He established laws, price regulations, and interest rates. He instituted remission of debts.[4] Westbrook says that "the king was the 'father of his people' in matters of social justice, a role to which being a redeemer was eminently suitable."[5]

---

1. *See infra* §§ 5.3 and 10.6 concerning slaves.
2. Roux, Ancient Iraq 129.
3. Oppenheim, Ancient Mesopotamia 98.
4. Samuel Greengus, *Legal and Social Institutions of Ancient Mesopotamia, in* 1 Civilizations of the Ancient Near East, *supra* ch. 1 note 14 at 469, 470–71; Oppenheim, Ancient Mesopotamia 102.
5. Westbrook, *Slave and Master*, 70 Chicago-Kent L. Rev. 1631, 1652 (1995) (footnote omitted).

The law collections of both Ur-Nammu and Lipit-Ishtar appear to recognize fundamentally two social classes: freemen and slaves.[6] Hammurabi's Laws indicate that the Old Babylonian society of his day had three distinct classes:[7] 1) *awilu* ("the ordinary citizens of Mesopotamian towns"[8]); 2) *mushkenu*[9] (a difficult term to translate that probably means "some kind of military or civilian 'state dependant' who submitted to certain obligations and restrictions in return for some kind of privileges"[10]); and 3) *wardu* (slaves).[11]

We know that the Mesopotamians developed a concept of citizenship related to the process of urbanization.[12] For some reason, the native-born citizens of Nippur, Babylon, and Sippar in Babylonia and the citizens of Assur and Harran in Assyria enjoyed special privileges of free citizens. They were exempt from *corveé* work, military service, and had some degree of tax exemption as well. For the citizens of these cities, then, citizenship bestowed significant privileges.[13] This unique, privileged legal status was called *kidinnutu*.[14] In addition, the citizens of Nippur, Babylon, and Sippar also had a

---

6. S.N. Kramer and A. Falkenstein, *Ur-Nammu Law Code*, 23 ORIENTALIA 40, 42 (1954).

7. *See generally* SAMUEL GREENGUS, *Legal and Social Institutions of Ancient Mesopotamia, in* 1 CIVILIZATIONS OF THE ANCIENT NEAR EAST, *supra* ch. 1 note 14 at 469, 475–78.

8. ROUX, ANCIENT IRAQ 204. *See also* WESTBROOK, OLD BABYLONIAN MARRIAGE LAW 67 ("The term *awīlum* is generally agreed to be used in three senses in CH: (i) a man (i.e. a person in general), (ii) a free man (as opposed to a slave), (iii) a nobleman.") (footnote omitted). *See also* SAMUEL GREENGUS, *Legal and Social Institutions of Ancient Mesopotamia, in* 1 CIVILIZATIONS OF THE ANCIENT NEAR EAST, *supra* ch. 1 note 14 at 469, 475–76.

9. *See* SAMUEL GREENGUS, *Legal and Social Institutions of Ancient Mesopotamia, in* 1 CIVILIZATIONS OF THE ANCIENT NEAR EAST, *supra* ch. 1 note 14 at 469, 476–77.

10. ROUX, ANCIENT IRAQ 191 (footnote omitted). *See* S.N. Kramer and A. Falkenstein, *Ur-Nammu Law Code*, 23 ORIENTALIA 40, 42 (1954). (Kramer and Falkenstein note that neither Ur-Nammu's law collection nor the collection of Lipit-Ishtar had a "social grouping corresponding to the *muškēnum* of the Hammurabi Code. (footnote incorporated))." For more on the social status of the *mushkenum, see* DRIVER & MILES, BABYLONIAN LAWS 93–95. According to Driver & Miles, for example, some documents show *mushkenu* owning land and houses, and making valid marriage contracts. DRIVER & MILES, BABYLONIAN LAWS 95. *See also* ROTH, LAW COLLECTIONS 14, 24, 36, 43, 46, 58, 72–73 (explaining the various social classes in the law collections).

11. SAMUEL GREENGUS, *Legal and Social Institutions of Ancient Mesopotamia, in* 1 CIVILIZATIONS OF THE ANCIENT NEAR EAST, *supra* ch. 1 note 14 at 469, 476–77; ROUX, ANCIENT IRAQ 191.

12. OPPENHEIM, ANCIENT MESOPOTAMIA 120. *See also generally* ELIZABETH C. STONE, *The Development of Cities in Ancient Mesopotamia, in* 1 CIVILIZATIONS OF THE ANCIENT NEAR EAST 235, 235–248 (Jack M. Sasson ed., 1995).

13. OPPENHEIM, ANCIENT MESOPOTAMIA 120–123.

14. *Id.* at 121.

privilege relating to lawsuits: the king was not permitted to fine them or imprison them, furthermore, he could not dismiss their legal claims. They also were exempt from taxes on their flocks.[15] In most ancient Mesopotamian towns, it is likely that all male citizens were members of the Assembly in its earliest stages, with the elders playing the most important roles.[16]

According to Westbrook, "[f]oreigners in the ancient Near East were in a precarious position. They had no legal rights outside of their own country or ethnic group unless they fell under the local rulers' protection."[17] But apparently non-citizens were permitted to have limited access to most Mesopotamian cities. Merchants, diplomats, and foreigners seeking political asylum could enter a city if they had royal permission. There is also evidence that, to a limited degree, non-citizens could actually reside in harbor areas (technically outside of the city).[18] A text from Ugarit mentions non-citizens in Carchemish who were allowed to live within the city gates. There was a certain area in the city called the *bit ub(a)ri* where foreign visitors and merchants could reside.[19]

Old Babylonian omen texts suggest that there was a significant degree of economic mobility. In these texts, the poor yearn for wealth but the wealthy fear they might lose their wealth and become poverty stricken.[20] For the most part, wealth determined status in ancient Mesopotamia. On the large estates, either slaves or serfs (people whose freedom was greatly restricted) did most of the manual labor. Some prisoners of war became slaves and, when famine struck, many poor citizens became serfs on landed estates just to survive.[21]

§ 5.2 Women

Women seem to have enjoyed more liberty and social status when Sumerian city-states were in their earliest stages of development than in some subsequent periods.[22] At the dawn of Sumerian civilization, women, for example, served temples in a variety of ways. They could receive grants of rations and allotments, and they could also serve as priestesses or, per-

---

15. *Id. See also Id.* at 103–104.
16. *Id.* at 111–112.
17. Westbrook, *Slave and Master*, 70 CHICAGO-KENT L. REV. 1631, 1639 (1995).
18. OPPENHEIM, ANCIENT MESOPOTAMIA 78.
19. *Id.*
20. *Id.* at 87.
21. *Id.* at 96.
22. SAGGS, BABYLON 187.

haps, temple prostitutes.[23] The priestesses "were drawn from all classes, from the king's daughter to the daughter of the humblest free man."[24] Importantly, it appears that they also participated in the general Assembly of all citizens.[25] Some Assyriologists even believe that early Sumerian women were permitted to have more than one husband at a time, but recent scholarship suggests that polyandry was unlikely.[26]

Later, by the time of the society depicted in the *Epic of Gilgamesh*,[27] it seems that women were no longer entitled to take part in the deliberations of the Assembly.[28] In Hammurabi's day (c. 1750 B.C.), a woman could enter into a binding agreement with her husband that his creditors would not be permitted to take her as a "debt-hostage."[29] Women could also own and sell property.[30] And women could serve as scribes.[31] Still, it is apparent that there was a certain degree of bias against women in Mesopotamian law and that "women and men stand differently in their interactions with the law."[32]

---

23. Marten Stol, *Private Life in Ancient Mesopotamia, in* 1 Civilizations of the Ancient Near East 485, 490–91, 493 (Jack M. Sasson ed., 1995); Saggs, Babylon 186. Regarding Hammurabi's Laws, Driver & Miles remark: "In the Laws there is nothing definite to show whether the various priestesses named in them were temple-prostitutes, but there can be little doubt that sacral prostitution existed in connexion with the temples...." Driver & Miles, Babylonian Laws 360. For a general overview of the different kinds of priestesses in Old Babylonian society, *see Id.* at 358–371.

24. Driver & Miles, Babylonian Laws 358.

25. Saggs, Babylon 37. *See also* Roux, Ancient Iraq 108–109 (explaining Jacobsen's theory of a "primitive democracy").

26. Saggs, Babylon 187 (stating that polyandry may have been practiced); Cooper, Royal Hymns at 70 ff. n. 8 (maintaining that the ancient Mesopotamians did not practice polyandry). *See also supra* ch. 2, note 25.

27. Gilgamesh was the legendary ruler of Uruk around 2600 B.C. *See* Dominique Charpin, *The History of Ancient Mesopotamia: An Overview, in* 2 Civilizations of the Ancient Near East, *supra* ch. 1 note 23 at 807, 809. *See* Nels Bailkey, *Early Mesopotamian Constitutional Development*, 72 American Hist. Rev. 1211, 1217 (1967).

28. Saggs, Babylon 39 (In the Epic of Gilgamesh, Gilgamesh "called together a general assembly of all male citizens (females no longer participated)....").

29. Hammurabi ¶ 151. *See* Driver & Miles, Babylonian Laws 230–233; Westbrook, Old Babylonian Marriage Law 50–51.

30. Hammurabi ¶¶ 39–40; Marten Stol, *Private Life in Ancient Mesopotamia, in* 1 Civilizations of the Ancient Near East, *supra* ch. 5 note 23, at 485, 490; Samuel Greengus, *Legal and Social Institutions of Ancient Mesopotamia, in* 1 Civilizations of the Ancient Near East, *supra* ch. 1 note 14 at 469, 479; Ellickson & Thorland, *Ancient Land Law*, 71 Chicago-Kent L. Rev. 321, 367 (1995).

31. Laurie E. Pearce, *The Scribes and Scholars of Ancient Mesopotamia, in* 4 Civilizations of the Ancient Near East 2265, 2266 (Jack M. Sasson ed., 1995); Marten Stol, *Private Life in Ancient Mesopotamia, in* 1 Civilizations of the Ancient Near East, *supra* ch. 5 note 23, at 485, 492; Saggs, Babylon 188.

32. Martha T. Roth, *Gender and Law: A Case Study From Ancient Mesopotamia, in* Gender and Law in the Hebrew Bible and the Ancient Near East, *supra* ch. 1

Regarding temple-women in general, Saggs states: "A great part of our knowledge of them comes from the laws of Hammurabi, and it has been suggested that the frequent mention in these laws of classes of temple-women indicates that they were in danger of becoming a depressed class, for whose protection Hammurabi, with his avowed purpose of succouring the weak, found it necessary to legislate."[33]

§ 5.3 Slaves[34]

It appears that there were basically three broad categories of slaves in ancient Mesopotamia: 1) debt-slaves (who owed their status to debt[35]); 2) chattel-slaves (who owed their status to birth, conquest,[36] or purchase); and 3) famine-slaves (who voluntarily entered servitude during periods of severe food shortage).[37] During the pinnacle of Sumerian culture, female slaves outnumbered male. Their owners used them primarily for spinning and weaving.[38] Saggs maintains that their owners also used them for sex,[39] but there is little actual evidence to support such a claim.

---

note 20 at 173, 183 (Victor H. Matthews, Bernard M. Levinson and Tikva Frymer-Kensky eds., 1997).

33. SAGGS, BABYLON 350. Of course "legislate" is an inaccurate term to describe the nature of Hammurabi's Laws. *See supra* §§ 2.1, 2.6.

34. Part of the discussion of slaves is included in the section on Status because some laws relate to slaves in terms of status. But much of the discussion about slaves is included in the section on Property law (*i.e., infra* § 10.6) because the majority of laws regarding slaves relate to them as property rather than as persons with a distinct status. *See* Good, 19 STAN. L. REV. 947, 962 (1967) ("With legislation relating to slaves we are perhaps closer to the law of property than to the law of persons. A slave was property....").

35. SAMUEL GREENGUS, *Legal and Social Institutions of Ancient Mesopotamia, in* 1 CIVILIZATIONS OF THE ANCIENT NEAR EAST, *supra* ch. 1 note 14 at 469, 477–78.

36. Westbrook, *Slave and Master*, 70 CHICAGO-KENT L. REV. 1631, 1641 (1995) (Westbrook notes: "Although war might be expected to be a prime source of slavery, there is very little mention of slaves from this source."). *See* SAMUEL GREENGUS, *Legal and Social Institutions of Ancient Mesopotamia, in* 1 CIVILIZATIONS OF THE ANCIENT NEAR EAST, *supra* ch. 1 note 14 at 469, 477.

37. Westbrook, *Slave and Master*, 70 CHICAGO-KENT L. REV. 1631, 1639, 1654–1656 (1995).

38. *See* SAMUEL GREENGUS, *Legal and Social Institutions of Ancient Mesopotamia, in* 1 CIVILIZATIONS OF THE ANCIENT NEAR EAST, *supra* ch. 1 note 14 at 469, 477; JOHN F. ROBERTSON, *The Social and Economic Organization of Ancient Mesopotamian Temples, in* 1 CIVILIZATIONS OF THE ANCIENT NEAR EAST 443, 445 (Jack M. Sasson ed., 1995); SAGGS, BABYLON 170; OPPENHEIM, ANCIENT MESOPOTAMIA 75.

39. SAGGS, BABYLON 170.

In the Early Dynastic period (c. 2900–2350 B.C.),[40] there were very few slaves, and those who were in Mesopotamia were mostly prisoners of war.[41] Extant documents from that time suggest that temples and the palace owned most of the slaves, and they lived in barracks. It was later that private individuals began owning slaves.[42] By the Third Dynasty of Ur (c. 2112–2004 B.C.),[43] it had become possible for free citizens to be enslaved either by being seized by their creditors or by being sold by their parents.[44] In Hammurabi's day, the majority of slaves were purchased abroad (*i.e.*, not captives of war).[45] A number of people entered slavery as a consequence of famine as well.[46] We also know that some persons could become slaves as a result of breach of contract.[47] For example, we have a marriage contract that punished the breaching wife with slavery, and a labor contract that invoked the same penalty for a worker who failed to perform his tasks according to his agreement.[48] If a slave owner accepted payment in an amount worth twice the value of his slave, that slave could legally gain his freedom.[49] A certain type of slave, called a *miqtu*, could not be sold if the *miqtu* had been given as a gift by the king.[50] Later, in the Neo-Babylonian period (612–539 B.C.),[51] it was possible for a slave to work independently, merely being obligated to pay his master a monthly fee.[52]

---

40. DOMINIQUE CHARPIN, *The History of Ancient Mesopotamia: An Overview, in* 2 CIVILIZATIONS OF THE ANCIENT NEAR EAST, *supra* ch. 1 note 23, at 807, 808.

41. SAGGS, BABYLON 169. *See* Westbrook, *Slave and Master*, 70 CHICAGO-KENT L. REV. 1631, 1640–41 (1995).

42. SAGGS, BABYLON 170.

43. DOMINIQUE CHARPIN, *The History of Ancient Mesopotamia: An Overview, in* 2 CIVILIZATIONS OF THE ANCIENT NEAR EAST, *supra* ch. 1 note 23, at 807, 808.

44. SAMUEL GREENGUS, *Legal and Social Institutions of Ancient Mesopotamia, in* 1 CIVILIZATIONS OF THE ANCIENT NEAR EAST, *supra* ch. 1 note 14 at 469, 477–78; SAGGS, BABYLON 169.

45. SAGGS, BABYLON 170. *See also* ROUX, ANCIENT IRAQ 191–92.

46. Westbrook, *Slave and Master*, 70 CHICAGO-KENT L. REV. 1631, 1639, 1645–46 (1995).

47. *Id.* at 1647.

48. *Id.*

49. LIPIT-ISHTAR ¶ 14 ("If a man's slave contests his slave status against his master, and it is proven that his master has been compensated for his slavery two-fold, that slave shall be freed.").

50. LIPIT-ISHTAR ¶ 15 ("If a *miqtu*-person is a gift of the king, he will not be appropriated.").

51. DOMINIQUE CHARPIN, *The History of Ancient Mesopotamia: An Overview, in* 2 CIVILIZATIONS OF THE ANCIENT NEAR EAST, supra ch. 1 note 23, at 807, 819, 826.

52. SAMUEL GREENGUS, *Legal and Social Institutions of Ancient Mesopotamia, in* 1 CIVILIZATIONS OF THE ANCIENT NEAR EAST, *supra* ch. 1 note 14 at 469, 477; OPPENHEIM, ANCIENT MESOPOTAMIA 76.

Hammurabi's Laws actually provide very little information regarding the status of slaves.[53] Slavery was a status subject to change. We know that a slave could marry a free woman,[54] but we know very little about the legal status of a free-woman and slave-male marriage.[55] And we can only surmise that the slave's master must have assented to a marriage of this type.[56] A slave could own property[57] and, in some instances, buy his own freedom with property that he had acquired. When a slave died, his master inherited the slave's property.[58] Slaves typically referred to their masters by the term *lugal* (literally "great man"), the same word used for "king."[59]

There seems to have been a meaningful difference between slaves owned privately in the home *versus* slaves owned by either the palace or temple.[60] According to Westbrook, "In Old Babylonian slave sales it was occasionally noted that a slave is 'house-born' (*wilid bitim*)."[61]

It seems likely that certain formalities had to be observed when a chattel-slave was manumitted in order for the transaction to be valid.[62] There is a reference in a document relating to manumission that the tablet itself was "kilnfired."[63] There are also references to smashing a pot and "clearing a man's forehead."[64] We hear of executing a certain document pertaining to manumission as well.[65] Driver and Miles explain that a religious ceremony—"cleansing of the brow"—was necessary both ritualistically and legally in order to validly manumit a slave,[66] but many details are still un-

---

53. DRIVER & MILES, BABYLONIAN LAWS 221 ("There is at the end of them a short group of sections setting out certain rules affecting the sale of slaves, and there are six sections which deal with fugitive slaves. The other references are incidental...." (footnotes omitted)). For a general summary of slavery in Hammurabi's Babylon, *see* DRIVER & MILES, BABYLONIAN LAWS 221–230.

54. WESTBROOK, OLD BABYLONIAN MARRIAGE LAW 66; SAGGS, BABYLON 170. *See* HAMMURABI ¶ 175. *See also* DRIVER & MILES, BABYLONIAN LAWS 354.

55. DRIVER & MILES, BABYLONIAN LAWS 354.

56. *Id.* at 355.

57. SAMUEL GREENGUS, *Legal and Social Institutions of Ancient Mesopotamia, in* 1 CIVILIZATIONS OF THE ANCIENT NEAR EAST, *supra* ch. 1 note 14 at 469, 477.

58. SAGGS, BABYLON 170.

59. *Id.* at 360.

60. DRIVER & MILES, BABYLONIAN LAWS 222.

61. Westbrook, *Slave and Master*, 70 CHICAGO-KENT L. REV. 1631, 1643 (1995) (footnote omitted).

62. SLHF (ii 4–6). *See also* SAGGS, BABYLON 63.

63. SAGGS, BABYLON 63.

64. SLHF (ii 7–9); SAMUEL GREENGUS, *Legal and Social Institutions of Ancient Mesopotamia, in* 1 CIVILIZATIONS OF THE ANCIENT NEAR EAST, *supra* ch. 1 note 14 at 469, 475.

65. SLHF (ii-10–13).

66. DRIVER & MILES, BABYLONIAN LAWS 225–230.

certain. We do not know, for example, whether some type of court order was needed, or whether a simple declaration of freedom by the slave's master was all that was necessary to finalize manumission. There is documentary evidence that suggests that the "cleansing of the brow" was not the final step. One text asserts that, *after* the "cleansing of the brow," a slave girl paid her mistress 10 shekels.[67]

It is likely that many slaves who were given their freedom were manumitted by a reciprocal agreement—the master agreeing to give the slave his freedom in return for the slave's promise to care for his master in old age.[68] In Hammurabi's Laws, "a master's slave-concubine and his issue by her were to be freed automatically upon his death."[69] A master could also manumit his slave by a contract of adoption.[70] For debt-slaves, manumission was possible through redemption—paying back the debt,[71] or, according to Hammurabi's Laws, a court might order release after three years.[72] Kings also could use their discretion and release debt-slaves either as a result of individual petitions[73] or by *misharum*.[74] Famine-slaves could gain their freedom by redemption too (probably stipulated in their contract).[75] Apparently, however, once manumitted, a former chattel-slave's status was

---

67. *Id.* at 229.

68. Westbrook, *Slave and Master*, 70 CHICAGO-KENT L. REV. 1631, 1648 (1995).

69. *Id.* at 1649. HAMMURABI ¶171.

70. Westbrook, *Slave and Master*, 70 CHICAGO-KENT L. REV. 1631, 1649–50 (1995); SAMUEL GREENGUS, *Legal and Social Institutions of Ancient Mesopotamia, in* 1 CIVILIZATIONS OF THE ANCIENT NEAR EAST, *supra* ch. 1 note 14 at 469, 477.

71. Westbrook, *Slave and Master*, 70 CHICAGO-KENT L. REV. 1631, 1651–53, 1675 (1995).

72. SAMUEL GREENGUS, *Legal and Social Institutions of Ancient Mesopotamia, in* 1 CIVILIZATIONS OF THE ANCIENT NEAR EAST, *supra* ch. 1 note 14 at 469, 477–78; Westbrook, *Slave and Master*, 70 CHICAGO-KENT L. REV. 1631, 1656 (1995) (citing HAMMURABI ¶117); RAYMOND WESTBROOK, *Social Justice in the Ancient Near East, in* SOCIAL JUSTICE IN THE ANCIENT WORLD 154.

73. Westbrook, *Slave and Master*, 70 CHICAGO-KENT L. REV. 1631, 1657 (1995) ("There is copious evidence of the king's exercise of this equitable role in individual cases, usually in response to petitions. We suspect, therefore, that the above limits on the length of debt-slavery represent criteria that the king might have applied in exercising his discretion in response to an individual petition." (footnote omitted)).

74. SAMUEL GREENGUS, *Legal and Social Institutions of Ancient Mesopotamia, in* 1 CIVILIZATIONS OF THE ANCIENT NEAR EAST, *supra* ch. 1 note 14 at 469, 478; Westbrook, *Slave and Master*, 70 CHICAGO-KENT L. REV. 1631, 1657–1660, 1675 (1995).

75. Westbrook, *Slave and Master*, 70 CHICAGO-KENT L. REV. 1631, 1655 (1995) ("In famine-slavery it appears that a person saved from famine had an underlying right to redeem himself from his benefactor's service. The terms of the right of redemption could be determined by contract."). *See also Id.* at 1675.

ambiguous. A manumitted chattel-slave in ancient Mesopotamia clearly did not enjoy the status of a free citizen.[76]

The Laws of Eshnunna contain a number of sections dealing with situations where a slave woman attempted—illegally—to find a way for her child to be raised as a free citizen. When a slave woman gave her child to an *awilu* woman to raise (apparently hoping to have her child grow up a free person), if the slave-mother's owner later discovered the child, even after the child had grown into adulthood, the owner was entitled to take the slave back as his property.[77] Similarly, when a palace slave gave her child "to a commoner (*mushkenum*) for rearing," the palace was entitled to reclaim the child.[78] But if someone actually "adopted" a "child of a slave woman of the palace" (perhaps this means instead of merely taking informal custody), then the adopter was required to give a slave of equal value to the palace in return.[79] In his article, "Literary Structure in the Laws of Eshnunna," B.I. Eichler presents a cogent analysis of these provisions:

> The legal statement made by both cases is that this special relationship created by sustaining and rearing a child does not take hold when the reception of the child was unlawful; even after the child has grown (i.e., is fully reared), the owner may claim him. Hence neither the daughter of the *mushkenum* nor the daughter of the freeman can claim any rights to this child. Furthermore, the daughter of the *mushkenum* is fined for taking part in this illegal act by having to return the child and deliver yet another, while the daughter of the freeman who had been duped must relinquish the child but without further penalty.[80]

Slaves were given a certain degree of freedom. For example, slaves were allowed to marry each other. There is a rather ambiguous Ur-Nammu law that addresses the status of a female slave when her husband later gains his freedom.[81] When a male slave married "a native woman [perhaps this means "free"]," the man was required to give his master one male child, but all other children were considered free.[82] When a male slave married an *awilu* woman, and she then bore children, the slave's owner was not enti-

---

76. DRIVER & MILES, BABYLONIAN LAWS 228–229.
77. ESHNUNNA ¶ 33.
78. ESHNUNNA ¶ 34.
79. ESHNUNNA ¶ 35.
80. Eichler, *Literary Structure* 79–80.
81. UR-NAMMU ¶ 4.
82. UR-NAMMU ¶ 5.

tled to take the children as slaves.[83] Children of concubines were considered slaves also unless the master acknowledged them as his legitimate off-spring.[84] Another example of a kind of quasi freedom afforded to slaves appears in the documents of the land owner, Balmunamhe. Apparently, during the winter months when grain prices were high and the need for agricultural labor ebbed, Balmunamhe occasionally released slaves to a third party (ordinarily a relative) for a kind of "furlough."[85]

The Laws of Eshnunna prohibited slaves from buying anything from either merchants or woman inkeepers.[86] Under certain circumstances, the Laws of Eshnunna required slaves "to bear fetters, shackles, or a slave hair-lock" to identify them as slaves.[87] A slave who bore fetters, shackles, or a slave hairlock was not permitted to "exit through the main city-gate of Eshnunna without his owner."[88] Hammurabi's Laws prohibited a barber from intentionally "shav[ing] off the slave-hairlock of a slave [*i.e.*, a slave not belonging to him] without the consent of the slave's owner."[89] The law pun-

---

83. According to Hammurabi's Laws, the owner in this circumstance: "will have no claims of slavery against the children...." Hammurabi ¶ 175.

84. Samuel Greengus, *Legal and Social Institutions of Ancient Mesopotamia, in* 1 Civilizations of the Ancient Near East, *supra* ch. 1 note 14 at 469, 477 ("Such offspring were slaves too, but here again, they could be freed or even adopted by their owners."); Saggs, Babylon 185.

85. Westbrook, *Slave and Master,* 70 Chicago-Kent L. Rev. 1631, 1669 (1995). *See* Samuel Greengus, *Legal and Social Institutions of Ancient Near East, in* 1 Civilizations of the Ancient Near East, *supra* ch. 1 note 14 at 469, 477.

86. Eshnunna ¶ 15 ("A merchant or a woman innkeeper will not accept silver, grain, wool, oil, or anything else from a male or female slave."). *See also* Finkelstein, *Ammisaduqa's Edict,* 15 J. Cuneiform Stud. 91, 99 (1961).

87. Eshnunna ¶ 52. *See* Samuel Greengus, *Legal and Social Institutions of Ancient Mesopotamia, in* 1 Civilizations of the Ancient Near East, *supra* ch. 1 note 14 at 469, 477 ("Slaves were marked either by tonsure or more permanently by tatoos or brands in order to distinguish them from free persons. * * * Unruly slaves could be encumbered by fetters...."); Saggs, Babylon 185 ("Slaves had a characteristic kind of tonsure, as did also priests and, apparently, doctors."); Oppenheim, Ancient Mesopotamia 75 ("The marking of slaves was rare in earlier periods—with the exception of slaves who were habitual runaways—but they seem to have had a characteristic hairdo. In certain regions, moreover, slaves outside their master's home had to wear fetters as a sign of bondage."). *See* Westbrook, *Slave and Master,* 70 Chicago-Kent L. Rev. 1631, 1667 (1995) ("[I]n Old Babylonian the *abbutum*...was the mark or tatoo applied to a slave's shaven head.... [B]y no means were all chattel-slaves so marked. It appears to have been used where the status or owner of the slave might be called into question, or where the slave was likely to run away.").

88. Eshnunna ¶ 51. *See* Westbrook, *Slave and Master,* 70 Chicago-Kent L. Rev. 1631, 1671 (1995).

89. Hammurabi ¶ 226. *See* Driver & Miles, Babylonian Laws 421–422; Westbrook, *Slave and Master,* 70 Chicago-Kent L. Rev. 1631, 1671 (1995).

ished the guilty barber by amputation of his hand (so that he could not re-
peat the offense).[90] If, however, someone deceived the barber, and induced
him under false pretenses to shave off a slave's slave-hairlock, the barber
was exonerated if he swore that he did not know that the person who deceived him was not the slave's owner.[91] In this case, the person who deceived the barber was executed and hanged "in his own doorway."[92]

---

90. Hammurabi ¶ 226. *See* Westbrook, *Slave and Master,* 70 Chicago-Kent L.
Rev. 1631, 1671 (1995).

91. Hammurabi ¶ 227. *See* Driver & Miles, Babylonian Laws 421–422; Westbrook, *Slave and Master,* 70 Chicago-Kent L. Rev. 1631, 1671 (1995).

92. Hammurabi ¶ 227. *See also* Westbrook, *Slave and Master,* 70 Chicago-Kent
L. Rev. 1631, 1671 (1995); Good, *Capital Punishment,* 19 Stan. L. Rev. 947, 962
(1967). Compare Hammurabi ¶ 21 (guilty defendant hanged in doorway) and Hammurabi ¶ 153 (adultress who has her husband killed is impaled). Driver & Miles conclude that the criminal barber was impaled and not buried. Driver & Miles, Babylonian Laws 424.

CHAPTER 6

The Family

§ 6.1 Introduction

As a general rule, the Mesopotamian family unit was relatively small.[1] The father was the head of the family and exercised significant control over his wife and children.[2] In the Old Babylonian period, it was possible for a man to have a primary wife and a secondary wife. Apparently, however, one wife was the norm and economic reality throughout most of Mesopotamian history.[3]

The ancient Mesopotamians used contracts to regulate many aspects of family law. We have cuneiform marriage contracts, adoption contracts, and divorce settlements. From the Old Babylonian period, we even have contracts for the nursing and upbringing of children.[4]

---

1. MARTEN STOL, *Private Life in Ancient Mesopotamia, in* 1 CIVILIZATIONS OF THE ANCIENT NEAR EAST, *supra* ch. 5 note 23, at 485, 488 ("The number of children surviving early childhood (the initial number born is unknown) was not high: the mean was two to four."); OPPENHEIM, ANCIENT MESOPOTAMIA 77.

2. SAMUEL GREENGUS, *Legal and Social Institutions of Ancient Mesopotamia, in* 1 CIVILIZATIONS OF THE ANCIENT NEAR EAST, *supra* ch. 1 note 14 at 469, 478; Ellickson & Thorland, *Ancient Land Law,* 71 CHICAGO-KENT L. REV. 321, 355–357 (1995). *See also* RAYMOND WESTBROOK, *Social Justice in the Ancient Near East, in* SOCIAL JUSTICE IN THE ANCIENT WORLD 149 (K.D. Irani and Morris Silver eds., 1995) ("The basic unit was the household, headed by a *paterfamilias* and containing wives, children, and slaves as subordinate members.").

3. MARTEN STOL, *Private Life in Ancient Mesopotamia, in* 1 CIVILIZATIONS OF THE ANCIENT NEAR EAST, *supra* ch. 5 note 23, at 485, 488, 489 ("The Babylonian and Assyrian man was monogamous in principle, but he was allowed to take a second wife if the first, the 'chosen,' did not bear children."); OPPENHEIM, ANCIENT MESOPOTAMIA 77.

4. OPPENHEIM, ANCIENT MESOPOTAMIA 283.

§6.2 Marriage

[A] Entering and Maintaining Marriage[5]

There is an obscure law from a Sumerian student text (*c.* 1800 B.C.) that seems to permit a man to marry a girl if: 1) he had sexual relations with her; and 2) he had not been identified by the girl's parents; and 3) he had declared that he would marry the girl.[6] Otherwise, most evidence suggests that the ancient Mesopotamians observed formalities, customs, ceremonies, and various legal requirements as antecedent to a valid marriage. The Old Babylonian term for husband was *mutum* and the term for wife was *aššatum*.[7] Contemporary documents, the Laws of Eshnunna, and Hammurabi's Laws used the verb *ahāzum* to express the concept "to take for marriage" or "to marry."[8] A couple was not legally considered husband and wife if the man had failed to obtain the consent of the bride's parents and also had failed to observe the nuptial feast.[9] This was the case even if they had lived together for as much as an entire year.[10] Many scholars have argued that Hammurabi's Laws required a contract (*riksātum*) of marriage in order for a marriage to be considered valid.[11] But Westbrook maintains that although "the contract is a necessary precondition to the marriage... [it] is nonetheless separate from it. Marriage, valid or no, is conceivable

---

5. For a general summary of the process of marriage formation, *see* DRIVER & MILES, BABYLONIAN LAWS 262–263.

6. SLEX ¶ 7' ("If he deflowers in the street the daughter of a man, her father and her mother do not identify(?) him, (but) he declares 'I will marry you'—her father and her mother shall give her to him in marriage."). Roth admits that this is a very difficult provision and notes that her translation is considerably different from previous attempts. ROTH, LAW COLLECTIONS 45, n.4.

7. WESTBROOK, OLD BABYLONIAN MARRIAGE LAW 18.

8. *Id.* at 10–16.

9. ESHNUNNA ¶ 27. *See* WESTBROOK, OLD BABYLONIAN MARRIAGE LAW 29–33, 62; DRIVER & MILES, BABYLONIAN LAWS 8; Finkelstein, *Sex Offenses in Sumerian Laws*, 86 J. OF THE AMERICAN ORIENTAL SOC. 355, 369 (1966).

10. ESHNUNNA ¶ 27-33. *See* WESTBROOK, OLD BABYLONIAN MARRIAGE LAW 29; DRIVER & MILES, BABYLONIAN LAWS 8; Finkelstein, *Sex Offenses in Sumerian Laws*, 86 J. OF THE AMERICAN ORIENTAL SOC. 355, 369 (1966).

11. HAMMURABI ¶ 128. Driver & Miles state that this contract is a "contract of marriage" (citing the work of Koschaker). DRIVER & MILES, BABYLONIAN LAWS 245. They say that the main verb in this provision refers to consummation of marriage, but that it means cohabitation and more than merely a sexual relationship. DRIVER & MILES, BABYLONIAN LAWS 246. *But see* WESTBROOK, OLD BABYLONIAN MARRIAGE LAW 61.

apart from the contract."[12] In any case, it seems quite clear that *riksātum* in this context does not mean a *written* contract but rather an "agreement" of the parties (*i.e.,* ordinarily the parents[13]) in a more abstract sense.[14]

In written marriage documents, the parties set forth summaries of the extensive negotiations that detailed the exchange of "gifts" and the *terhatum* (payment).[15] Such documents, apparently, "record important transactions which could affect the status and rights of husbands or wives" but were not intended as records or "contracts" of marriage.[16] Both husband and wife were responsible for debts incurred after the wife "enters the man's house."[17]

---

12. Westbrook, Old Babylonian Marriage Law 31.

13. *Id.* ("It is therefore with the parents that the contract must be made before a valid marriage can take place."). *See also* Marten Stol, *Private Life in Ancient Mesopotamia, in* 1 Civilizations of the Ancient Near East, *supra* ch. 5 note 23, at 485, 488.

14. Samuel Greengus, *The Old Babylonian Marriage Contract,* 89 J. of the American Oriental Soc. 505–514 (1969). Greengus persuasively argues this point. *See Id.* at 506 ("In legal contexts one may reasonably translate *riksātum* as "binding agreement, pact, covenant," or in a broad sense "contract;' but *prima facie* there is nothing in the terms *riksātum* or *rakāsum* to indicate a written document." (footnote omitted)), *Id.* at 508 ("[T]his term never denotes a written document in the Old Babylonian period."), 510 ("In all these documents the term *riksātum* need not refer to written documents and can be well translated as agreements or contracts in the abstract sense."), *Id.* at 513 ("It is therefore our conclusion that CE §§ 27–28 and CH § 128 do not state a need for written marriage documents; rather *riksātum šakānum* denotes the making of a contract, agreement, or pact which did not have to be in writing in order to have legal validity."). According to Driver & Miles, this law does not mean that a marriage without a contract is null and void, but rather that the woman does not acquire the special rights and liabilities of a distinct kind of wife—an *aššat awīlum*—unless her husband gives her a contract (*riksātum*). Driver & Miles, Babylonian Laws 247. *But see* Westbrook, Old Babylonian Marriage Law 13 (characterizing Driver & Miles's conclusion as "untenable"). *See also* Driver & Miles, Babylonian Laws 249 ("[T]he *riksātum* proves that a lawful marriage has taken place, while the bringing and accepting of the various gifts by the parties concerned effect an inchoate marriage which the *copula carnalis* completes.").

15. *See infra* ch. 6 note 23 and accompanying text. *See also* JJ. Finkelstein, *The Laws of Ur-Nammu,* 22 J. of Cuneiform Stud. 66, 75, n. 5 (1969). Driver & Miles describe these as the *biblum* ("betrothal gift") and *tirhâtum* ("bridal gift"). Driver & Miles, Babylonian Laws 249–250. Later in their text, Driver & Miles expand upon their definition of *tirhâtum,* suggesting "that its meaning is a marriage gift or a gift given to secure a marriage with a view to procreation...." Driver & Miles, Babylonian Laws 264. For amplification and clarification of these terms, *see* Roth, Law Collections 270–71 (definition of "marriage prestations" in the *glossary*).

16. Greengus, *The Old Babylonian Marriage Contract,* 89 J. of the American Oriental Soc. 505, 512 (1969).

17. Hammurabi ¶ 152. *See* Driver & Miles, Babylonian Laws 230–233.

The girl, usually in her teens,[18] was ordinarily not a party to the marriage contract. Usually her father fashioned the agreement on her behalf.[19] If a father died before his daughter married, the girl's brothers inherited the obligation to "give her in marriage."[20] Contemporary marriage documents show that it was ordinarily the would-be groom who approached the father of the girl whom he wished to marry. He then gave the marriage gifts and payment to the girl's father.[21]

The two most prominent marriage gifts were called the *biblum* and the *terhatum*. The *biblum* probably was comprised of provisions for the marriage feast or "a gift made by the groom's party to the bride's party on the occasion of marriage."[22] The *terhatum* appears to have been a sum that the groom brought to the bride's father which gave the groom "the right to claim the bride in marriage."[23] Technically, once the *biblum* and *terhatum* had been brought to the girl's father, Old Babylonian law considered the marriage "inchoate," and it could then be "completed by the delivery of the

---

18. MARTEN STOL, *Private Life in Ancient Mesopotamia, in* 1 CIVILIZATIONS OF THE ANCIENT NEAR EAST, *supra* ch. 5 note 23, at 485, 488.

19. *Id.*; DRIVER & MILES, BABYLONIAN LAWS 248. Greengus provides the following summary regarding contemporary documents from the Ur III period: "The Ur III marriage agreements are promissory statements…most typically uttered by the father of the groom to the father of the bride; in some cases, the groom's mother spoke on his behalf, while at other times the prospective groom spoke for himself." Greengus, *The Old Babylonian Marriage Contract*, 89 J. OF THE AMERICAN ORIENTAL SOC. 505, 524 (1969).

20. LIPIT-ISHTAR ¶ 23 ("If a daughter is not given in marriage while her father is alive, her brothers shall give her in marriage."); MARTEN STOL, *Private Life in Ancient Mesopotamia, in* 1 CIVILIZATIONS OF THE ANCIENT NEAR EAST, *supra* ch. 5 note 23, at 485, 488 ("[I]f the father was no longer alive, the mother or brother took care of this for a girl, serving as her guardian."); SAMUEL GREENGUS, *Legal and Social Institutions of Ancient Mesopotamia, in* 1 CIVILIZATIONS OF THE ANCIENT NEAR EAST, *supra* ch. 1 note 14 at 469, 479 ("Women were given in marriage by their fathers or, if the father was deceased, by their brother.").

21. DRIVER & MILES, BABYLONIAN LAWS 249.

22. WESTBROOK, OLD BABYLONIAN MARRIAGE LAW 65 and 101–102. See SAMUEL GREENGUS, *Legal and Social Institutions of Ancient Mesopotamia, in* 1 CIVILIZATIONS OF THE ANCIENT NEAR EAST, *supra* ch. 1 note 14 at 469, 480.

23. WESTBROOK, OLD BABYLONIAN MARRIAGE LAW 59 ("[T]he *terhatum* was a real price for a right over the bride, but one less than ownership."); *Id.* at 60 ("Where the parents demand it, the *terhatum* is nothing other than payment for the right to control over their daughter."). Westbrook explains that this is clearly not a sum used for a "purchase and sale" of the bride: "[T]he amount of the *terhatum* at its highest is too low to constitute a real purchase-price of a wife—it would not suffice to purchase a slave, and in particular is often lower than the dowry given by the father to the bride." WESTBROOK, OLD BABYLONIAN MARRIAGE LAW 55 (footnotes omitted). *See also Id.* at 56, 66.

bride to the bridegroom…."[24] But we are not certain of precisely what act or acts constituted the "completion" of marriage.[25] Depending on the circumstances, it appears that a marriage could be completed by: 1) the bride physically moving into the husband's home (*domum deductio*); 2) intercourse (*copula carnalis*); or 3) the recitation of certain spoken words by the groom (*verba solemnia*).[26]

If the bride and groom were minors, the marriage contracted-for was considered "inchoate," and there were two possible scenarios: "standard inchoate marriage" and "*kallūtum* inchoate marriage."[27] "Standard inchoate marriage" occurred when the groom brought the *terhatum* to the father-in-law's house but the girl remained in her own house; and then later, when she was older, she moved in with her new husband's family.[28] The "*kallūtum* inchoate marriage" occurred when the groom brought the *terhatum* to the father-in-law's house and subsequently the girl went to live in her father-in-law's house, and lived there as a quasi daughter until she was older and able to formally become a wife.[29] In the latter case, the young girl was referred to as a *kallatum* and the marriage was called "a *kallâtūtu* marriage."[30] Finally, when the bride left her home to enter the groom's, the bride's father gave her (for the groom to keep in his possession) a dowry.[31]

24. MARTEN STOL, *Private Life in Ancient Mesopotamia, in* 1 CIVILIZATIONS OF THE ANCIENT NEAR EAST, *supra* ch. 5 note 23, at 485, 489; DRIVER & MILES, BABYLONIAN LAWS 249–250. Driver & Miles suggest that the *biblum* may have been "the provisions for the marriage-feast which presumably…were given while the marriage was still inchoate." *Id.* at 250. *See also* WESTBROOK, OLD BABYLONIAN MARRIAGE LAW 8 (characterizing Driver & Miles's term "inchoate marriage" as a "major contribution to the general understanding of OB [*i.e.,* Old Babylonian] marriage…."), and *Id.* at 29.

25. *See generally* WESTBROOK, OLD BABYLONIAN MARRIAGE LAW 48–53.

26. *Id.*

27. *Id.* at 34.

28. *Id.* at 34–36.

29. *Id.* at 36–38; DRIVER & MILES, BABYLONIAN LAW 251–252.

30. HAMMURABI ¶¶ 155–156. WESTBROOK, OLD BABYLONIAN MARRIAGE LAW 17–18, 36; DRIVER & MILES, BABYLONIAN LAWS 251–252; MARTEN STOL, *Private Life in Ancient Mesopotamia, in* 1 CIVILIZATIONS OF THE ANCIENT NEAR EAST, *supra* ch. 5 note 23, at 485, 489.

31. Contemporary documents show that the mother could also give the dowry. WESTBROOK, OLD BABYLONIAN MARRIAGE LAW 89. In addition, if the father had died before giving his daughter a dowry, it was the brothers of the bride who were responsible for providing her with the dowry (at least in the case of a *šugītum* priestess). HAMMURABI ¶ 184. *See* WESTBROOK, OLD BABYLONIAN MARRIAGE LAW 89; MARTEN STOL, *Private Life in Ancient Mesopotamia, in* 1 CIVILIZATIONS OF THE ANCIENT NEAR EAST, *supra* ch. 5 note 23, at 485, 489; SAMUEL GREENGUS, *Legal and Social Institutions of Ancient Mesopotamia, in* 1 CIVILIZATIONS OF THE ANCIENT NEAR EAST, *supra* ch. 1 note 14 at 469, 479–80.

It is likely that the content of the dowry had been agreed upon during negotiations at the time of betrothal.[32] In Hammurabi's Laws, the word used for dowry is *šeriktum* but in some contemporary documents the word used for dowry appears to have been *nudunnûm*.[33] The precise meaning of *nudunnûm* is unclear. As was noted, some documents use it as a synonym for dowry[34] but others seem to indicate that the *nudunnûm* was some kind of gift given by the husband to the wife at the beginning of marriage.[35] In his book, *Old Babylonian Marriage Law*, Westbrook hypothesizes:

> The term *nudunnûm* means a wife's marital property, comprising the dowry given to her by members of her own family and gifts from her husband. The term can refer to either of the individual components or both together. In [Hammurabi's Laws], one of these components, the dowry, is referred to by a special term: *šeriktum*. It is thus distinguished from the rest of the *nudunnûm*....[36]

The *nudunnûm* was used to support the wife in the event that her husband should predecease her, and then, upon her death, it devolved to her children.[37] Contemporary documents demonstrate that the most common form of dowry was movable goods. There were instances where land was included as well, but not money.[38] Some items given as part of Old Babylonian dowries were personal items such as "clothing, jewellery, toilet articles of the bride, together with quantities of oil..., a large number of household utensils, in particular kitchen utensils such as millstones and cooking-pots and often a substantial amount of furniture, such as tables, chairs and (more than one) bed."[39]

---

32. WESTBROOK, OLD BABYLONIAN MARRIAGE LAW 90.

33. *Id.* at 24, 89; DRIVER & MILES, BABYLONIAN LAWS 271–272; SAMUEL GREEN-GUS, *Legal and Social Institutions of Ancient Mesopotamia, in* 1 CIVILIZATIONS OF THE ANCIENT NEAR EAST, *supra* ch. 1 note 14 at 469, 479.

34. DRIVER & MILES, BABYLONIAN LAWS 265.

35. WESTBROOK, OLD BABYLONIAN MARRIAGE LAW 24–25; DRIVER & MILES, BABYLONIAN LAWS 271.

36. WESTBROOK, OLD BABYLONIAN MARRIAGE LAW 25. *See also Id.* at 27 ("In summary, we would argue that the difference in terminology between the law-codes and the documents of practice does not reflect a contradiction but merely different approaches to expressing the same concept, conditioned by the different nature of the two sources.").

37. *Id.* at 99.

38. *Id.*; DRIVER & MILES, BABYLONIAN LAWS 274; MARTEN STOL, *Private Life in Ancient Mesopotamia, in* 1 CIVILIZATIONS OF THE ANCIENT NEAR EAST, *supra* ch. 5 note 23, at 485, 489; SAMUEL GREENGUS, *Legal and Social Institutions of Ancient Mesopotamia, in* 1 CIVILIZATIONS OF THE ANCIENT NEAR EAST, *supra* ch. 1 note 14 at 469, 479.

39. WESTBROOK, OLD BABYLONIAN MARRIAGE LAW 90; MARTEN STOL, *Private*

During the marriage, the husband possessed and controlled the dowry but, technically speaking, the wife had a life estate in it.[40] When the husband died, if they had had children, the widow retained the dowry.[41] When she died, it passed to her sons (if any), or, if she had no sons, it devolved to her father's house.[42] In addition, if her husband divorced her because she had no sons (or in circumstances where she was otherwise innocent), she was entitled to take her dowry with her.[43] If he divorced her in circumstances where she was the guilty party, the husband retained the dowry.[44]

In a situation where a man promised to marry a woman and brought marriage gifts (*biblum* and *terhatum*) to her father, he was required to forfeit the marriage gifts if he thereafter changed his mind and decided to marry another.[45] But if, instead, the bride's father changed his mind and de-

---

Life in Ancient Mesopotamia, in 1 CIVILIZATIONS OF THE ANCIENT NEAR EAST, *supra* ch. 5 note 23, at 485, 489.

40. WESTBROOK, OLD BABYLONIAN MARRIAGE LAW 25, 93–94, 99; DRIVER & MILES, BABYLONIAN LAWS 352–353; MARTEN STOL, *Private Life in Ancient Mesopotamia, in* 1 CIVILIZATIONS OF THE ANCIENT NEAR EAST, *supra* ch. 5 note 23, at 485, 489; SAMUEL GREENGUS, *Legal and Social Institutions of Ancient Mesopotamia, in* 1 CIVILIZATIONS OF THE ANCIENT NEAR EAST, *supra* ch. 1 note 14 at 469, 480; Ellickson & Thorland, *Ancient Land Law*, 71 CHICAGO-KENT L. REV. 321, 368–69 (1995). *See infra* § 7.3 [A].

41. HAMMURABI ¶ 171. WESTBROOK, OLD BABYLONIAN MARRIAGE LAW 91 ("Since the dowry is part of her marital property, the widow is entitled to separate it from the mass of the husband's estate which is to be divided among his heirs or other claimants. The rule is expressed in CH 171b and again in 176. . . ."); SAMUEL GREENGUS, *Legal and Social Institutions of Ancient Mesopotamia, in* 1 CIVILIZATIONS OF THE ANCIENT NEAR EAST, *supra* ch. 1 note 14 at 469, 480.

42. ESHNUNNA ¶ 18. WESTBROOK, OLD BABYLONIAN MARRIAGE LAW 25, 91–92, 97; SAMUEL GREENGUS, *Legal and Social Institutions of Ancient Mesopotamia, in* 1 CIVILIZATIONS OF THE ANCIENT NEAR EAST, *supra* ch. 1 note 14 at 469, 480; DRIVER & MILES, BABYLONIAN LAWS 353 ("Until a woman had sons her *šeriktum* was due to pass to her brothers, but sons, when born, took the place of her brothers. Whilst she and her husband were alive he administered it.").

43. HAMMURABI ¶¶ 138, 149, 163–164. WESTBROOK, OLD BABYLONIAN MARRIAGE LAW 72, 91–93, 97; DRIVER & MILES, BABYLONIAN LAWS 272, 344.

44. WESTBROOK, OLD BABYLONIAN MARRIAGE LAW 92; SAMUEL GREENGUS, *Legal and Social Institutions of Ancient Mesopotamia, in* 1 CIVILIZATIONS OF THE ANCIENT NEAR EAST, *supra* ch. 1 note 14 at 469, 480.

45. HAMMURABI ¶ 159. WESTBROOK, OLD BABYLONIAN MARRIAGE LAW 72 ("The *terhatum* is thus the measure of damages for breach, but the injured party is now the wife and not the father."). Driver & Miles draw an analogy between this measure of damages and our modern "liquidated damages, *i.e.* a pre-estimate by the parties of the damage which would be caused if either broke his contract." DRIVER & MILES, BABYLONIAN LAWS 261. Westbrook discusses actual documents of contemporary practice that are analogous to HAMMURABI ¶ 159. *See* WESTBROOK, OLD BABYLONIAN MARRIAGE LAW 29, 34, 43–45. Owen and Westbrook recount one document in particular (CT 45,86) where "the groom in a *kallūtum* inchoate marriage refuses to marry the

cided to reject the would-be the groom, then the bride's father had to pay the groom twice the value of the marriage gifts that he had brought ("twofold everything that had been brought to him").[46] If the bride's father changed his mind due to a slanderous accusation by one of the groom's "comrades," then it was the comrade who committed the slander who was liable to the groom for twice the value of his marriage gifts.[47] The same law also provided that the slanderous comrade was not allowed to marry the bride who was involved. Presumably, the law was intended to prevent a man from slandering a groom in hopes of getting the bride for himself.

[B] Protection of Marriage for Soldiers

Under Eshnunna's Laws, if a man was taken as a prisoner, no matter how long he was absent, and even if another man married his wife and fathered

---

bride chosen for him by his father and is ordered by the court to restore her dowry in full." D.I. Owen and R. Westbrook, *Tie Her Up and Throw Her Into the River! An Old Babylonian Inchoate Marriage on the Rocks*, 82 ZEITSCHRIFT FÜR ASSYRIOLOGIE UND VORDERASIATISCHE ARCHÄOLOGIE 203 (1992). They summarize another case (FLP 1340—which they ascribe to the 15th year of Hammurabi) which is similar but with an interesting twist:

> The present text concerns litigation between a groom and his father-in-law. The groom has refused to complete the inchoate marriage, evidently alleging justification, since he claims the return of his *terhatum* in the form of a house. The father-in-law counters that he acquired the house through purchase and not as a *terhatum* and is therefore not obliged to return it. He takes the oath to this effect, thereby blocking the groom's claim to the *terhatum*, but without broaching the question of fault.
>
> The groom, however, maintains his position, which is that his refusal to marry is justified by the bride's *implied* misconduct. Accordingly, he insists that she be punished by drowning, as in CH § 143. This may be an astute move since, if the groom can prove his allegations, he may be able to force the father-in-law to pay him ransom-money to forego his right to demand the bride's death.

Id. at 203–204 (footnote omitted).

46. HAMMURABI ¶ 160; UR-NAMMU ¶ 15; LIPIT- ISHTAR ¶ 29; ESHNUNNA ¶ 25. *See also* WESTBROOK, OLD BABYLONIAN MARRIAGE LAW 34, 39–43; SAMUEL GREENGUS, *Legal and Social Institutions of Ancient Mesopotamia, in* 1 CIVILIZATIONS OF THE ANCIENT NEAR EAST, *supra* ch. 1 note 14 at 469, 480; DRIVER & MILES, BABYLONIAN LAWS 252, 322–323; Eichler, *Literary Structure* 76. A contemporary document shows a payment of merely restitution (*in simplum*) rather than double. WESTBROOK, OLD BABYLONIAN MARRIAGE LAW 42.

47. HAMMURABI ¶ 161; LIPIT-ISHTAR ¶ 29. WESTBROOK, OLD BABYLONIAN MARRIAGE LAW 34, 42–43; DRIVER & MILES, BABYLONIAN LAWS 252, 322–323. Westbrook explains that the comrade whom this law contemplates "has…a special status, he is one of a group with particular functions in the wedding celebrations." WESTBROOK, OLD BABYLONIAN MARRIAGE LAW 42.

children by her during his absence, upon his return, he was entitled to "take back his wife."[48] However, if instead a man intentionally repudiated his city and fled, he was not entitled to reclaim his wife upon his return.[49]

Hammurabi's Laws take these basic principles and add more. If a man was taken prisoner, his wife was not permitted to move in with another man so long as she had "sufficient provisions" in her house.[50] But if provisions were insufficient, she could move in with another man with impunity.[51] In such a case, even if the woman had children by the second man, if the original husband returned home, the woman was legally bound to return to him. Her children "inherit[ed] from their father."[52] Thus, the second marriage was, in essence, valid. It was merely voidable in the event that the first husband returned.[53] If, on the other hand, a man simply deserted his city—as opposed to having been taken prisoner—his wife was permitted to move in with another man, and was not required to go back to her original husband in the event that he later returned from his desertion.[54] In any event, it is likely that the "second husband" was indeed considered married to the woman. In other words, the woman who left her first husband on account of insufficient provisions or on account of his desertion was deemed married to the man with whom she lived.[55] In fact, the second hus-

---

48. ESHNUNNA ¶ 29. *See* WESTBROOK, OLD BABYLONIAN MARRIAGE LAW 51, 86–88; Finkelstein, *Sex Offenses in Sumerian Laws*, 86 J. OF THE AMERICAN ORIENTAL SOC. 355, 369 (1966); SAMUEL GREENGUS, *Legal and Social Institutions of Ancient Mesopotamia, in* 1 CIVILIZATIONS OF THE ANCIENT NEAR EAST, *supra* ch. 1 note 14 at 469, 481.

49. ESHNUNNA ¶ 30. *See* WESTBROOK, OLD BABYLONIAN MARRIAGE LAW 51, 86–88. *See also* Finkelstein, *Sex Offenses in Sumerian Laws*, 86 J. OF THE AMERICAN ORIENTAL SOC. 355, 369 (1966); Eichler, *Literary Structure* 75.

50. HAMMURABI ¶ 133a. *See* WESTBROOK, OLD BABYLONIAN MARRIAGE LAW 51, 86–88; DRIVER & MILES, BABYLONIAN LAWS 284–285.

51. HAMMURABI ¶ 134. *See* WESTBROOK, OLD BABYLONIAN MARRIAGE LAW 51, 86–88; DRIVER & MILES, BABYLONIAN LAWS 286.

52. HAMMURABI, ¶ 135. WESTBROOK, OLD BABYLONIAN MARRIAGE LAW 87 ("It is essentially the same as CE 29—a husband who has been absent due to captivity abroad can reclaim his wife on his return in spite of an intervening marriage. But a distinction is inserted: the intervening marriage is valid by reason of the wife's lack of means of support."). *See also* DRIVER & MILES, BABYLONIAN LAWS 286 ("[T]he sons borne to the second man (the only sons mentioned in the section) follow their father, i.e. cannot be claimed by the first husband."); SAMUEL GREENGUS, *Legal and Social Institutions of Ancient Mesopotamia, in* 1 CIVILIZATIONS OF THE ANCIENT NEAR EAST, *supra* ch. 1 note 14 at 469, 481.

53. WESTBROOK, OLD BABYLONIAN MARRIAGE LAW 87.

54. HAMMURABI ¶ 136; ESHNUNNA ¶ 30. *See* WESTBROOK, OLD BABYLONIAN MARRIAGE LAW 51, 88; DRIVER & MILES, BABYLONIAN LAWS 285–286.

55. DRIVER & MILES, BABYLONIAN LAWS 287–290.

band is referred to by a special term, *hāwirum*, to distinguish his role from that of the original husband.[56] Thus, Driver and Miles summarize these provisions as follows: "[I]f a woman has been left without maintenance by her first husband, she may remarry and, although if her husband returns, she may have to return to him, her sons by the second husband are the lawful sons of their father."[57]

[C] Polygamy & Fidelity in Marriage

In ancient Mesopotamia men ordinarily were monogamous.[58] A man usually married only one wife who shared his social status. There were some exceptions, however, that permitted polygamy.[59] In particular, Hammurabi's Laws provide that a man could marry more than one woman under at least three circumstances: 1) when his wife was a priestess who, by virtue of her status as a priestess, was not allowed to bear children;[60] 2) when his wife was extremely ill;[61] and, 3) when his wife was guilty of severe misconduct (but not adultery).[62] Contemporary documents indicate that the two wives ordinarily had one of two legal relationships: mistress/slave or sisterhood. There are a number of texts that show that the second wife was often the first wife's slave.[63] There are also several records indicating that the co-wives were actually blood-relative sisters or else had "adopted" one another as sisters.[64]

---

56. Westbrook, Old Babylonian Marriage Law 18–19.

57. Driver & Miles, Babylonian Laws 290.

58. Samuel Greengus, *Legal and Social Institutions of Ancient Mesopotamia, in* 1 Civilizations of the Ancient Near East, *supra* ch. 1 note 14 at 469, 478.

59. *See generally* Westbrook, Old Babylonian Marriage Law 103–111; Samuel Greengus, *Legal and Social Institutions of Ancient Mesopotamia, in* 1 Civilizations of the Ancient Near East, *supra* ch. 1 note 14 at 469, 478.

60. Hammurabi ¶¶ 144–145; Westbrook, Old Babylonian Marriage Law 107–108; Samuel Greengus, *Legal and Social Institutions of Ancient Mesopotamia, in* 1 Civilizations of the Ancient Near East, *supra* ch. 1 note 14 at 469, 478.

61. Hammurabi ¶ 148; Lipit-Ishtar ¶ 28; Westbrook, Old Babylonian Marriage Law 108; Samuel Greengus, *Legal and Social Institutions of Ancient Mesopotamia, in* 1 Civilizations of the Ancient Near East, *supra* ch. 1 note 14 at 469, 479.

62. Hammurabi ¶ 141; Westbrook, Old Babylonian Marriage Law 108; Samuel Greengus, *Legal and Social Institutions of Ancient Mesopotamia, in* 1 Civilizations of the Ancient Near East, *supra* ch. 1 note 14 at 469, 479.

63. Westbrook, Old Babylonian Marriage Law 103–107; Samuel Greengus, *Legal and Social Institutions of Ancient Mesopotamia, in* 1 Civilizations of the Ancient Near East, *supra* ch. 1 note 14 at 469, 478.

64. Westbrook, Old Babylonian Marriage Law 103–107.

In an ordinary, monogamous marriage, an ancient Mesopotamian husband was permitted to have sex with temple prostitutes.[65] Adultery was "an offence against a husband but not against a wife."[66] As a general rule, prostitution in the ancient Near East was legal.[67]

[D] Special Marriage Rights of Certain Women

There were certain classes of women who had special marriage rights. Two such groups of women were temple dedicatees named *šugitu* and *naditu*. When a *šugitu* or *naditu* married and had children, if her husband decided to divorce her, she was entitled: 1) to have her dowry returned; 2) to have one-half of her husband's "field, orchard, and property"; and, 3) later, after her children had grown, she was entitled to a share of property equal to that of her sons.[68]

§ 6.3 Divorce[69]

[A] General

Driver and Miles maintain that Babylonian marriage and divorce were quite distinct from present-day "Christian" marriage and divorce: "Nothing there is sacred or perpetual about the marriage tie; if a woman has a right to leave her husband, he cannot complain if she remarries and, if he cannot complain, it is no one else's business to do so."[70] The verb for "to divorce" in Old Babylonian laws and documents is *ezēbum*.[71] The Sumerian equivalent

---

65. Marten Stol, *Private Life in Ancient Mesopotamia, in* 1 Civilizations of the Ancient Near East, *supra* ch. 5 note 23, at 485, 493; Saggs, Babylon 185.

66. Driver & Miles, Babylonian Laws 286. *See also* Finkelstein, *Sex Offenses in Sumerian Laws*, 86 J. of the American Oriental Soc. 355, 366 n. 34 (1966). *See infra* § 8.4 [B] concerning adultery as a crime.

67. Marten Stol, *Private Life in Ancient Mesopotamia, in* 1 Civilizations of the Ancient Near East, *supra* ch. 5 note 23, at 485, 493; Good, *Capital Punishment*, 19 Stan. L. Rev. 947, 959 (1967); Saggs, Babylon 351.

68. Hammurabi ¶ 137. *See also* Westbrook, Old Babylonian Marriage Law 20–21, 60–61, 73–75; Driver & Miles, Babylonian Laws 335, 372; Roux, Ancient Iraq 200.

69. *See generally* Greengus, *The Old Babylonian Marriage Contract*, 89 J. of the American Oriental Soc. 505, 532 n. 141 (1969) and accompanying text.

70. Driver & Miles, Babylonian Law 303.

71. Westbrook, Old Babylonian Marriage Law 20–21.

was *tag*.[72] When a marriage was in its "inchoate" stage,[73] a "mere declaration seems to have been sufficient for...dissolution...."[74] When a marriage had been completed (*i.e.*, it had gone beyond the inchoate stage), the most common means of effectuating a divorce was for the husband to declare a symbolic phrase (*verba solemnia*) to his wife: "You are not my wife."[75] It is likely that the husband was required to make this declaration in the presence of his wife and witnesses, but apparently court proceedings were not mandatory. Some Old Babylonian documents mention this formal language, settlement money, and the symbolic act of "cutting the fringe of her garment" (*sissiktam batāqum*).[76] According to Westbrook, the "cutting the fringe of her garment" seems to have been performed when the divorce was "before a court."[77] In addition, it appears that this act "symbolises the fact that the wife...departs without her dowry...."[78]

A man was required to leave his house if he divorced his wife after having had children by her, and then remarried.[79] It seems likely that children ordinarily stayed with their mother in cases where the husband divorced his wife without justification.[80] The converse appears to have been true as well: when a man divorced his wife for a good reason, the children probably went with him.[81] In Lipit-Ishtar's Laws, after a young married man visited a prostitute, the judges could forbid him to revisit the prostitute.[82] If he then divorced his wife and paid her a divorce settlement, he still was not allowed to marry the prostitute.[83] Scholars disagree as to whether a wife had the legal capacity to divorce her husband.[84] If wives were legally permitted to

---

72. *Id.* at 20, n. 86.

73. *See supra* ch. 6 note 24 and accompanying text.

74. DRIVER & MILES, BABYLONIAN LAWS 290. HAMMURABI ¶ 159.

75. WESTBROOK, OLD BABYLONIAN MARRIAGE LAW 69; DRIVER & MILES, BABYLONIAN LAWS 292–292.

76. DRIVER & MILES, BABYLONIAN LAWS 292.

77. WESTBROOK, OLD BABYLONIAN MARRIAGE LAW 69 ("The phrase is attested in five OB documents.")(footnote omitted).

78. *Id.* at 70.

79. ESHNUNNA ¶ 59. *See* WESTBROOK, OLD BABYLONIAN MARRIAGE LAW 21, 72–73, 97; SAMUEL GREENGUS, *Legal and Social Institutions of Ancient Mesopotamia, in* 1 CIVILIZATIONS OF THE ANCIENT NEAR EAST, *supra* ch. 1 note 14 at 469, 480.

80. WESTBROOK, OLD BABYLONIAN MARRIAGE LAW 73, 85.

81. *Id.* at 85.

82. LIPIT-ISHTAR ¶ 30.

83. *Id.*; MARTEN STOL, *Private Life in Ancient Mesopotamia, in* 1 CIVILIZATIONS OF THE ANCIENT NEAR EAST, *supra* ch. 5 note 23, at 485, 493.

84. *See* WESTBROOK, OLD BABYLONIAN MARRIAGE LAW 79–85; SAMUEL GREENGUS, *Legal and Social Institutions of Ancient Mesopotamia, in* 1 CIVILIZATIONS OF THE ANCIENT NEAR EAST, *supra* ch. 1 note 14 at 469, 480.

do so, apparently it was a right that they had merely in the abstract; for as a matter of practice, they did not.[85]

[B] Grounds for Divorce

It may have been a criminal offense for a wife to appropriate goods, squander household possessions, or disparage her husband, and then to leave him. In these circumstances, a husband could divorce his wife and not have to pay her anything.[86] Even if he decided not to divorce her, he was still permitted to marry another, and the first wife was allowed to "reside in her husband's house as a slave woman."[87]

A wife was entitled to repudiate her husband if he was "wayward" and if she was "circumspect and without fault." In that case, she was allowed to take her dowry and return to her father's house.[88] On the other hand, if an investigation revealed that she was not circumspect but instead it was *she* who was "wayward," she was "cast...into the water."[89]

In Lipit-Ishtar's Laws, a man was allowed to marry a second wife if his first wife "lost her attractiveness" or became "paralytic." Under these circumstances, however, the first wife stayed in the home and the second wife helped care for her.[90] As a general rule, a divorced woman was entitled to remarry.[91]

According to the Laws of Hammurabi, although a man was not permitted to divorce his wife if she contracted *la'bum* (some kind of severe disease, perhaps malaria),[92] he was, apparently, allowed to marry a second

---

85. Westbrook, Old Babylonian Marriage Law 82–85.

86. Hammurabi ¶ 141. *See* Westbrook, Old Babylonian Marriage Law 76–77.

87. Hammurabi ¶141. *See* Westbrook, Old Babylonian Marriage Law 76–77; Driver & Miles, Babylonian Laws 298–299; Westbrook, *Slave and Master*, 70 Chicago-Kent L. Rev. 1631, 1635 (1995); Finkelstein, *Sex Offenses in Sumerian Laws*, 86 J. of the American Oriental Soc. 355, 362–63 (1966).

88. Hammurabi ¶ 142. Westbrook, Old Babylonian Marriage Law 45–48, 61, 81. (Westbrook thinks it unlikely that this law is evidence that a wife could divorce her husband. (*Id.* at 81)). Driver & Miles, Babylonian Laws 299 (Driver & Miles note that this provision appears to give a wife the power to divorce her husband but that it does not: "she cannot start proceedings but must wait until her husband applies...for restitution of conjugal rights." (footnote omitted)).

89. Hammurabi ¶ 143. Westbrook, Old Babylonian Marriage Law 45–47. *See* Good, *Capital Punishment* 19 Stan. L. Rev. 947, 958 (1967); Finkelstein, *Sex Offenses in Sumerian Laws*, 86 J. of the American Oriental Soc. 355, 362–63 (1966).

90. Lipit-Ishtar ¶ 28. *See* Westbrook, Old Babylonian Marriage Law 77.

91. Driver & Miles, Babylonian Laws 298, 303.

92. *Id.* at 309 (Driver & Miles describe the disease as being "of such a nature that she ceases to be fitted for married life; he is consequently permitted to marry another woman."). They, however, express the opinion that it was not a contagious disease, since she was permitted to go wherever she pleased. "The only thing positive is that it

wife. But in these circumstances, he was required to care for his sick wife in special quarters built for her.[93] This provision seems to apply whether the diseased wife had borne children.[94] If the diseased wife refused to stay with her husband, he was required to return her dowry, and she could leave.[95] It is curious that the law treats a wife who contracts *la'bum* better than a wife who cannot bear children (as in HAMMURABI ¶ 138). Driver and Miles suggest a contract-like explanation for the difference: the disease is something that strikes the wife after the marriage, whereas the inability to bear children is more like a "latent defect" which renders the woman unfit for her particular purpose (child-bearing), thereby giving the husband the right to revoke his acceptance.[96] A standard legal form book from about 1700 B.C. provides that a husband who "despised" his wife was permitted to divorce her so long as he paid "a divorce settlement in silver."[97]

[C] Divorce Payments

Under Ur-Nammu's Laws, a man could divorce "his first-ranking wife," but he had to pay her 60 shekels of silver as a divorce settlement.[98] Many Old Babylonian marriage contracts contain provisions that established a payment (usually a fixed sum between 10 shekels and one mina) that the husband had to make if he divorced his wife.[99] A husband did not have to make that payment if he divorced his wife for sufficient cause.[100] If a man divorced a woman who had previously been a widow (so that this was her second marriage), he had to pay her 30 shekels of silver as a divorce settlement.[101] But a man who only had had "sexual relations with the widow

---

must be incurable, and presumably it makes cohabitation impossible as the sufferer is replaced by another wife." *Id.* at 310.

93. HAMMURABI ¶ 148. *See* WESTBROOK, OLD BABYLONIAN MARRIAGE LAW 21, 77–78.

94. DRIVER & MILES, BABYLONIAN LAWS 310.

95. HAMMURABI ¶ 149. *See* WESTBROOK, OLD BABYLONIAN MARRIAGE LAW 77–78. Apparently, she did not have to return to her father's house. But, like the infertile wife in HAMMURABI ¶ 138, it does not appear likely that she will find another husband. DRIVER & MILES, BABYLONIAN LAWS 309.

96. DRIVER & MILES, BABYLONIAN LAWS 311.

97. SLHF (iv 12–14).

98. UR-NAMMU ¶ 9.

99. WESTBROOK, OLD BABYLONIAN MARRIAGE LAW 78. *See* SAMUEL GREENGUS, *Legal and Social Institutions of Ancient Mesopotamia, in* 1 CIVILIZATIONS OF THE ANCIENT NEAR EAST, *supra* ch. 1 note 14 at 469, 480.

100. WESTBROOK, OLD BABYLONIAN MARRIAGE LAW 78.

101. UR-NAMMU ¶ 10.

without a formal written contract [of marriage]," did not have to pay any-thing to her if they separated.[102] Old Babylonian documents refer to the lump sum of money that a husband paid to his wife upon divorce as *uzub-bûm*.[103]

A man of the upper class in Hammurabi's day could divorce his "first-ranking wife who did not bear him children."[104] In order to do so, he had to give her a settlement payment consisting of her dowry plus silver equal to the money and property that he had given his wife's family as "bridewealth" (*terhatum*) prior to their marriage.[105] If he had not given any *terhatum*, then he had to pay "60 shekels of silver as a divorce settlement."[106] A "com-moner" could divorce his wife by paying her 20 shekels of silver.[107] West-brook takes the position that "this arrangement—dowry plus divorce-money—represents the standard settlement of an ordinary marriage where there is not the complication of children."[108] According to Driver and Miles, "the money...which the husband must give his wife...provide[s] the woman with a maintenance...and...protect[s] her from capricious di-vorce."[109] But clearly the disposition of payments to a wife upon divorce is a complicated matter and apparently it depended on a number of factors—not all of which are completely understood.[110]

In the the Early Dynastic period (c. 2900–2350 B.C.),[111] upon his divorce, a man was required to pay a fee to the government—actually he paid the fee to an inspector who was responsible to the Ensi. So not only did he pay a settlement to his wife, but he also had to pay a government fee.[112]

---

102. UR-NAMMU ¶ 11.

103. WESTBROOK, OLD BABYLONIAN MARRIAGE LAW 23.

104. HAMMURABI ¶ 138.

105. HAMMURABI ¶ 138. WESTBROOK, OLD BABYLONIAN MARRIAGE LAW 71, 97. Driver & Miles assert that the settlement payment "protects such a wife from capri-cious divorce." DRIVER & MILES, BABYLONIAN LAWS 293. *See also* OPPENHEIM, AN-CIENT MESOPOTAMIA 87.

106. HAMMURABI ¶ 139. WESTBROOK, OLD BABYLONIAN MARRIAGE LAW 62 (not-ing that this law suggests that the *terhatum* was not mandatory ("a legal necessity") for marriage). *See also Id.* at 71.

107. HAMMURABI ¶ 140. *See* WESTBROOK, OLD BABYLONIAN MARRIAGE LAW 71.

108. WESTBROOK, OLD BABYLONIAN MARRIAGE LAW 72 (footnote omitted).

109. DRIVER & MILES, BABYLONIAN LAWS 296.

110. *Id.* at 296–297.

111. DOMINIQUE CHARPIN, *The History of Ancient Mesopotamia: An Overview, in* 2 CIVILIZATIONS OF THE ANCIENT NEAR EAST, *supra* ch. 1 note 23, at 807, 808.

112. SAGGS, BABYLON 234.

§6.4 Parents, Children, & Caregivers

[A] Child Custody & Adoption[113]

Ancient Mesopotamians customarily adopted infant children, although occasionally adults were adopted as well.[114] Generally speaking, they adopted for a number of practical reasons. A couple might adopt a child to procure a son for the following reasons: 1) so that the family itself could be perpetuated; 2) so that there would be someone to carry on a family business; 3) so that there would be someone to care for the parents when they were elderly; or 4) so that there would be someone to perform religious rites when the parents died.[115] A well-to-do childless couple could adopt an orphan or child of a poor family. Saggs translates an adoption document of this sort:

> Yahatti-Il is the son of Hillalum and of the lady Alitum. He shall benefit by their benefits and suffer ill by their ills. If Hillalum his father or the lady Alitum his mother say to their son Yahatti-Il 'You are not our son', they shall forfeit house and furniture. If Yahatti-Il says to Hillalum his father or the lady Alitum his mother 'You are not my father' or 'You are not my mother', they shall shave his head and sell him for silver.
>
> (In respect to) Hillalum and the lady Alitum, however many sons they acquire, Yahatti-Il is the heir. From the house of Hallalum his father he shall receive a double share (at the division of the paternal property) and his junior brethren shall share (the rest) equally.[116]

Upon their adoption, children legally lost the right to inherit from their biological parents.[117] Rather, adopted children had roughly the same legal

---

113. *See generally* Driver & Miles, Babylonian Laws 383–405.

114. Marten Stol, *Private Life in Ancient Mesopotamia, in* 1 Civilizations of the Ancient Near East, *supra* ch. 5 note 23, at 485, 491–92; Samuel Greengus, *Legal and Social Institutions of Ancient Mesopotamia, in* 1 Civilizations of the Ancient Near East, *supra* ch. 1 note 14 at 469, 479 (Greengus thinks that adult adoption is more common: "Sometimes this involved the legal transfer of a newborn or infant child; but more frequently, adoption was arranged between adults."); Driver & Miles, Babylonian Laws 388.

115. Marten Stol, *Private Life in Ancient Mesopotamia, in* 1 Civilizations of the Ancient Near East, *supra* ch. 5 note 23, at 485, 492; Samuel Greengus, *Legal and Social Institutions of Ancient Mesopotamia, in* 1 Civilizations of the Ancient Near East, *supra* ch. 1 note 14 at 469, 479; Driver & Miles, Babylonian Laws 383.

116. Saggs, Babylon 171.

117. Driver & Miles, Babylonian Laws 387.

rights as any natural children of their adoptive parents.[118] If adoptive parents failed to treat them as equals, the adopted children returned to their biological parents.[119] Interestingly, in Hammurabi's Laws, parents who adopted a child could legally "disinherit" that child later if they had children of their own. But in that case, the disinheritance was not complete, for the adopted child was entitled to a one-third share of his adoptive parents' estate.[120] It is probable that the departing adopted son received his one-third share immediately upon his departure—not having to wait until his adoptive father's demise.[121] Possibly, this law was only applicable in situations where the adopted son had already reached the age of majority and was eligible to move into a house of his own and marry.[122]

Hammurabi's Laws provided that if a child was adopted *at birth* and then raised by his adoptive parents, the biological parents were not later permitted to reclaim the child.[123] However, if a child was adopted as "a young child" (*i.e.,* later than "at birth"), and the child engaged in "seeking his father and mother," then the adoptive parents were required to return the child to his biological parents.[124]

Adoptive parents were required to sell their adopted son into slavery (and he thus lost all rights to their property) if he repudiated them and declared that they were not his father and mother.[125] By the same token, if it was the adoptive parents who said to the adopted son "You are not our son," they forfeited their estate (to him?).[126]

---

118. *Id.*

119. HAMMURABI ¶ 190. *See* DRIVER & MILES, BABYLONIAN LAWS 390 (Driver & Miles suggest that this law "must describe a privilege of the child." (footnote omitted). Thus they maintain that this law is "one of the few humanitarian provisions of the Laws" because it shows genuine concern for the child's feelings.). *See also Id.* at 395–396.

120. HAMMURABI ¶ 191. *See* DRIVER & MILES, BABYLONIAN LAWS 397 ("here it is a question not of the adoptive son leaving his adoptive father but of the adoptive father getting rid of his adoptive son."). *See also Id.* at 398–399 (Stating that the adopter must give the adoptee one-third of his heritage but he does not get any of the "ancestral property.").

121. DRIVER & MILES, BABYLONIAN LAWS 400–401.

122. *Id.* at 398.

123. HAMMURABI ¶ 185. *See* DRIVER & MILES, BABYLONIAN LAWS 388.

124. HAMMURABI ¶ 186. *See* DRIVER & MILES, BABYLONIAN LAWS 389.

125. SLEX ¶ 4'. DRIVER & MILES, BABYLONIAN LAWS 386 (According to Driver & Miles, adoption contracts in the Old Babylonian period stipulate punishment for adopted children who deny their adoptive parents; and vice versa.). *See* MARTEN STOL, *Private Life in Ancient Mesopotamia, in* 1 CIVILIZATIONS OF THE ANCIENT NEAR EAST, *supra* ch. 5 note 23, at 485, 492.

126. SLEX ¶¶ 5', 6'. MARTEN STOL, *Private Life in Ancient Mesopotamia, in* 1 CIVILIZATIONS OF THE ANCIENT NEAR EAST, *supra* ch. 5 note 23, at 485, 492.

Children reared by members of a group of temple dedicatees were not permitted to claim openly that those who raised them were not their parents. If such children denied that those who reared them were their parents, the penalty was to have their tongues cut out.[127] If such a child left his home and returned to his biological father, the penalty was to have his eye plucked out.[128]

When a craftsman took on a young apprentice, once the boy learned his master's craft, his parents were no longer entitled to reclaim him.[129] However, if the craftsman failed to teach the child his craft (or if the boy could not or would not learn it), then the child had to "return to his father's house."[130] Apparently, these laws envision that a craftsman would adopt a boy with the specific intent that he would learn his adoptive father's business and later inherit it.[131] If a father failed to "give the food, oil, and clothing rations (to the caregiver)" to whom he had entrusted his child for three years, he was required to pay the caregiver 10 shekels of silver and was also required to take back his child.[132]

[B] Child Conduct & Property of Children

The first time that a son committed "a grave offense deserving the penalty of disinheritance," he was pardoned; a father was allowed to disinherit his son the second time.[133] A child was not permitted to strike his father. The penalty was to "cut off his hand."[134]

A widow with young children was allowed to move in with another man if the judges first approved the move. However, the widow and new husband were required to write down an inventory of the deceased husband's

---

127. HAMMURABI ¶ 192. *See* DRIVER & MILES, BABYLONIAN LAWS 368, 401–405.

128. HAMMURABI ¶ 193. *See* DRIVER & MILES, BABYLONIAN LAWS 401–405.

129. HAMMURABI ¶ 188 ("If a craftsman takes a young child to rear and then teaches him his craft, he will not be reclaimed."). *See* DRIVER & MILES, BABYLONIAN LAWS 392.

130. HAMMURABI ¶ 189. DRIVER & MILES, BABYLONIAN LAWS 390. *See also Id.* at 392, and 394 (Driver & Miles contend "that a provision was included or implied in the contract enabling the craftsman to send the boy back to his home if he could not or would not learn.").

131. DRIVER & MILES, BABYLONIAN LAWS 393.

132. ESHNUNNA ¶ 32. For an interesting discussion of this section, *see* Eichler, *Literary Structure* 78.

133. HAMMURABI ¶ 169; SAMUEL GREENGUS, *Legal and Social Institutions of Ancient Mesopotamia, in* 1 CIVILIZATIONS OF THE ANCIENT NEAR EAST, *supra* ch. 1 note 14 at 469, 479.

134. HAMMURABI ¶ 195.

estate. They acted as trustees of that estate on behalf of the widow's children by her first marriage.[135] If someone bought "household goods of the children of a widow," that transaction was considered void. The buyer had to return the property but was not allowed to recover his purchase price.[136]

---

135. *See* WESTBROOK, OLD BABYLONIAN MARRIAGE LAW 60; DRIVER & MILES, BABYLONIAN LAWS 356.

136. HAMMURABI ¶ 177.

CHAPTER 7

Inheritance & Succession

§ 7.1 Introduction[1]

Curiously, Hammurabi's Laws only indirectly mention the law of succession.[2] In actual Old Babylonian practice, a person's estate was usually divided shortly after death. Temple judges presided over the distribution.[3] A person's heirs even inherited the obligation to pay the deceased's debts.[4] Obviously, it is not always easy to divide possessions in such a way that shares turn out equally. In fact, some property is basically indivisible merely by its very nature. According to Driver and Miles,

> When property of an indivisible nature was included, the person who took it had to compensate the other parties to the division for any excess value; sometimes such a piece of property was exempted from the division and remained the joint property of the family.[5]

It is likely that at some early time in Sumer, only males — sons — inherited.[6] But by the Old Babylonian period, "both the widow and the daughters had certain claims to inherit."[7] As a general rule, Mesopotamian law provided that all heirs, no matter how many, shared equally an inherited estate.[8] But in southern Mesopotamia, the eldest son was entitled to a share of

---

1. *See generally* DRIVER & MILES, BABYLONIAN LAWS 324–358.
2. Id. at 324.
3. Id. at 333.
4. Id.
5. Id. at 334.
6. Id. at 328–329.
7. Id. at 331; MARTEN STOL, *Private Life in Ancient Mesopotamia, in* 1 CIVILIZATIONS OF THE ANCIENT NEAR EAST, *supra* ch. 5 note 23, at 485, 494–95; SAMUEL GREENGUS, *Legal and Social Institutions of Ancient Mesopotamia, in* 1 CIVILIZATIONS OF THE ANCIENT NEAR EAST, *supra* ch. 1 note 14 at 469, 478.
8. SLHF (iv 31–34). SAMUEL GREENGUS, *Legal and Social Institutions of Ancient Mesopotamia, in* 1 CIVILIZATIONS OF THE ANCIENT NEAR EAST, *supra* note 14 at 469, 478; DRIVER & MILES, BABYLONIAN LAWS 331.

his father's estate superior to that of his siblings.[9] In addition, inheritance laws provided resources for dowries for daughters and financing for weddings for younger brothers. It was usual for brothers to inherit real property as tenants in common so that it could not be broken into smaller parcels.[10]

§7.2 Order of Succession: Sons First

Sons were first in line to inherit.[11] We know that at certain times political offices were hereditary. For example, the Ensi in Lagash was probably elected by citizens at first, but by about 2500 B.C., it was passed from father to son.[12] In the Old Babylonian period, a son's share of his father's estate was determined by lot. The sons simply had to accept that the gods were deciding their shares by sortition.[13] A man's brothers inherited his property if he died "leaving no descendants either male or female...."[14] But what happened to a son's inheritance if he predeceased his father? Suppose a son (A) was born to a father (B), and suppose that A had two brothers, C and D. Suppose, in addition, that A himself had sons X and Y. If son A were to die before his father, B, then when B died, A's sons (X and Y) were entitled to split their father's (A's) share. A's sons stood in the shoes of their father. In this simple example, C would receive one-third share of B's estate, D would receive one-third share of B's estate, and X and Y each would receive one-sixth (*i.e.*, one-half of their father's (A's) one-third share) of B's estate.[15]

If a man's sons were minors at his death, the widow administered the sons' estate.[16] If she remarried, both she and her new husband jointly took

---

9. DRIVER & MILES, BABYLONIAN LAWS 331; SAMUEL GREENGUS, *Legal and Social Institutions of Ancient Mesopotamia, in* 1 CIVILIZATIONS OF THE ANCIENT NEAR EAST, *supra* ch. 1 note 14 at 469, 478.

10. OPPENHEIM, ANCIENT MESOPOTAMIA 77.

11. DRIVER & MILES, BABYLONIAN LAWS 331; SAMUEL GREENGUS, *Legal and Social Institutions of Ancient Mesopotamia, in* 1 CIVILIZATIONS OF THE ANCIENT NEAR EAST, *supra* ch. 1 note 14 at 469, 478.

12. SAGGS, BABYLON 46, 67. *See also* ROUX, ANCIENT IRAQ 162.

13. OPPENHEIM, ANCIENT MESOPOTAMIA 208–209.

14. DRIVER & MILES, BABYLONIAN LAWS 341–342.

15. Id. at 331 ("If a son has predeceased his father and has left sons, these take their father's place *per repraesentationem* and divide the property *per stirpes* with their father's surviving brothers, i.e. their surviving uncles." (footnote omitted)).

16. MARTEN STOL, *Private Life in Ancient Mesopotamia, in* 1 CIVILIZATIONS OF THE ANCIENT NEAR EAST, *supra* ch. 5 note 23, at 485, 495.

the responsibility to administer the sons' estate. The sons took possession of their shares when they reached the age of majority. It was then, also, that their mother became entitled to her share (if she had one). Generally speaking, the mother was entitled to a share only if she had no *nudunnûm*.[17] In any event, her share was a life estate that passed to her sons upon her death or remarriage.[18]

If a man had failed to provide a bridewealth (*terhatum*)[19] for his youngest son (assuming that his older sons had already married), upon his death, the older brothers were required to give to their youngest brother both the amount for his *terhatum* and also his share of the paternal estate.[20] Later in Mesopotamian history, the Assyrian Laws do not permit a boy to marry—even inchoately—until age ten.[21] Thus, this provision would control situations where a father died but still had an unmarried son, perhaps under age ten.

In both Lipit-Ishtar's Laws and Hammurabi's, a father, "during his lifetime," was permitted to give a gift in "a sealed document" to "his favored son."[22] If he did so, after his death, his other heirs were not permitted to contest the gift that he gave to his favored son.[23] Clearly, a father was not allowed to give his favorite the entire family estate. The effect of a gift of that magnitude would be to disinherit his other sons.[24] Driver and Miles assert that this law "shows that a father could, to some extent, alter the general rule that all sons share the inheritance equally."[25]

A father could only disinherit his son for cause.[26] Apparently, this was true whether the son in question was biological or adopted.[27] A father was entitled to disinherit a son only if "the judges" investigated and determined

---

17. *See supra* ch. 6 notes 33–37 and accompanying text. *See also* HAMMURABI ¶ 172.

18. WESTBROOK, OLD BABYLONIAN MARRIAGE LAW 60; DRIVER & MILES, BABYLONIAN LAWS 334; MARTEN STOL, *Private Life in Ancient Mesopotamia, in* 1 CIVILIZATIONS OF THE ANCIENT NEAR EAST, *supra* ch. 5 note 23 at 485, 495.

19. *See supra* ch. 6 note 23 and accompanying text.

20. HAMMURABI ¶ 166. *See* WESTBROOK, OLD BABYLONIAN MARRIAGE LAW 34, 38.

21. DRIVER & MILES, BABYLONIAN LAWS 346–347.

22. LIPIT-ISHTAR ¶ 31; HAMMURABI ¶ 165 (same). *See* WESTBROOK, OLD BABYLONIAN MARRIAGE LAW 98; DRIVER & MILES, BABYLONIAN LAWS 345–346.

23. Id.

24. DRIVER & MILES, BABYLONIAN LAWS 346.

25. Id.

26. SAMUEL GREENGUS, *Legal and Social Institutions of Ancient Mesopotamia, in* 1 CIVILIZATIONS OF THE ANCIENT NEAR EAST, *supra* ch. 1 note 14 at 469, 479.

27. DRIVER & MILES, BABYLONIAN LAWS 349.

that the son was twice "guilty of a grave offense deserving the penalty of disinheritance."[28] For the first such offense, the judges merely gave the son a warning.[29] It seems strange that these laws (HAMMURABI ¶¶ 168–169) fail to specify the nature of the offenses that could give rise to disinheritance.[30] In addition, a son could be disinherited by operation of law: if a man was caught having sexual relations with his father's "principal wife" after his father's death, that man was "disinherited from the paternal estate."[31]

§ 7.3 Inheritance by a Wife

[A] Death of Husband—Wife Inherits Life Estate

After a woman's husband died, she was permitted to live in her husband's house.[32] She was not, however, allowed to sell the house. She retained only a life-estate. In the Old Babylonian period, it seems doubtful that their concept of "life-estate" was exactly analogous to our modern notion. "The Babylonians did not create life interests, with remainders. They gave a life estate, but after the life the property reverted to the donor's family by operation of the law and not by the grant of the donor."[33] Upon the widow's death, only her own children inherited her estate.[34] Even if she married again and had children by a second husband, only *her* children (including children of both marriages—but not her husband's children from a previous marriage [*i.e.*, not step-children]) were entitled to inherit her dowry.[35] All of her own children inherited equally.[36]

---

28. HAMMURABI ¶¶ 168–69. DRIVER & MILES, BABYLONIAN LAWS 348–350; Westbrook, *Slave and Master,* 70 CHICAGO-KENT L. REV. 1631, at 1635 (1995).

29. HAMMURABI ¶ 169.

30. *See* DRIVER & MILES, BABYLONIAN LAWS 349.

31. HAMMURABI ¶ 158. DRIVER & MILES, BABYLONIAN LAWS 321 (Driver & Miles maintain "that the woman was a wife or concubine of the father of the offender but not his mother, since § 157 deals with that offence.") .

32. HAMMURABI ¶ 171. *See* Ellickson & Thorland, *Ancient Land Law,* 71 CHICAGO-KENT L. REV. 321, 368–69 (1995).

33. DRIVER & MILES, BABYLONIAN LAWS 324.

34. HAMMURABI ¶ 171. *See* DRIVER & MILES, BABYLONIAN LAWS 332–333, 351.

35. HAMMURABI ¶¶ 173–174. WESTBROOK, OLD BABYLONIAN MARRIAGE LAW 93; SAMUEL GREENGUS, *Legal and Social Institutions of Ancient Mesopotamia, in* 1 CIVILIZATIONS OF THE ANCIENT NEAR EAST, *supra* ch. 1 note 14 at 469, 480 ("When she died, her dowry was inherited by her children, both male and female. If her husband had children from another marriage, they had no claim on her dowry.").

36. HAMMURABI ¶¶ 173–174.

[B] "Sealed Document"

Hammurabi's Laws permitted a husband to execute "a sealed document" in favor of his wife granting to her "a field, house, or movable property."[37] The effect of such a property transfer was to shield that property from the widow's children after her husband's death. The widow, however, was not allowed to give her estate "to an outsider." Rather, she was legally bound to give it only "to whichever of her children she love[d]."[38]

[C] A Special Circumstance

When an *awilu* man was engaged, and if he had already brought the bridewealth (*terhatum*) to his prospective father-in-law's house, if either he or his bride died, the *terhatum* was returned to "the widower or his heir."[39] If, on the other hand, one of them died *after* the marriage and *after* the couple had begun living together, then the widow or his heir took back only a specified portion of the bridewealth, not all of it.[40]

§ 7.4 Inheritance by Female Child

The Laws of Lipit-Ishtar allowed that when a man died "without male offspring, an unmarried daughter...be[came] his heir."[41] When a girl be-

---

37. HAMMURABI ¶ 150. *See* Ellickson & Thorland, *Ancient Land Law*, 71 CHICAGO-KENT L. REV. 321, 366 (1995); WESTBROOK, OLD BABYLONIAN MARRIAGE LAW 95–96, 98; MARTEN STOL, *Private Life in Ancient Mesopotamia, in* 1 CIVILIZATIONS OF THE ANCIENT NEAR EAST, *supra* ch. 5 note 23, at 485, 495 ("A husband could take care of this situation by a donation to his wife, a 'gift in contemplation of death.'").

38. HAMMURABI ¶ 150. *See* DRIVER & MILES, BABYLONIAN LAWS 311–312.

39. ESHNUNNA ¶ 17. *See* WESTBROOK, OLD BABYLONIAN MARRIAGE LAW 38, 47, 91; Raymond Westbrook, *A Death in the Family: Codex Eshnunna 17–18 Revisited*, 29 ISRAEL L. REV. 32–42 (1995).

40. ESHNUNNA ¶ 18. *See* WESTBROOK, OLD BABYLONIAN MARRIAGE LAW 97. The law is unclear. Contemporary scholars acknowledge that the text fails to reveal exactly how much the widow or his heir was entitled to have returned. Roth suggests that it might have been the "'excess' — of bridewealth over...dowry...." ROTH, LAW COLLECTIONS 69, n.6 (1995). *See also* WESTBROOK, OLD BABYLONIAN MARRIAGE LAW 51; Raymond Westbrook, *A Death in the Family: Codex Eshnunna 17–18 Revisited*, 29 ISRAEL L. REV. 32–42 (1995).

41. LIPIT-ISHTAR ¶ b. *See* Westbrook, *Biblical and Cuneiform Law Codes* 262 (discussing the similarity between this provision and the inheritance law articulated in the Biblical story of Zelophehad in *Numbers* XXVII, 1–11).

came a member of one of three special temple groups (*ugbabtu, naditu,* or *qadištu*) while her father was alive, she was considered "an equal heir" along with her brothers.[42] In Hammurabi's Laws, there were a number of special inheritance laws that granted preferred inheritance rights and privileges to daughters who became members of special temple or priestess groups such as *ugbabtu, naditu, sekretu, qadištu, kulmašitu,* and *šugitu*.[43] Ancient documents bolster the argument that these special laws were not merely hypothetical or abstract legal provisions introduced by Hammurabi, but, rather, that they "were based on earlier laws or customs that were observed long before the time of Hammura[b]i and then incorporated by him into his code."[44] It appears from Old Babylonian documents that a daughter did not necessarily have to be a priestess in order to be able to inherit a share of her father's estate.[45] According to Driver and Miles, "The relevant sections of the Laws deal mainly with the inheritance of priestesses but the documents show other daughters apparently joining with their brothers in the division of their father's estate."[46] It is likely that only unmarried daughters had these inheritance rights.[47] Thus, an unwed daughter probably was entitled to either a dowry or a share of her father's estate.[48] The ancient documents, however, do not say whether the daughter's share was equal to that of her brothers.[49] These laws confirm that women could own property and that daughters could have a life estate in their inheritance share.[50] As a practical matter, though, it is possible that the majority of girls either married or became priestesses prior to their fathers' deaths. Thus, the issue of whether a

---

42. LIPIT-ISHTAR ¶ 22.

43. *See* HAMMURABI ¶¶ 178–184. *See* DRIVER & MILES, BABYLONIAN LAWS 273, 368, 374–376. ("[T]he *šeriktum* of a priestess was regarded as a portion given in satisfaction of her right of inheritance." (*Id.* at 374)). *See also generally* Rivkah Harris, *The nadītu Laws of the Code of Hammurapi in Praxis,* 30 ORIENTALIA 163 (1961).

44. Rivkah Harris, *The nadītu Laws of the Code of Hammurapi in Praxis,* 30 ORIENTALIA 163, 169 (1961).

45. DRIVER & MILES, BABYLONIAN LAWS 335. *But see* SAMUEL GREENGUS, *Legal and Social Institutions of Ancient Mesopotamia, in* 1 CIVILIZATIONS OF THE ANCIENT NEAR EAST, *supra* ch. 1 note 14 at 469, 478.

46. DRIVER & MILES, BABYLONIAN LAWS 335, 337 ("[I]n certain documents of the first dynasty daughters who are not described as priestesses not infrequently share with their brothers and are assigned a share by them.").

47. *Id.* at 337.

48. *Id.* at 336. *Id.* at 338 ("It may then be conjectured that a daughter who is neither married nor a priestess receives a share of her father's property....").

49. *Id.* at 337.

50. Driver & Miles also raise the possibility that the words for "sons" (*mārū*) and "brothers" (*ahhū*) refer to daughters and sisters as well in the context of inheritance law. DRIVER & MILES, BABYLONIAN LAWS 338–341.

daughter had a right of inheritance was probably relevant mostly if she was an infant at the time of her father's death.[51]

§ 7.5 Death of Wife — Inheritance by Her Children

Once a wife bore children, when she died, her children — not her father — were entitled to her dowry.[52] If, on the other hand, a wife died without having children, her dowry was returned to her father upon the condition that he, in turn, was to return to his son-in-law the bridewealth (*terhatum*) that he (*i.e.,* the son-in-law/husband) had brought to his father-in-law at the inception of the marriage.[53] Driver and Miles suggest that there is a logical reason why the husband should get back the *terhatum* in this circumstance: "the husband has had the expense of keeping a woman who has not done her part by providing him with sons. He has to give back her *šeriktum*, and so the lawgiver thinks it equitable that he should at any rate be compensated up to the amount of the *terhatum* which he gave for her."[54]

If a man married a second time, his children by his first wife were not entitled to any of the dowry of his second wife (it belonged "only to her children").[55] In essence, a dowry was considered property that was owned as a life estate that passed to a woman's offspring.[56] When the father died,

---

51. Id. at 337.

52. HAMMURABI ¶ 162. *See* WESTBROOK, OLD BABYLONIAN MARRIAGE LAW 93, 97; DRIVER & MILES, BABYLONIAN LAWS 344; SAMUEL GREENGUS, *Legal and Social Institutions of Ancient Mesopotamia, in* 1 CIVILIZATIONS OF THE ANCIENT NEAR EAST, *supra* ch. 1 note 14 at 469, 480.

53. HAMMURABI ¶ 163. DRIVER & MILES, BABYLONIAN LAWS 252, 344. *See* WESTBROOK, OLD BABYLONIAN MARRIAGE LAW 72, 92, 97.

54. DRIVER & MILES, BABYLONIAN LAWS 253. (However, contemporary marriage documents appear to contradict the rules stated in ¶ 163 of Hammurabi's Laws. According to these documents, the bridal gift is "to be restored to the bride's father-in-law or to the bridegroom at the time of marriage; such an arrangement, as there cannot as yet be any sons of the marriage, seems not to harmonize with the provisions of § 163 under which the *tirhâtum* is restored to the husband only if the wife dies without sons."). Driver & Miles transcribe, translate, and discuss three such documents. DRIVER & MILES, BABYLONIAN LAWS 253–259. *See also Id.* at 344.

55. LIPIT-ISHTAR ¶ 24; HAMMURABI ¶ 167. SAMUEL GREENGUS, *Legal and Social Institutions of Ancient Mesopotamia, in* 1 CIVILIZATIONS OF THE ANCIENT NEAR EAST, *supra* ch. 1 note 14 at 469, 480; DRIVER & MILES, BABYLONIAN LAWS 347–48.

56. *See supra* §§ 6.2 [A] and 7.3.

the children by both wives divided their father's property equally.[57] As Westbrook succinctly puts it, "while the children of one father by different mothers are each entitled to a *pro-rata* share of the whole paternal estate, they are not entitled to such a share of the dowries of the marriage, but only of their own mother's dowry."[58]

§ 7.6 Inheritance by Children Where Remarriage Occurs

If a man's wife died, he was permitted to marry a slave woman who had borne his children.[59] In that case, the children by his first wife were considered his primary heirs, but his children by the slave were entitled to a share of his estate and were "considered equal to a native free born son."[60]

According to Hammurabi's Laws, when a man married a second time, his second wife's dowry (*šeriktum*) was considered the property of only the children that she bore him (not the children of his first wife). The children of the first wife and the children of the second wife divided the father's estate equally (presumably upon his death).[61] Thus, the dowry was considered property capable of being possessed as a life estate; and it passed to the mother's offspring.

§ 7.7 Children of Female Slaves & Free Males

It was possible for a free man to father children by both his wife and a slave woman. In Hammurabi's Laws, if the man acknowledged his children by the slave by calling them "my children," and treated them as his children

---

57. LIPIT-ISHTAR ¶ 24; HAMMURABI ¶ 167. Driver & Miles summarize HAMMURABI ¶ 167 as follows:

> This section aims at setting out the inheritance of the sons of two marriages and therefore takes no trouble about the life-interest of the widow in her *šeriktum* or in her *nudunnûm*; the former being derived from the wife's family, must go only to her own sons or revert to her father's house, but the latter, coming from the husband's house, descends to his sons by any wife.

DRIVER & MILES, BABYLONIAN LAWS 271 (footnote omitted).

58. WESTBROOK, OLD BABYLONIAN MARRIAGE LAW 93.

59. LIPIT-ISHTAR ¶ 26.

60. *Id.*

61. HAMMURABI ¶ 167; LIPIT-ISHTAR ¶ 24. *See* WESTBROOK, OLD BABYLONIAN MARRIAGE LAW 27–28, 93; DRIVER & MILES, BABYLONIAN LAWS 347–348.

while he was alive, then, after his death, both the children by his wife and the children by the slave were entitled to equal shares of their father's estate.[62] Although the shares may have been equal, we do not know how the shares were determined or the order of distribution (*e.g.*, by seniority or sortition).[63] It was, nevertheless, a son by his wife who was considered "the preferred heir."[64] The preferred heir was permitted to "select and take a share first."[65] If, on the other hand, the father did not acknowledge the slave's children as his, then those children were not entitled to any of their father's estate upon his death.[66] In that case, however, both the slave woman and her children were given their freedom upon his death.[67]

Under the Laws of Lipit-Ishtar, when a married man had children by both his wife and also by a slave, he was required to free the slave woman and her children. The children of his legitimate wife, however, were not required to share their father's estate with the children of the slave woman.[68] Also, according to Lipit-Ishtar's Laws, when a man had no children by his wife but did father a child by a prostitute, the prostitute's child was considered his heir, and he was required to "provide grain, oil, and clothing rations for the prostitute."[69] But in this situation, as long as the man's wife was alive, the prostitute was not allowed to live in the man's house.[70]

§ 7.8 Wills

Although we have some wills that may be from the Old Babylonian period, most inheritance law in ancient Mesopotamia seems to have been

62. HAMMURABI ¶ 170. *See* WESTBROOK, OLD BABYLONIAN MARRIAGE LAW 12, 50; DRIVER & MILES, BABYLONIAN LAWS 222, n. 12, 332–333; SAMUEL GREENGUS, *Legal and Social Institutions of Ancient Mesopotamia, in* 1 CIVILIZATIONS OF THE ANCIENT NEAR EAST, *supra* ch. 1 note 14 at 469, 477.

63. DRIVER & MILES, BABYLONIAN LAWS 350–351 ("There is, however, nothing to show in what way the shares are determined nor the order, whether by seniority or by lot, in which the members of the two families *inter se* choose their respective shares." (footnote omitted)).

64. HAMMURABI ¶ 170. *See* WESTBROOK, OLD BABYLONIAN MARRIAGE LAW 50; DRIVER & MILES, BABYLONIAN LAWS 332–333.

65. HAMMURABI ¶ 170.

66. HAMMURABI ¶ 171. *See* DRIVER & MILES, BABYLONIAN LAWS 222, n. 12, 332–333, 351.

67. HAMMURABI ¶ 171. *See* DRIVER & MILES, BABYLONIAN LAWS 332–333, 351.

68. LIPIT-ISHTAR ¶ 25.

69. LIPIT-ISHTAR ¶ 27.

70. *Id.*

controlled by operation of law.[71] Marten Stol bluntly asserts: "Drawing up wills was not done in Babylonia...."[72] Greengus relates that only in lands neighboring Mesopotamia were wills used to distribute property after death: "In some areas *outside* Mesopotamia, one finds the practice of making out a will (*šīmtu*) prior to the father's death."[73] According to Driver and Miles, "Testate succession in the strict sense did not exist...; there was no such instrument as a will or testament by which a revocable disposition to take effect after the testator's death is made a part or the whole of his estate."[74] They explain:

> The Babylonian view is that a gift is a gift for life (or less), and in fact no mortal can enjoy a gift for a longer period. It is the law, and not the donor, which decides to whom the gift shall pass on the death of the donee. The Babylonians did not recognize the 'dead hand' of a testator, nor did they enjoy the benefit of the complicated English system of future interests and estates.[75]

The ancient Mesopotamians used other forms of conveyance to accomplish many of the same objectives that modern legal systems achieve with a will. For example, a man could adopt another in order to transfer wealth.[76] An adoptee then inherited as a son. During his life a man could also grant property to his wife. She then had a life estate in that property after his death.[77] In addition, a man could grant property to his favorite son on the condition that the son would take possession upon his father's death.[78]

---

71. OPPENHEIM, ANCIENT MESOPOTAMIA 87.
72. MARTEN STOL, *Private Life in Ancient Mesopotamia, in* 1 CIVILIZATIONS OF THE ANCIENT NEAR EAST, *supra* ch. 5 note 23, at 485, 494.
73. SAMUEL GREENGUS, *Legal and Social Institutions of Ancient Mesopotamia, in* 1 CIVILIZATIONS OF THE ANCIENT NEAR EAST, *supra* ch. 1 note 14 at 469, 478 (emphasis added).
74. DRIVER & MILES, BABYLONIAN LAWS 343 (footnote omitted).
75. Id. at 270–271. *See also Id.* at 381 ("In Babylon a man had his property during his lifetime and had no interest or control over it after his death.").
76. MARTEN STOL, *Private Life in Ancient Mesopotamia, in* 1 CIVILIZATIONS OF THE ANCIENT NEAR EAST, *supra* ch. 5 note 23, at 485, 492; DRIVER & MILES, BABYLONIAN LAWS 343.
77. MARTEN STOL, *Private Life in Ancient Mesopotamia, in* 1 CIVILIZATIONS OF THE ANCIENT NEAR EAST, *supra* ch. 5 note 23, at 485, 495; DRIVER & MILES, BABYLONIAN LAWS 343.
78. DRIVER & MILES, BABYLONIAN LAWS 343.

CHAPTER 8

Criminal Law

§8.1 Introduction

Westbrook notes that criminal law in ancient Mesopotamia was very different from modern criminal law:

> Crimes such as murder, adultery, rape, and theft, which in modern law are prosecuted and punished by the state, were dealt with on an entirely different basis in the ancient systems. Such crimes gave rise to a dual right on the part of the victim or his family: to revenge or to accept payment in lieu of revenge.[1]

There are very few actual texts that record the results or proceedings of ancient Mesopotamian criminal trials.[2] We have one Sumerian text that records a murder trial and the murderer's execution; but that may be merely a literary exercise. There is another noteworthy Sumerian text that describes a murder trial in which the murderer was convicted but died before he could be executed. Thus, the court ordered the wife and daughters of the convicted murderer to be given as slaves to the victim's sons. In addition, the victim's sons also divided the murderer's property.[3] Otherwise, there are: 1) an Old Babylonian text regarding a strangled slave and a kidnapped infant; and 2) a number of texts from Mari that mention a political homicide, a dead child whose body had been mutilated, and merchants who had been murdered. Beyond these, reports of other crimes—such as

---

1. RAYMOND WESTBROOK, *Social Justice in the Ancient Near East, in* SOCIAL JUSTICE IN THE ANCIENT WORLD 157.

2. SAMUEL GREENGUS, *Legal and Social Institutions of Ancient Mesopotamia, in* 1 CIVILIZATIONS OF THE ANCIENT NEAR EAST, *supra* ch. 1 note 14 at 469, 474–75.

3. Good, *Capital Punishment*, 19 STAN. L. REV. 947, 974 (1967) ("The rationale apparently was that the court had to find a way to do justice for the victim's family since the guilty party could not be brought to justice.").

treason, theft and burglary—come from periods after the Old Babylonian period.[4]

In his book, *The Greatness That Was Babylon*, Saggs describes rituals performed by the king during the Akitu Festival: "The king knelt down before the god, and recited a negative confession in which he claimed not to have offended against the god in certain specific ways: "I have not smitten the cheek of the people under (your) protection, I have not occasioned their humiliation...."[5] These phrases suggest that the king is disclaiming wrongful acts (either criminal or tortious). He first disclaims an act that we would characterize as battery and the second appears to disclaim some kind of defamation or injury to a person's reputation. It is significant that these words appear to recognize not only physical injury as a wrong but intangible, psychological injury as well.

The paucity of contemporary documents forces us to rely on the law collections for most of our information regarding criminal law. The collections contain laws that deal with many specific types of crimes, such as murder, rape, robbery, forgery, and embezzlement.[6] But, perhaps the most curious and enigmatic criminal law in the ancient Mesopotamian law collections is the second of Ur-Nammu's Laws: "If a man acts lawlessly(?), they shall kill him."[7] What makes this law so difficult to interpret, of course, is that we have not a clue as to what "lawlessly" means. Presumably, it must have encompassed serious misconduct, since other laws in Ur-Nammu's collection make it clear that minor transgressions were not considered capital offenses.[8]

§ 8.2 Homicide

One of Ur-Nammu's laws tersely states: "If a man commits a homicide, they shall kill that man."[9] In the Laws of Lipit-Ishtar, a person found guilty of striking a woman in such a way that the blow caused her both to mis-

---

4. OPPENHEIM, ANCIENT MESOPOTAMIA 283–84. *See also* ROUX, ANCIENT IRAQ 203.

5. SAGGS, BABYLON 386. *See also* J.N. Postgate, *Royal Ideology and State Administration in Sumer and Akkad, in* 1 CIVILIZATIONS OF THE ANCIENT NEAR EAST 395, 399 (Jack. M. Sasson ed., 1995).

6. SAGGS, BABYLON 193, 202, 217.

7. UR-NAMMU ¶ 2.

8. *See e.g.,* UR-NAMMU ¶¶ 13, 14, 18, 19, *etc.*

9. UR-NAMMU ¶ 1.

carry and to die, herself, received a death penalty.[10] Hammurabi's Laws do not overtly state that homicide was a crime punishable by death, but the very first law in the great collection directs that when a man accused another of homicide and failed to "bring proof," the accuser was put to death.[11] By implication it is, therefore, logical to assume that homicide itself was also punished with execution. Scholars have remarked that it seems odd that Hammurabi's Laws do not directly address murder as a crime *per se*.[12] But they also note that "it seems clear from other sections of the Laws that a distinction between 'murder' and 'manslaughter' was to some extent recognized by him [*i.e.*, Hammurabi]...."[13]

In Hammurabi's Laws, it was a capital crime for a woman to arrange to have her husband killed. The law contemplates a circumstance where a wife had her husband murdered "on account of (her relationship with) another male...."[14] It is possible that this law refers to a situation where a woman murdered her husband (or had him murdered) by poisoning him.[15] Driver and Miles remark that this law is unusual because we cannot tell what kind of proof was necessary to convict.[16] The method of execution for this crime was impalement.[17]

We possess an account of a homicide trial, the famous Nippur Homicide Trial, in which a widow is accused of conspiring in her husband's murder.[18] Roth states that the texts recording this case were "written in the early part of the second millennium BCE, in Sumerian on cuneiform clay tablets."[19] The widow was convicted and sentenced to death for her conspiracy along

---

10. LIPIT-ISHTAR ¶¶ d–e.
11. HAMMURABI ¶ 1. *See* DRIVER & MILES, BABYLONIAN LAWS 59–60, 314–315.
12. DRIVER & MILES, BABYLONIAN LAWS 59 ("It is strange that Hammurabi gives no description of the crime of murder...."). Also, regarding the absence of any laws relating directly to homicide, Driver & Miles state: "it is remarkable that there is no direct prohibition of homicide and no discussion of that crime in these Laws." "[I]t may be...that homicide in Babylonia still gave rise to a blood feud...." Id. at 314.
13. *Id.* at 59 (citing to HAMMURABI ¶¶ 116, 207–210, and 229–230). *See generally Id.* at 314–317.
14. HAMMURABI ¶ 153.
15. DRIVER & MILES, BABYLONIAN LAWS 313.
16. *Id.*
17. HAMMURABI ¶ 153. Driver & Miles suggest that the guilty widow may have been executed by some other means prior to impalement, and that she would not have been buried in a case such as this. DRIVER & MILES, BABYLONIAN LAWS 314.
18. *See generally* MARTHA T. ROTH, *Gender and Law: A Case Study From Ancient Mesopotamia* 173, *in* GENDER AND LAW IN THE HEBREW BIBLE AND THE ANCIENT NEAR EAST, supra ch. 1 note 20 at 173–184 (Victor H. Matthews, Bernard M. Levinson and Tikva Frymer-Kensky eds., 1997).
19. *Id.* at 175.

with the three men who actually murdered the husband: "As men who have killed, they should not be allowed to live. Those...males and that woman shall be killed...."[20] Interestingly, one judge characterized the widow's culpability—as a conspirator—as greater than even that of the murderers themselves: "It is she who (as good as) killed her husband; her guilt exceeds even that of those who (actually) kill a man."[21]

It was not uncommon for a creditor to take a family member of a debtor as a "debt-hostage."[22] It was, however, also possible for someone to be "pseudo-creditor" who did not actually have a claim against another. If such a pseudo-creditor took a family member as a "debt-hostage" and caused that family member's death, he was punished by death.[23]

When one considers the Mesopotamian law collections as a whole, it seems odd that so few laws relate to murder. It is likely that numerous murder cases were actually tried in ancient Mesopotamia, though "very few court records of murder cases are to be found."[24] It is possible that extensive laws relating to murder were unnecessary because, like the ancient Athenians,[25] Mesopotamian law considered murder "a private affair to be handled by the victim's family, coming into the courts only when some peculiar situation warranted public attention."[26]

Two additional crimes that are theoretically related to homicide are worth considering at this point: abortion and suicide. There is not a great deal of information regarding the "legality" of either. Driver and Miles claim that, if a *nadîtum* priestess became pregnant, the "birth would be prevented by abortion, which...was doubtless practiced in Babylonia."[27] In Assyria, abortion was a capital offense. But, according to tradition, the mother of Sargon the Great rid herself of her unwanted child by setting

---

20. *Id.* at 176 (footnotes omitted).
21. *Id.* at 177.
22. SAMUEL GREENGUS, *Legal and Social Institutions of Ancient Mesopotamia, in* 1 CIVILIZATIONS OF THE ANCIENT NEAR EAST, *supra* ch. 1 note 14 at 469, 478 ("In the face of debt, a father could give his creditor not only a slave, but any member of his family in order to satisfy unpaid obligations. The father had the right but not the duty to redeem them."). *See infra* § 11.3 [C].
23. ESHNUNNA ¶ 24. *See also* Eichler, *Literary Structure* 76–78.
24. Good, *Capital Punishment,* 19 STAN. L. REV. 947, 951 (1967). Driver & Miles mention a document that records a murder trial that takes place in the 30th year of Rîm-Sin of Larsa. The victim was a slave girl who was strangled. DRIVER & MILES, BABYLONIAN LAWS 61.
25. *See* DOUGLAS M. MACDOWELL, THE LAW IN CLASSICAL ATHENS 111 (1978).
26. Good, *Capital Punishment,* 19 STAN. L. REV. 947, 952 (1967). *See also* DRIVER & MILES, BABYLONIAN LAWS 314–315.
27. DRIVER & MILES, BABYLONIAN LAWS 366–367 (footnote omitted).

him free on a small raft in the river (a form of exposure).[28] Many have speculated that the dead buried in the "so-called royal tombs of Ur" (*c.* 2600 B.C.)[29] committed suicide. If that is the case, it is possible—although only a possibility—that suicide was not necessarily considered a criminal offense.

§ 8.3 Theft Crimes[30]

[A] Introduction & General Provisions

Most criminal law systems treat theft, robbery, and burglary differently. As a general rule, "theft" is stealing during daylight. "Burglary" is nocturnal stealing. "Robbery" is stealing that involves some opportunity for confrontation between the robber and the victim. Since the degree of risk to human life is considered greater for robbery and burglary, they, as a general rule, bear more severe penalties than theft.[31] The Reforms of Urukagina (Uru-inimgina) contained some provisions that related to theft. For example, priests were prohibited from entering a commoner's garden and chopping down a tree or removing produce.[32] There was also a provision in Urukagina's (Uru-inimgina's) Reforms that forbade a person of the upper class from taking fish from a commoner's artificial fish pond.[33]

---

28. SAGGS, BABYLON 349–50.

29. *See* ROUX, ANCIENT IRAQ 131–32; JAMES D. MUHLY, *Mining and Metalwork in Ancient Western Asia, in* 3 CIVILIZATIONS OF THE ANCIENT NEAR EAST 1501, 1508 (Jack M. Sasson ed., 1995); ANN C. GUNTER, *Material, Technology, and Techniques in Artistic Production, in* 3 CIVILIZATIONS OF THE ANCIENT NEAR EAST 1539, 1548 (Jack M. Sasson ed., 1995); SAGGS, BABYLON 374.

30. *See generally* JACKSON, ESSAYS, (ch. 3 "Principles and Cases: The Theft Laws of Hammurabi") 64–74 (1975).

31. W.F. Leemans has argued that the Akkadian verbs that scholars usually translate "steal" and "rob" are not well differentiated in the Old Babylonian laws. Leemans states: "As a rule, no clear cut distinction between the two ideas was made in the Old-Babylonian period, probably because robbery usually includes theft, robbery to be defined as stealing by violence or intimidation from a person who is present at the taking." W.F. Leemans, *Some Aspects of Theft and Robbery in Old Babylonian Documents, in* SCRITTI IN ONORE DI GIUSEPPE FURLANI 661 (1957). Leemans notes, however, that the Laws of Hammurabi *do* distinguish between these two concepts. But Leemans says that the concepts do not translate readily into modern legal doctrine: "[N]either *šarāqu*, nor *habātu* seem to coincide with modern concepts of theft and robbery; *šarāqu* appears to imply misappropriation, *habātu* perhaps breaking and entering with intent to steal." *Id.* (citations and footnotes omitted).

32. SAGGS, BABYLON 47.

33. *Id.*

One example of an ancient case involving robbery comes from the trial testimony of witnesses establishing that the defendant had beaten the plaintiff and stolen his oxen. After the defendant refused to take an oath alledging that the witnesses had lied, he admitted the crime, and as a penalty had to pay the plaintiff 30 shekels of silver.[34] In the Sumerian Law Handbook of Forms, many thefts carried with them penalties based on the value of the property stolen. Ordinarily, the thief was ordered to pay a factor of the value of the object(s) taken as compensation to the property owner. For example, a thief had to pay double the value of a boat or pig.[35] In Hammurabi's Laws, some sections establish a fixed amount of compensation for theft; such as the theft of agricultural implements (*e.g.*, 5 shekels for theft of a plow).[36] Driver and Miles suggest that the reason why this penalty for theft is relatively lenient is because such implements might have been either left out in a field and then taken (*i.e.*, the finder may have presumed them abandoned) or the "thief" may have borrowed them to begin with (a bailment).[37] A shepherd, who was found guilty of altering the brand on sheep or cattle and selling them, paid ten-times their value as recompense.[38] Even though this offense is described as a theft, this law treats the shepherd's crime more like that of the bailee in HAMMURABI ¶¶ 253–255[39] where compensatory payment is made—not the death penalty.[40]

It is interesting and unusual that these thefts were punished not by incarceration or physical punishment, but rather merely by monetary compensation. Yet for the shepherd who altered the cattle brand, damages

---

34. Saggs translates this example of a case where one party refused to swear an oath:

> The witnesses of A recounted before the judges, 'B beat A and took oxen away from him'. So the judges said to B, 'Take the oath of the gods against the witnesses'. And this is the declaration of B; before the judges he admitted 'I did strike A': B was afraid of the gods. A won the case and the judges made B pay 30 shekels of silver to A.

Id. at 219.

35. SLHF (iii 10–12), (iii 13–15).

36. HAMMURABI ¶¶ 259–260 (5 shekels for a plow stolen "from the common irrigated area"; 3 shekels for theft of "a clod-breaking plow or harrow").

37. DRIVER & MILES, BABYLONIAN LAWS 80–81, 450.

38. HAMMURABI ¶ 265. *See* Raymond Westbrook and Claus Wilcke, *The Liability of an Innocent Purchaser of Stolen Goods in Early Mesopotamian Law*, 113 [hereinafter "Westbrook and Wilcke, *Liability of an Innocent Purchaser of Stolen Goods*"], 25 ARCHIV FÜR ORIENTFORSCHUNG 111, 113 (1974–1977).

39. *See infra* § 8.3 [D].

40. DRIVER & MILES, BABYLONIAN LAWS 457.

amounting to a factor of ten times their value is decidedly punitive. Perhaps damages are higher in this instance because trust is broken. This was an injury caused in a situation where a relationship was involved—not merely an injury between strangers. A similar law that imposed punitive payment in another situation pertaining to a broken trust involved consignment. If a consignee failed to deliver goods as promised for his consignor, the consignee was liable to his consignor for five times the amount of property that had been consigned to him.[41] Driver and Miles suggest that this law, like HAMMURABI ¶ 120 (involving "theft" of grain by a bailee), is similar in many respects to the English common law. "The principle seems the same: the thief is one who wrongfully takes property from the possession of another man without his knowledge or consent, and the bailee therefore is not a thief."[42] In most instances of theft, it was the victim who initiated legal proceedings, not the government.[43] This may be another reason why monetary compensation was the ordinary punishment for theft instead of incarceration or corporal punishment.

In Hammurabi's Laws, ¶ 6 punishes theft of "valuables" from a temple or a palace, or receiving "valuables" stolen from a temple or palace, by death.[44] On the other hand, ¶ 8 provides that when someone steals "an ox, a sheep, a donkey, a pig, or a boat" from a temple or palace, his penalty is not death, but to pay back thirty times that which he stole.[45] Obviously there is an apparent inconsistency between ¶ 6 and ¶ 8.[46] It is possible that the livestock enumerated in ¶ 8 were considered less dear than the valuables in ¶ 6.[47] But probably these two provisions evolved from two separate legal traditions:

---

41. HAMMURABI ¶ 112. See DRIVER & MILES, BABYLONIAN LAWS 208.

42. DRIVER & MILES, BABYLONIAN LAWS 452.

43. W.F. Leemans, *Some Aspects of Theft and Robbery in Old Babylonian Documents, in* SCRITTI IN ONORE DI GIUSEPPE FURLANI 661 (1957).

44. HAMMURABI ¶ 6. See also Good, *Capital Punishment*, 19 STAN. L. REV. 947, 963 (1967) (Good suggests that these were "probably sacred and valuable objects belonging to the temple or palace....").

45. HAMMURABI ¶ 8. See Good, *Capital Punishment*, 19 STAN. L. REV. 947, 963 (1967). For additional commentary on these provisions, see JACKSON, ESSAYS (ch. 3 "Principles and Cases: The Theft Laws of Hammurabi") 65–74 (1975).

46. See DRIVER & MILES, BABYLONIAN LAWS 82.

47. Westbrook and Wilcke, *Liability of an Innocent Purchaser of Stolen Goods,* 25 ARCHIV FÜR ORIENTFORSCHUNG 111, 112 (1974–1977) ("[C]ommentators have sought to explain the different provisions of §6 and §8 in terms of the different kinds of temple/state goods involved, since they are described as *NING.GA* (=*makkurum/namkurum*) in §6 but by way of enumeration of movable goods in §8.") (footnote omitted). *See also* BOTTÉRO, WRITING, REASONING, AND THE GODS 162 (noting the apparent inconsistencies of these provisions).

one based on capital punishment and one based on monetary damages.[48] If the theft-victim was a commoner instead of a temple or palace, the thief was required to pay back only ten times what he stole.[49] But if the thief in either case did not have sufficient resources to pay back the livestock or boat, the penalty was death.[50]

There was a special provision in Hammurabi's Laws dealing with fire-fighters who stole goods from a burning house. If a volunteer firefighter stole belongings from a house where he was fighting a fire, his punishment was to be put to death by throwing him into the very fire that he was helping to extinguish.[51]

Two striking provisions in Hammurabi's Laws furnished a kind of social theft insurance and life insurance for victims of robbery.[52] One law established that if the robber was not apprehended, "the city and governor in whose territory and district the robbery was committed" will replace the stolen property to the victim, provided that he was able to "establish the extent of his lost property before the god...."[53] The other law mandated that the city and the governor had to pay 60 shekels of silver to the victim's family in the event that someone was killed in the course of a robbery.[54] There are, in addition, actual documents (one is a tablet from Nuzi) that corroborate "that the city or local officers are responsible for paying compensation for offences committed in their districts...."[55]

---

48. Westbrook and Wilcke, *Liability of an Innocent Purchaser of Stolen Goods,* 25 ARCHIV FÜR ORIENTFORSCHUNG 111, 113 (1974–1977) ("Our conclusion is that we are indeed faced with two separate sets of laws dealing with theft and related offences: §6(-7) and §§9–11, which are based on the death penalty, and the other §8 and §12(-13), which are based on a scheme of multiple damages."). *See also* JACKSON, ESSAYS (ch. 3 "Principles and Cases: The Theft Laws of Hammurabi") 73 ("The solution must be an historical one. LH 6 and LH 8 represent differing traditions, whether from different times, places, or schools." (footnote omitted)).

49. HAMMURABI ¶ 8.

50. *Id.* For a discussion of the apparent contradiction between this provision and HAMMUARABI ¶¶ 9–11, *see* Westbrook and Wilcke, *The Liability of an Innocent Purchaser of Stolen Goods,* 25 ARCHIV FÜR ORIENTFORSCHUNG 111–120 (1974–1977). *See also* DRIVER & MILES, BABYLONIAN LAWS 81, 95–105.

51. HAMMURABI ¶ 25. DRIVER & MILES, BABYLONIAN LAWS 111. *See also* Good, *Capital Punishment,* 19 STAN. L. REV. 947, 963 (1967).

52. HAMMURABI ¶¶ 23–24.

53. HAMMURABI ¶ 23. Driver & Miles suggest that the city pays because its officials "failed to maintain law and order." DRIVER & MILES, BABYLONIAN LAWS 109. This law offers the same kind of protection that the Prince of Dor offered to the Egyptian named Wenamon circa 1100 B.C. *See* THE LITERATURE OF ANCIENT EGYPT 142 (William Kelly Simpson ed., 1978).

54. HAMMURABI ¶ 24. DRIVER & MILES, BABYLONIAN LAWS 109.

55. DRIVER & MILES, BABYLONIAN LAWS 110.

[B] Selling Goods Under False Pretenses & Theft by Fraud

Hammurabi's Laws recognized that sales transactions were suspicious when the seller was either a minor ("a son of a man") or a slave. It was, of course, possible that the youth or the slave did not have the authority to sell the man's goods (*i.e.* he had essentially stolen them to sell).[56] Therefore, when either a minor or a slave tried to sell goods, the Laws of Hammurabi required that there be either witnesses to the sale or a written contract as evidence of the sale.[57] If the buyer had neither witnesses nor a written contract to such a sale, the law considered *him* a thief and imposed a death penalty.[58] Here we see the importance that the ancients placed on evidence to corroborate the truth: either something in writing or the testimony of witnesses.[59]

The ancient Mesopotamians also appreciated that taking possession of another's property by fraudulent means was a kind of theft. One of the Laws of Eshnunna provides that for theft of a boat "under fraudulent circumstances" the guilty party was required to pay 10 shekels (and presumably he also had to return the boat).[60]

[C] Black Market Resale

In the ancient world, like the modern, some unscrupulous characters made a living by stealing goods and then reselling them on the black market. Legal systems throughout the ages have experimented with different solutions to the problems that arise when an innocent purchaser buys stolen goods.[61] On the one hand, the good faith purchaser believes that he has a right to the goods that he has bought. On the other hand, the original

---

56. Good, *Capital Punishment*, 19 STAN. L. REV. 947, 963 (1967). DRIVER & MILES, BABYLONIAN LAWS 84.

57. HAMMURABI ¶ 7. *See generally* DRIVER & MILES, BABYLONIAN LAWS 82–86. *See also* Good, *Capital Punishment*, 19 STAN. L. REV. 947, 963 (1967).

58. HAMMURABI ¶ 7. According to Driver & Miles, "[t]he text does not say that the goods in question have been stolen, but the penalty of death and the position of the section between two sections dealing with theft make this practically certain." DRIVER & MILES, BABYLONIAN LAWS 84. *See also* BOTTÉRO, WRITING, REASONING, AND THE GODS 163.

59. *See also* HAMMURABI ¶ 105 (law requiring trading agents to obtain written receipts of transactions in order to be eligible for reimbursement).

60. ESHNUNNA ¶ 6.

61. Westbrook and Wilcke, *Liability of an Innocent Purchaser of Stolen Goods,* 25 ARCHIV FÜR ORIENTFORSCHUNG 111 (1974–1977).

owner whose goods were stolen and resold feels that he has a superior claim to his property since his property was taken illegally. One of the longest provisions in Hammurabi's Laws, ¶ 9, addresses this situation. This law required both the original owner and the good faith purchaser to provide witnesses. The owner's witnesses must identify the goods as his. The purchaser's witnesses, on the other hand, must declare that they were witnesses to the purchaser's sale. The parties were given up to six months to bring their witnesses. The one who failed to bring his witnesses within six months was "assessed the penalty for that case."[62] Furthermore, the purchaser had to "produce the seller." If the judges believed all of the witnesses of both parties, Hammurabi's law dispensed justice as follows: 1) the stolen goods were returned to their original owner; 2) the aggrieved purchaser recouped his purchase price "from the seller's estate"; and, 3) the criminal seller was given a death sentence.[63] It was, however, essential that the purchaser either produce the seller or the witnesses who observed the sale. Otherwise *he* was treated as the thief and given the death penalty ("then it is the buyer who is the thief, he shall be killed").[64] Similarly, if the man claiming to be the original owner was unable to produce witnesses authenticating his prior ownership, then it was he who was executed.[65]

Several documents exist that record the legal proceedings of cases involving an innocent purchaser of stolen goods.[66] These documents are not entirely consistent in themselves nor do they uniformly reflect the law as

---

62. HAMMURABI ¶ 13. *See* DRIVER & MILES, BABYLONIAN LAWS 81, 95–105.

63. HAMMURABI ¶ 9. W.F. Leemans has shown, however, that in one actual court case of this kind "the theft was settled by means of an indemnification, with, perhaps, an additional fine." W.F. Leemans, *Some Aspects of Theft and Robbery in Old Babylonian Documents, in* SCRITTI IN ONORE DI GIUSEPPE FURLANI 661, 665 (1957) (footnote omitted). The modern law of the Uniform Commercial Code reaches a result different from Hammuarabi's Laws; giving possession to the good faith purchaser for value. The original owner must seek damages from the thief-seller. In terms of policy, the UCC tries to encourage commercial transactions. Thus the UCC opts not to punish the good faith purchaser for value. *See* UNIFORM COMMERCIAL CODE § 2-403. *See also* DRIVER & MILES, BABYLONIAN LAWS 81, 95–105; and, Good, *Capital Punishment*, 19 STAN. L. REV. 947, 963 (1967).

64. HAMMURABI ¶ 10; ESHNUNNA ¶ 40 (the buyer must "establish the identity of the seller."). Such a rule would encourage written contracts, since writing would allow a buyer to "establish the identity of the seller." This is a normative rule that encouraged buyers to obtain either witnesses or written contracts. *See also* DRIVER & MILES, BABYLONIAN LAWS 81, 95–105.

65. HAMMURABI ¶ 11. According to Driver & Miles, "one who brings a false accusation of theft is liable to the penalty for theft, namely death." DRIVER & MILES, BABYLONIAN LAWS 62 (footnote omitted). *See also Id.* at 81, 95–105.

66. Westbrook and Wilcke, *Liability of an Innocent Purchaser of Stolen Goods*, 25 ARCHIV FÜR ORIENTFORSCHUNG 111, 115–117 (1974–1977).

described in Hammurabi's Laws. Westbrook and Wilcke have analyzed these documents, compared them to the relevant Hammurabi provisions, and have suggested the following model of the law of the good faith innocent purchaser:

> [T]he innocent purchaser in whose hands stolen property was found was primarily liable, apart from specific restitution, to pay multiple damages for the theft. He could shift this liability to the actual thief or possibly the handler, who was usually (though not necessarily) the person who sold the goods to him, but the burden of proof would be on the purchaser. The purchaser might well be reluctant to make an accusation of theft against the seller if there were insufficient evidence, in which case he might face a further penalty for false accusation, or if the seller were someone with whom he had long-standing commercial relations. In such circumstances he would prefer to accept liability as a «constructive thief» and seek to recoup his losses in a contractual action against the seller for failing to pass good title, assuming that his contract of purchase allowed for such a possibility.[67]

Westbrook and Wilcke then conclude: "[T]he purchaser's strict liability is tempered by his ability either (i) to avoid the penalty altogether by producing the real thief in his place, or (ii) to sue the seller to recoup the payment of the penalty, or (iii) where specially decreed or even by contractual agreement, to require the seller, thief or not, to replace him as defendant."[68] They take the position that the norm was for the innocent purchaser to pay multiple damages.[69] They believe that the provisions in the Laws of Hammurabi which impose a death penalty (in the presence of the purchaser's insolvency) are either academic extrapolations or come from a legal tradition that was either geographically or temporally removed from that of Old Babylonia.[70]

[D] Embezzlement

Embezzlement is a kind of theft. Embezzlement occurs when someone who is entitled to possession of another's property appropriates the property in a manner that manifests an intent to take title to it (not mere pos-

---

67. *Id.* at 117 (footnote omitted).
68. *Id.* at 118 (footnote omitted).
69. *Id.* at 119.
70. *Id.* For more about punishments in situations such as this and other thefts, *see Id.* at 119, nn. 35–36.

session). For example, a bank teller is legally entitled to possess your cash deposit. If, however, the teller pockets your money, that is embezzlement. Hammurabi's Laws criminalized embezzlement in the context of a cultivator.[71] The particular provision deals with a situation where a property owner contracts with another to care for his property (*i.e.,* cultivating fields, caring for cattle, storing grain, etc.). In other words, the cultivator has legal *possession* of the owner's property. If, however, the cultivator embezzled "seed or fodder," he was punished by amputation a hand.[72] In one actual case of a man who embezzled grain, the perpetrator was punished by: 1) being forced to repay the sum plus interest; and 2) having to pay the profit he had made when he sold the grain.[73]

§ 8.4 Sex Offenses[74]

[A] Rape & Incest

As a general rule, a man received capital punishment for rape when the victim was either married or contracted-for-marriage at the time of the rape.[75] After a man had delivered marriage gifts to his fiance's father, it was a capital offense for another man to abduct and rape her.[76] The woman who was the victim of rape was released.[77]

Hammurabi's Laws made incest with one's daughter a criminal offense. A man found guilty of incest with his daughter was banished from his

---

71. HAMMURABI ¶ 253.

72. *Id. See* DRIVER & MILES, BABYLONIAN LAWS 445 (discussing the difficulties of specific vocabulary in this provision). *See also Id.* at 446–448.

73. SAGGS, BABYLON 193.

74. *See* Good, *Capital Punishment*, 19 STAN. L. REV. 947, 956 (1967) (Good comments: "Of all the capital crimes, those dealt with most thoroughly and in the most detail involve sexual relations and marriage.")(footnote omitted).

75. Id. at 947, 956, 975.

76. ESHNUNNA ¶ 26; HAMMURABI ¶ 130; UR- NAMMU ¶ 6. *See* WESTBROOK, OLD BABYLONIAN MARRIAGE LAW 29, 35, 48; DRIVER & MILES, BABYLONIAN LAWS 277, 282 (Driver & Miles explain that the girl in this provision "is still living in her father's house and is inchoately married and a mere child." (footnote omitted)). *See also* Eichler, *Literary Structure* 76; Finkelstein, *Sex Offenses In Sumerian Laws* 86 J. OF THE AMERICAN ORIENTAL SOC. 355, 356 (1966).

77. HAMMURABI ¶ 130. *See* WESTBROOK, OLD BABYLONIAN MARRIAGE LAW 35, 48; Finkelstein, *Sex Offenses in Sumerian Laws*, 86 J. OF THE AMERICAN ORIENTAL SOC. 355, 356 (1966).

city.[78] Apparently, the daughter was not punished.[79] If a man was found guilty of having sexual relations with his mother (after his father's death), both he and his mother received capital punishment by burning.[80] A father-in-law who was caught having sexual relations with his daughter-in-law suffered the death penalty ("they shall bind that man and cast him into the water").[81]

[B] Adultery

The Laws of Eshnunna provided that a married woman found guilty of adultery ("seized in the lap of another man") received capital punishment.[82] Ur Nammu's Laws were more specific, imposing the death penalty where the married woman herself "initiate[d] sexual relations."[83] One of Hammurabi's Laws stipulated that a woman caught in adultery was to be bound and "cast…into the water" along with her lover.[84] If the woman's husband wished to spare her, however, he could. In that case, the king also spared her lover.[85] That does not necessarily mean that the man escaped

---

78. HAMMURABI ¶ 154. See DRIVER & MILES, BABYLONIAN LAWS 318 ("This penalty of banishment will include loss of family and property as well as of citizenship and is perhaps more severe than that prescribed in § 158, where the offender is driven from his ancestral home."(footnote omitted)).

79. DRIVER & MILES, BABYLONIAN LAWS 318.

80. HAMMURABI ¶ 157. See also Good, Capital Punishment, 19 STAN. L. REV. 947, 959 (1967). It is possible that burning as a penalty has a connection to the concept of religious sacrifice and was intended to eradicate "pollution". DRIVER & MILES, BABYLONIAN LAWS 206, 320 (remarking that this is also the penalty in ¶ 110 for "a priestess who frequents or opens a wine-shop…." (footnote omitted)).

81. HAMMURABI ¶ 155. See DRIVER & MILES, BABYLONIAN LAWS 318.

82. ESHNUNNA ¶ 28. See also WESTBROOK; OLD BABYLONIAN MARRIAGE LAW 29–33, 75; DRIVER & MILES, BABYLONIAN LAWS 8; Finkelstein, Sex Offenses in Sumerian Laws, 86 J. OF THE AMERICAN ORIENTAL SOC. 355, 369 (1966); Eichler, Literary Structure 75; MARTEN STOL, Private Life in Ancient Mesopotamia, in 1 CIVILIZATIONS OF THE ANCIENT NEAR EAST, supra ch. 5 note 23, at 485, 494.

83. UR-NAMMU ¶ 7.

84. HAMMURABI ¶ 129. See WESTBROOK, OLD BABYLONIAN MARRIAGE LAW 35, 75; DRIVER & MILES, BABYLONIAN LAWS 281. See also Good, CAPITAL PUNISHMENT, 19 STAN. L. REV. 947, 957, 973–74 (1967); Finkelstein, Sex Offenses in Sumerian Laws, 86 J. OF THE AMERICAN ORIENTAL SOC. 355, 370–72 (1966).

85. HAMMURABI ¶ 129. See WESTBROOK, OLD BABYLONIAN MARRIAGE LAW 35, 75; MARTEN STOL, Private Life in Ancient Mesopotamia, in 1 CIVILIZATIONS OF THE ANCIENT NEAR EAST, supra ch. 5 note 23, at 485, 494; Good, CAPITAL PUNISHMENT, 19 STAN. L. REV. 947, 957, 973–74 (1967); Finkelstein, Sex Offenses in Sumerian Laws, 86 J. OF THE AMERICAN ORIENTAL SOC. 355, 370–72 (1966). Driver & Miles deem it "remarkable" that "it is not the aggrieved husband but the king who spares the life of the adulterer." DRIVER & MILES, BABYLONIAN LAWS 281 (footnote omitted).

scot-free. But it is possible that both received some lesser punishment.[86] It is likely that in such a case the husband would have been the party to initiate the lawsuit, for it appears that the "state" did not prosecute adultery as a capital crime on its own behalf.[87]

An adultress whose husband had been taken as a prisoner of war may have received a lesser penalty. Hammurabi's Laws state that if a woman whose husband was taken prisoner did "not keep herself chaste," she would be "cast...into the water."[88] It is unclear whether this provision is tantamount to a death penalty or whether it is the equivalent, instead, of submitting to the Divine River Ordeal.[89] It may be that the law viewed her husband's having been taken prisoner as a mitigating circumstance.

In Hammurabi's Laws, we learn that if a husband accused his wife of adultery (but she has not been caught in the act), the wife may swear an oath to her innocence. Then, she may "return to her house."[90] If a third party accused a woman of adultery (but she has not been caught in the act), "she shall submit to the divine River Ordeal for her husband."[91] These two laws are very interesting. The first leads us to believe that, when a husband accused his wife of adultery, so long as she swore an oath of innocence, she could not be convicted in the absence of eyewitness testimony. The second, however, says that she will have to submit to the divine River Ordeal if the accuser is someone other than her husband. The presumption operating here seems to be that a husband is more likely to fabricate an accusation of his own wife's adultery than a third party. Driver and Miles submit that, in the case of accusation by a third party, "the evidence against her is much stronger...since 'a finger has been pointed at her on account of another male....'"[92]

---

86. DRIVER & MILES, BABYLONIAN LAWS 281.

87. Id. at 277. *See also* Finkelstein, *Sex Offenses in Sumerian Laws*, 86 J. OF THE AMERICAN ORIENTAL SOC. 355, 371–72 (1966).

88. HAMMURABI ¶ 133b. This provision should be read in conjunction with § 133a and §§ 134–135 which permit a woman to seek the protection of another man in certain circumstances. *See supra* § 6.2[B].

89. *See supra* § 4.3.

90. HAMMURABI ¶ 131. *See* DRIVER & MILES, BABYLONIAN LAWS 277, 283–284. (Driver & Miles express the opinion that, in this case of accusation by the husband, the wife ordinarily would be "ordered to an ordeal by oath. If she fails to perform this ordeal, she will be convicted and drowned...." (*Id.* at 284)). *See* Finkelstein, *Sex Offenses in Sumerian Laws*, 86 J. OF THE AMERICAN ORIENTAL SOC. 355, 367 (1966).

91. HAMMURABI ¶ 132. *See* DRIVER & MILES, BABYLONIAN LAWS 277, 284; Good, *Capital Punishment*, 19 STAN. L. REV. 947, 973 (1967); Finkelstein, *Sex Offenses in Sumerian Laws*, 86 J. OF THE AMERICAN ORIENTAL SOC. 355, 367, 371 (1966).

92. DRIVER & MILES, BABYLONIAN LAWS 284.

In his article "Sex Offenses in Sumerian Laws,"[93] Finkelstein concludes that there are two issues that are most important in analyzing "all of the extant 'statutory' rules dealing with extramarital (hetero-) sexual activity...."[94] These are whether the victim was married or unmarried and whether she consented.[95] Finkelstein summarizes the laws as follows:

> [A]dultery...is treated with the utmost gravity[;] the death penalty often being faced by the adultress, her lover, or both, depending on the circumstances. By contrast, even rape of an unmarried woman seems to have been treated as a relatively mild offense, and....was considered only an economic injury to the girl's father—or master, where the victim was a slave-girl. The only penal element that may come into force in such instances is the right of the girl's parents to insist that the attacker/seducer marry her with forfeiture of the future right of divorce, and the possibly penal assessment of triple the standard "bride-price."[96]

Finkelstein also interprets these laws as showing two legal presumptions: 1) young girls are unlikely to consent to sex; 2) adult women are generally more likely to consent than young girls.[97]

In his conclusion, however, Finkelstein states:

> [A]dultery...in ancient Mesopotamia was not quite the serious offence it would seem at first glance from a reading of the "codes." It was at bottom a civil invasion of a husband's domain, and it was left to him to take as serious or as lenient a view of the matter as he chose; in practice the inclination was towards the less severe view.[98]

In his essay "Private Life in Ancient Mesopotamia," Stol notes that adultery was an offense that could only be committed by a woman, not a man: "A husband's extramarital liasons were not punishable as adultery. Adultery could be committed only by a married woman: it was an offense by the wife against her husband."[99]

---

93. Finkelstein, *Sex Offenses in Sumerian Laws*, 86 J. OF THE AMERICAN ORIENTAL SOC. 355 (1966).

94. Id. at 366.

95. *Id.*

96. Id. at 366–67.

97. Id. at 368.

98. Id. at 372 (footnote omitted).

99. MARTEN STOL, *Private Life in Ancient Mesopotamia, in* 1 CIVILIZATIONS OF THE ANCIENT NEAR EAST, *supra* ch. 5 note 23, at 485, 494.

§ 8.5 Military Crimes

Under Hammurabi's Laws, it was a capital offense for either a soldier or a fisherman to hire a substitute to go on a royal campaign on his behalf.[100] An individual who informed the authorities of a soldier's or fisherman's deception was granted "full legal possession of his [the soldier's or fisherman's] estate."[101] It was also a capital offense for "either a captain or a sergeant" to accept and employ either substitutes or deserters.[102]

There are provisions in Hammurabi's Laws prohibiting officers from abusing their power by taking things that rightfully belong to their soldiers, oppressing soldiers, or hiring out their soldiers to influential persons.[103] The penalty for such an abuse of power is death.[104] In the Laws of Eshnunna, military officials along with "any person in a position of authority" could be charged with theft for taking possession of a fugitive slave or stray ox or donkey without bringing it to the capital city within the period of one month.[105]

§ 8.6 "Criminal" Trespass & "Criminal" Negligence

Trespass and negligence are ordinarily dealt with in Tort law. Nevertheless, in certain situations, the culpability involved is so egregious or severe, that the law treats the offense with heightened severity. Such is the case in ancient Mesopotamia with trespass and negligence.

The Laws of Eshnunna made it illegal for someone to trespass in another's field or house.[106] One can only assume that these laws were—at

---

100. HAMMURABI ¶ 26. Driver & Miles describe the "soldier" in Hammurabi's Laws as "a member of the military force but whose main duty is to preserve public order and generally act as a policeman." DRIVER & MILES, BABYLONIAN LAWS 114 (footnote omitted). They say that the "fishermen" were employees of the crown. Id. at 115.

101. HAMMURABI ¶ 26. See Good, Capital Punishment, 19 STAN. L. REV. 947, 967 (1967). See also DRIVER & MILES, BABYLONIAN LAWS 116.

102. HAMMURABI ¶ 33. See Good, Capital Punishment, 19 STAN. L. REV. 947, 967 (1967). See also DRIVER & MILES, BABYLONIAN LAWS 121–122.

103. HAMMURABI ¶ 34. See also DRIVER & MILES, BABYLONIAN LAWS 121–122.

104. HAMMURABI ¶ 34. See Good, Capital Punishment, 19 STAN. L. REV. 947, 967 (1967). See also DRIVER & MILES, BABYLONIAN LAWS 121–122.

105. ESHNUNNA ¶ 50.

106. ESHNUNNA ¶¶ 12–13. See also Good, Capital Punishment, 19 STAN. L. REV. 947, 963 (1967).

least in part—intended to curb theft.[107] The penalty for trespass during the daytime was 10 shekels.[108] Trespass at night, however, was considered a capital offense.[109] It is likely that nocturnal trespass was considered a more serious offense because of the perceived higher risk of injury to a property owner under cover of darkness. This is analogous to the distinction recognized in many legal systems between theft (stealing in the daytime) *versus* burglary (stealing at night).[110] Hammurabi's Laws dealt with breaking and entering very strictly: "If a man breaks into a house, they shall kill him and hang(?) him in front of that very breach."[111]

Hammurabi's Laws contain two laws that are arguably criminal negligence. These provisions imposed severe penalties on a contractor who constructed a house so poorly that it collapsed and killed someone.[112] If the collapse killed the owner, the contractor himself received the death penalty.[113] If the collapse killed the owner's son, it was the contractor's son who was put to death.[114] In addition, two of the Laws of Eshnunna treated negligence as so severe that it was considered a capital offense.[115] In each case, the negligence involved a person's failure to prevent injury. One law dealt with the situation where the owner of a wall ignored the warning of municipal officials that his wall was buckling and in need of repair.[116] When the wall collapsed and killed "a member of the *awilu*-class," the law states

---

107. *See* LIPIT-ISHTAR ¶ 9 (apparently combining the concepts of trespass and theft in one provision).

108. ESHNUNNA ¶¶ 12–13. *See also* Good, *Capital Punishment*, 19 STAN. L. REV. 947, 963 (1967), and LIPIT-ISHTAR ¶ 9.

109. ESHNUNNA ¶¶ 12–13. *See also* Good, *Capital Punishment*, 19 STAN. L. REV. 947, 963 (1967); Ellickson & Thorland, *Ancient Land Law*, 71 CHICAGO-KENT L. REV. 321, 343 (1995).

110. *See supra* § 8.3 [A].

111. HAMMURABI ¶ 21. *See* Ellickson & Thorland, *Ancient Land Law*, 71 CHICAGO-KENT L. REV. 321, 343 (1995). This is a unique punishment in Hammurabi's Laws and in Mesopotamian law in general. Driver & Miles observe: "The punishment then reflects the crime: as he has made a hole in the wall of the house, so a hole is made in his body." DRIVER & MILES, BABYLONIAN LAWS 108. Compare HAMMURABI ¶ 227 (guilty defendant is hanged in the doorway).

112. HAMMURABI ¶¶ 229–230. *See* DRIVER & MILES, BABYLONIAN LAWS 426; Good, *Capital Punishment*, 19 STAN. L. REV. 947, 954 (1967).

113. HAMMURABI ¶ 229. *See* Ellickson & Thorland, *Ancient Land Law*, 71 CHICAGO-KENT L. REV. 321, 348–49 (1995).

114. HAMMURABI ¶ 230. *See* DRIVER & MILES, BABYLONIAN LAWS 426; Ellickson & Thorland, *Ancient Land Law*, 71 CHICAGO-KENT L. REV. 321, 349 (1995).

115. ESHNUNNA ¶ 58, ¶ 60.

116. ESHNUNNA ¶ 58. *See* Good, *Capital Punishment*, 19 STAN. L. REV. 947, 954 (1967).

that it was "a capital case" that must be "decided by a royal decree."[117] A related law mandated a death penalty for a guard whose negligence allowed a burglar to break into a house.[118]

§ 8.7 False Witness/Perjury

Ur-Nammu's Laws imposed a fine of 15 shekels on a witness who committed perjury.[119] If a witness refused "to take the oath," his penalty was to "make compensation of whatever was the object of the case."[120] The very first law in Hammurabi's Laws makes it a capital offense to accuse another of homicide falsely: "If a man accuses another man and charges him with homicide but cannot bring proof against him, his accuser shall be killed."[121] The third of Hammurabi's Laws provides that when someone "cannot bring evidence for his accusation" in a capital case, his punishment is death.[122] Edwin Good has suggested, regarding these two laws, that "[i]n both cases, the penalty may be an application of the punishment which would be imposed if the case were proved true and may therefore be an instance of *lex talionis*."[123] Hammurabi's Laws also penalized someone who accused either a certain kind of priestess called an *ugbabtu* or a married woman and failed "to bring proof."[124] This law does not specify just what the accusation had to concern. The penalty for an unsubstantiated claim under this provision was flogging and having half his hair shaved off.[125]

---

117. ESHNUNNA ¶ 58. *See* Ellickson & Thorland, *Ancient Land Law*, 71 CHICAGO-KENT L. REV. 321, 348 (1995).

118. ESHNUNNA ¶ 60.

119. UR-NAMMU ¶ 28.

120. UR-NAMMU ¶ 29.

121. HAMMURABI ¶ 1.

122. HAMMURABI ¶ 3.

123. Good, *Capital Punishment*, 19 STAN. L. REV. 947, 968 (1967).

124. HAMMURABI ¶ 127. DRIVER & MILES, BABYLONIAN LAWS 278 (Driver & Miles express the opinion that "these words refer to the failure to justify his slander in the proceeding whether brought by him or by the slandered woman or by persons acting on her behalf.").

125. HAMMURABI ¶ 127. DRIVER & MILES, BABYLONIAN LAWS 279 (Driver & Miles assert that shaving half of a person's head was a form of public ridicule, causing shame and embarrassment.). *See* Finkelstein, *Sex Offenses in Sumerian Laws*, 86 J. OF THE AMERICAN ORIENTAL SOC. 355, 371 (1966).

§ 8.8 Miscellaneous "Crimes"

[A] Religious Offenses

Certain classes of priestesses were prohibited from either opening a tavern or entering one "for some beer."[126] The penalty was apparently death by burning.[127] This law was probably intended to keep the priestesses from associating with prostitutes, since the tavern was either a place where prostitutes gathered or it may have been a brothel itself.[128]

[B] Witchcraft

There were laws prohibiting some brand of witchcraft, but "we have no evidence for witches being actually criminally prosecuted...."[129] Hammurabi's Laws used the divine River Ordeal as a means to determine whether someone was guilty of witchcraft.[130] If the accused was overwhelmed by the water (and therefore adjudged guilty), his accuser was granted "full legal possession of his estate."[131] On the other hand, if the accused survived the divine River Ordeal, the accuser was put to death and the accused was granted "full legal possession of his accuser's estate."[132]

[C] False Imprisonment/Kidnapping

One of Ur-Nammu's Laws appears to have prohibited an individual from restricting another's freedom of movement. Perhaps this was a law prohibiting false imprisonment: "If a man detains(?) (another), that man

---

126. HAMMURABI ¶ 110. *See* DRIVER & MILES, BABYLONIAN LAWS 364.

127. HAMMURABI ¶ 110. DRIVER & MILES, BABYLONIAN LAWS 206 (Driver & Miles suggest that burning as a punishment is based on religious sacrifice).

128. MARTEN STOL, *Private Life in Ancient Mesopotamia, in* 1 CIVILIZATIONS OF THE ANCIENT NEAR EAST, *supra* ch. 5 note 23, at 485, 493. *See* DRIVER & MILES, BABYLONIAN LAWS 206; Good, *Capital Punishment,* 19 Stan. L. Rev. 947, 959 (1967).

129. WALTER FARBER, *Witchcraft, Magic, and Divination in Ancient Mesopotamia, in* 3 CIVILIZATIONS OF THE ANCIENT NEAR EAST 1895, 1898 (Jack M. Sasson ed., 1995); SAGGS, BABYLON 317.

130. HAMMURABI ¶ 2.

131. *Id.*

132. *Id.* For more about this provision, *see* DRIVER & MILES, BABYLONIAN LAWS 61–62. *See also* Good, *Capital Punishment,* 19 STAN. L. REV. 972 (1967).

shall be imprisoned and he shall weigh and deliver 15 shekels of silver."[133] In Hammurabi's Laws, kidnapping was a capital offense.[134]

[D] Harboring Criminals

A woman innkeeper was required to turn in criminals who congregated in her house. If she failed to do so, she received the death penalty.[135]

[E] Bribery

In the time of Hammurabi, we have evidence that a person found guilty of bribery was taken to the king for punishment; but details are unclear.[136]

§ 8.9 Punishments

The most common penalties for conduct that we would characterize as criminal are: 1) death[137] (by drowning, burning,[138] or impalement[139]); 2)

---

133. UR-NAMMU ¶ 3.

134. HAMMURABI ¶ 14. *See also* Westbrook, *Slave and Master*, 70 CHICAGO-KENT L. REV. 1631, 1642 (1995); Good, *Capital Punishment*, 19 STAN. L. REV. 947, 953 (1967); and DRIVER & MILES, BABYLONIAN LAWS 105 (Driver & Miles say that the law about kidnapping is placed among theft laws because it was considered a kind of theft).

135. HAMMURABI ¶ 109. *See also* DRIVER & MILES, BABYLONIAN LAWS 205; Good, *Capital Punishment*, 19 STAN. L. REV. 947, 967 (1967); MARTHA T. ROTH, *Gender and Law: A Case Study From Ancient Mesopotamia* in GENDER AND LAW IN THE HEBREW BIBLE AND THE ANCIENT NEAR EAST *supra* ch. 1 note 20 at 173, 178–179 (Victor H. Matthews, Bernard M. Levinson and Tikva Frymer-Kensky eds., 1997).

136. SAGGS, BABYLON 73.

137. DRIVER & MILES, BABYLONIAN LAWS 494 ("The capital penalty is most often expressed by saying that the offender 'shall be killed' ...; this occurs seventeen times in the first thirty-four sections. A second form of expression, which occurs five times, is that 'they shall kill' ... the offender.").

138. Burning as a penalty was probably based on the concept of religious sacrifice. DRIVER & MILES, BABYLONIAN LAWS 206. *See also Id.* at 495–496 (identifying specific provisions in Hammurabi's Laws in which death by burning is the punishment: ¶ 25 (for looting during a fire); ¶ 110 (for a priestess who operates or frequents an inn); and ¶ 157 (for a man and his mother who commit incest with one another after the father/husband's death)).

139. *See* DRIVER & MILES, BABYLONIAN LAWS 496 (identifying specific provisions in Hammurabi's Laws where impalement is the punishment: ¶ 153 (for a woman who kills her husband on account of her lover); ¶ 21 (for a burglar who breaks into a house) (this reference appears to be erroneous since ¶ 21 clearly refers to "hanging" as

mutilation (such as amputation of a limb or appendage);[140] 3) payment of compensation,[141] multiple damages, or fines;[142] 4) banishment;[143] and, 5) public flogging.[144] The punishment of being "cast into the water" poses some problems of interpretation. If the criminal was bound (as was the case for all men cast into the water in Hammurabi's Laws), it is unlikely that he would have had any chance for escape.[145] If, on the other hand, the criminal was not bound, apparently escape and exoneration were possible.[146] In Hammurabi's Laws, women are cast into the water as a penalty in four laws[147] but are only described as "bound" in one (¶ 129) — where an adultress has been caught *in flagrante delicto* with her lover.[148] Driver and Miles conclude that drowning is actually employed as a punishment five times[149] for three kinds of offenses in Hammurabi's Laws: 1) for adultery;[150] 2) for incest with a daughter-in-law;[151] and, 3) for a woman inkeeper (alewife) cheating her customers.[152]

Mesopotamian laws do not employ incarceration as a punishment. But debtors or members of their families could be taken as "debt hostages" for limited periods of time.[153] Although retributive punishment — *lex*

---

the punishment); ¶ 227 for an "*awīlum* who has wrongfully procured the removal of the owner's mark from a slave....")).

140. *See Id.* at 499 (Driver & Miles identify specific provisions in Hammurabi's Laws where particular parts of the body are mutilated or amputated: hand (¶¶ 195, 218, 226, 253); ear (¶¶ 205, 282); tongue (¶ 192); breast (¶ 194); eye (¶ 193)).

141. *Id.* at 500 (According to Driver & Miles, the goal of monetary compensation in Hammurabi's Laws is restitution: "The law requires restitution and, so far as possible seeks to make the injured party as well off as he was before the injury and by so doing causes the offender to suffer equally with the injured party, whereby equilibrium is obtained.").

142. Driver & Miles conclude that all monetary damages in the Old Babylonian period went to the injured party, and were not fines payable to the state. DRIVER & MILES, BABYLONIAN LAWS 500–501.

143. HAMMURABI ¶ 154 ("If a man should carnally know his daughter, they shall banish that man from the city.").

144. HAMMURABI ¶ 202 ("If an *awīlu* should strike the cheek of an *awīlu* who is of status higher than his own, he shall be flogged in the public assembly with 60 stripes of an ox whip.").

145. DRIVER & MILES, BABYLONIAN LAWS 282.

146. SAMUEL GREENGUS, *Legal and Social Institutions of Ancient Mesopotamia, in* 1 CIVILIZATIONS OF THE ANCIENT NEAR EAST, *supra* ch. 1 note 14 at 469, 474.

147. HAMMURABI ¶¶ 108, 129, 133, 143.

148. DRIVER & MILES, BABYLONIAN LAWS 282.

149. *Id.* at 495.

150. HAMMURABI ¶¶ 129, 133, 143.

151. HAMMURABI ¶ 155.

152. HAMMURABI ¶ 108.

153. SAGGS, BABYLON 194.

talionis—is common in Hammurabi's Laws, it is either non-existent or rare in other—earlier—Sumerian law collections where money damages and fines are the ordinary punishments.[154] In addition to the evidence in the law collections, there is evidence in actual legal documents dating from the Ur III period (*c.* 2100 B.C.) indicating that multiple damages were the common punishment for theft.[155]

---

154. *Id.* at 200.

155. Westbrook and Wilcke, *Liability of an Innocent Purchaser of Stolen Goods,* 25 Archiv für Orientforschung 111, 114 (1974–1977) (mentioning cases involving stolen: sheep—a factor of 10—; fish—a factor of 14—; and, asses owned by the temple—"restoration of an unknown amount of money.").

CHAPTER 9

Torts

§ 9.1 The Problem of Categorization (Battery, Negligence, Strict Liability)

In Hammurabi's Laws, there are a number of provisions that cover situations that we today might be tempted to classify as battery, but it is not always entirely clear.[1] This ambiguity arises because many of the provisions which at first appear to be straight forward instances of battery are unclear as to whether the conduct described in them is intentional, negligent, or neither. For example, one famous law states: "If an *awīlum* should blind the eye of another *awīlum*, they shall blind his eye."[2] The law that immediately follows is of the same ilk: "If he should break the bone of another *awīlum*, they shall break his bone."[3] Under modern tort law, the acts described in these provisions would be classified as batteries only if the tortfeasor *intentionally* caused the harmful or offensive contact (*i.e.*, the physical contact that caused the blindness or the broken bone) with the victim. Modern tort law would characterize these acts as negligent only if the tortfeasor's conduct that caused the blindness or broken bone failed to conform to the standard of what a reasonable person would have done under similar circumstances. For example, arguably it would not be negligent for an individual to strike another acidentally with a stick (causing blindness or a fracture) if he was in the process of defending himself from an attacking dog; especially if a reasonable person in the position of the man being attacked by the dog would have been unaware of the victim's presence (for example, if the victim had walked up from behind just as the dog began its attack).

---

1. HAMMURABI ¶¶ 195–208. *See also* DRIVER & MILES, BABYLONIAN LAWS 409 (listing these laws in a table giving the Aggressor, Offence, Victim, and Penalty).
2. HAMMURABI ¶ 196.
3. HAMMURABI ¶ 197. *See also* HAMMURABI ¶ 200 (knocking out a tooth).

As these two laws are written, they seem to describe situations where liability would be imposed in a *strict liability sense* (*i.e.*, merely because an actor *caused* personal injury). These laws do not say that the blinding or fracture need have been intentional. Nor do they require that the conduct involved was negligent (*i.e.*, failing to act like a reasonable person would have under the circumstances). Rather, these laws appear to impose liability regardless of whether the tortfeasor intended the injury, caused the injury negligently, or did so accidentally—like the example of the person defending himself with a stick. We would call this liability—liability based on causation alone—*strict liability*.

Driver and Miles examine the provisions in Hammurabi's Laws that overtly include "negligence," and conclude that "there is no general law of negligence, but certain acts or results which are due to negligence must be proved."[4] Nevertheless, they acknowledge that many provisions in Hammurabi's Laws contain concepts that are very similar to our modern notion of negligence.[5] In Hammurabi's Laws, according to Driver and Miles, "[t]he law of torts…is fair and equitable, and traces of the conception of negligence are to be found."[6] For example, when boats collided on a river, Mesopotamian law imposed liability on the upstream boat.[7] The legal presumption operating is that the upstream captain has a greater opportunity to avoid a collision than a downstream captain because he has more control, since he travels at a slower speed.[8] Another law that appears to rely on the concept of negligence is HAMMURABI ¶ 267. According to this law, if a shepherd negligently allowed mange to spread within an enclosure, he had to replace the sheep, goats, or cattle that were damaged by the mange.[9] Presumably, this situation involves negligence on the part of the shepherd, unlike the situation in HAMMUARABI ¶ 266 where the shepherd takes an oath claiming no responsibility, and the property owner (*i.e.*, the owner of the enclosure) is adjudged liable for the injury to the animal.[10]

---

4. DRIVER & MILES, BABYLONIAN LAWS 462. *See also generally Id.* at 461–466.

5. Id. at 465 (specifically identifying HAMMURABI ¶¶ 245, 236–237, 240, 53, and 55).

6. DRIVER & MILES, BABYLONIAN LAWS 57.

7. HAMMURABI ¶ 240; SLHF (v 27–31), (v 32–36). Driver & Miles argue that the boats in this provision are special, and that they are not just "any kind of ship going upstream" or "any kind of ship going downstream." DRIVER & MILES, BABYLONIAN LAWS 433.

8. DRIVER & MILES, BABYLONIAN LAWS 431–432.

9. HAMMURABI ¶ 267.

10. *See infra* § 10.5; DRIVER & MILES, BABYLONIAN LAWS 461 (regarding the concept of negligence). *See also Id.* at 459 (Driver & Miles note that this same principle is found in contemporary contracts where the shepherd warrants "against scab and

Still, since it is often unclear whether many of the provisions in the ancient Mesopotamian law collections address situations that involve what we would characterize as "fault" (*i.e.*, either intentional or negligent conduct), absent evidence to the contrary, it may simply be best to admit that many of these laws *could* refer to situations involving any of the three: 1) intent (liability based on the tortfeasor's deliberate attempt to strike or harm the victim); 2) negligence (liability based on the tortfeasor's failure to act like a reasonable person under the circumstances); or 3) strict liability (liability based on mere causation).[11]

§ 9.2 The Influence of "Status" on Tort Damages

Class — or personal status — made a significant difference in how Hammurabi's Laws assessed damages for torts.[12] When a member of the *awilu* class injured a commoner or a slave (*i.e.*, not another *awilu*), damages were ordinarily monetary compensation rather than *lex talionis* (retribution).[13] For example, when an *awilu* either blinded a commoner's eye or broke a commoner's bone, he paid 60 shekels of silver as compensation.[14] If it was a slave whose eye had been blinded or bone broken by an *awilu*, then the compensation was one-half of the slave's value (no doubt paid to the owner).[15] But the payments for compensation are not mathematically consistent across the board. There are some puzzling inconsistencies.[16]

---

loss." According to them, "in the view of the legislator, this occurs only with a lazy or incompetent shepherd.").

11. *See* Driver & Miles, Babylonian Laws 406 ("no general rule is laid down but a number of individual instances are given....."). Regarding this issue, Driver & Miles conclude:

> The Babylonian lawgiver realized that an injury may be caused by intention or by negligence, but he contents himself with specifying typical acts of intention or of negligence and, if a recognized injury is committed, he is indifferent as to the manner in which it is caused. It looks as if Babylonian law was in a transitional stage and was becoming conscious of the principle that a man should not be responsible unless he was in fault but had not yet worked out the principle sufficiently to make it safe to put it in practice.

Id. at 465–466.

12. *See supra* § 5.1 regarding legal status. Driver & Miles, Babylonian Laws 409–410.

13. Samuel Greengus, *Legal and Social Institutions of Ancient Mesopotamia*, in 1 Civilizations of the Ancient Near East, *supra* ch. 1 note 14 at 469, 476.

14. Hammurabi ¶ 198. *See also* Hammurabi ¶ 201 ("If he should knock out the tooth of a commoner, he shall weigh and deliver 20 shekels of silver.").

15. Hammurabi ¶ 199.

16. Driver & Miles, Babylonian Laws 410–411.

One act that seems to have special significance is a "strike" on the cheek.[17] When an *awilu* struck the cheek of another *awilu* who was "of status higher than his own," Hammurabi's Laws treated the offense more like a criminal matter than a tort: the perpetrator was "flogged in the public assembly with 60 stripes of an ox whip."[18] If, instead, the victim was "his equal," then compensation was 60 shekels.[19] The pattern with respect to status that prevails for other torts holds true in the case of a slap to the cheek: the penalty was milder when a commoner was the victim and it was more severe if the perpetrator was from a class lower than his victim. For example, a commoner who struck another commoner's cheek paid only 10 shekels as compensation.[20] If a slave struck an *awilu*'s cheek, Hammurabi's Laws provided mutilation as a penalty: "they shall cut off his ear."[21]

§ 9.3 Catalogue of Torts & Compensation

There were a number of laws that established compensation for causing a woman to miscarry.[22] The compensation varied depending on the status of the woman and on the degree of fault involved (*i.e.*, an intentional act carried a stiffer penalty than one simply involving negligence).[23] The student exercise tablet of Bēlshunu (*c.* 1800 B.C.) provides that compensation for causing a miscarriage was 20 shekels if the tortfeasor's act was intentional ("strikes")[24] and only 10 shekels if the act was negligent ("jostles").[25]

---

17. For a perceptive analysis of the cheek-slapping provisions in the Laws of Hammurabi and other documents related to this offense, *see* Martha T. Roth, *Mesopotamian Legal Traditions and the Laws of Hammurabi*, 71 CHICAGO-KENT L. REV. 13, 26–37 (1995).

18. HAMMURABI ¶ 202.

19. HAMMURABI ¶ 203.

20. HAMMURABI ¶ 204.

21. HAMMURABI ¶ 205.

22. *See* DRIVER & MILES, BABYLONIAN LAWS 413–416. *See also* Lafont, *Continuity and Pluralism* 108; Good, *Capital Punishment* 19 STAN. L. REV. 947, 953 (1967) ("Five separate codes envision the situation of a blow to a pregnant woman resulting in a miscarriage. Code of Hammurabi sections 209–14 deal with six separate possibilities.").

23. *See* Good, *Capital Punishment*, 19 STAN. L. REV. 947, 954 (1967) ("The little extant material from Lipit-Ishtar calls for fines the amounts of which depend on whether the blow was intentional or unintentional.").

24. SLEX ¶ 2'.

25. SLEX ¶ 1'. *Cf.* Lafont, *Continuity and Pluralism* 112 (Lafont states that "all the cuneiform sources…assume the intentional nature of the blows suffered by the woman….").

These two provisions reveal a sharp distinction between injuries caused intentionally versus injuries caused negligently. In Lipit-Ishtar's Laws, striking "the daughter of a man" and causing a miscarriage cost the tortfeasor 30 shekels.[26] If it was "the slave woman of a man" instead of a daughter who miscarried because of a blow, the damages were set at 5 shekels. Curiously, by the time of Hammurabi's Laws, damages for this type of intentional tort decreased. If a member of the *awilu* class caused an *awilu* woman to miscarry, he was required to pay 10 shekels.[27] If the woman was a commoner, the penalty was only 5 shekels.[28] If the woman was a slave, he paid only 2 shekels. But the stakes were proportionately higher in the event that the woman, herself, in addition to losing her fetus, also died. If the woman was of the *awilu* class, the law imposed a death sentence on the tortfeasor's daughter.[29] If the offender did not have a daughter, it is reasonable to assume that a money damage could be used as a substitute.[30] If the woman involved was a commoner, the guilty party had to pay 30 shekels.[31] If the woman was an *awilu*'s slave, the tortfeasor paid 20 shekels.[32]

In Ur-Nammu's Laws, many torts involving personal injury that we would probably classify either as types of battery or negligence[33] had fixed amounts of compensation. It is instructive to recognize that the general rule was for the tortfeasor to pay money damages to the victim. These laws were not laws of *lex talionis*, where brutality was punished with the same brand of brutality (*e.g.,* "an eye for an eye"). For example, when someone cut off another's foot, he had to pay 10 shekels of silver as compensation to the victim.[34] When someone broke another's bone with a club, he paid 60 shekels.[35] It cost the tortfeasor 40 shekels for cutting off someone's nose[36] and 2 shekels for knocking out someone's tooth.[37]

---

26. LIPIT-ISHTAR ¶ d.
27. HAMMURABI ¶ 209. *See* DRIVER & MILES, BABYLONIAN LAWS 413–416.
28. HAMMURABI ¶ 211. *See* DRIVER & MILES, BABYLONIAN LAWS 413–416.
29. HAMMURABI ¶ 210. The imposition of a death penalty makes this law seem more criminal in nature than tortious. *See* DRIVER & MILES, BABYLONIAN LAWS 413–416.
30. *See* Lafont, *Continuity and Pluralism* 115 ("Since fulfillment of these punishments might sometimes raise problems, as when the guilty party has no daughter or no wife, it has to be assumed that these penalties were convertible into money.").
31. HAMMURABI ¶ 212. *See* DRIVER & MILES, BABYLONIAN LAWS 413–416.
32. HAMMURABI ¶ 214. *See* DRIVER & MILES, BABYLONIAN LAWS 413–416.
33. The classification would depend primarily upon whether the tortfeasor acted intentionally or negligently. *See supra* § 9.1.
34. UR-NAMMU ¶ 18.
35. UR-NAMMU ¶ 19.
36. UR-NAMMU ¶ 20.
37. UR-NAMMU ¶ 22.

The Laws of Eshnunna regarding personal injury were similar: the tort-feasor paid money damages to the victim. The amount was established by the Laws and varied depending upon which body part had been injured and how severe the injury was.[38] The following are the injuries covered by these Laws:

biting off a nose	60 shekels[39]
an eye	60 shekels[40]
a tooth	30 shekels[41]
an ear	30 shekels[42]
a slap to the cheek	10 shekels[43]
cutting off a finger	20 shekels[44]
knocking someone down in the street and thereby breaking his hand	30 shekels[45]
knocking someone down in the street and thereby breaking his foot	30 shekels[46]
injuries inflicted "in the course of a fray"	10 shekels[47]
breaking a collarbone	20 shekels[48]

§ 9.4 Actual Warnings of Foreseen Dangers

A number of laws from ancient Mesopotamia imposed liability in instances where a tortfeasor received a warning, putting him on notice that his property posed a danger to others. In modern tort terminology, we refer to this as not just *foreseeable* but actually a *foreseen* danger. Presumably,

---

38. They look something like a modern workers' compensation table.
39. ESHNUNNA ¶ 42.
40. *Id.*
41. *Id.*
42. *Id.*
43. *Id.*
44. ESHNUNNA ¶ 43.
45. ESHNUNNA ¶ 44.
46. ESHNUNNA ¶ 45.
47. ESHNUNNA ¶ 47.
48. ESHNUNNA ¶ 46.

when one has been warned of a foreseen, dangerous situation, a reasonable person should take reasonable steps to reduce the likelihood of injury. Thus, Mesopotamian law held warned persons responsible for the resulting injuries when they failed to take remedial measures. For example, suppose that a property owner warned his neighbor that he (the neighbor) was neglecting his property in such a manner that a robber could gain access to his (the complaining property owner's) house: "Your fallow land has been neglected; someone could break into my house. Fortify your property!"[49] If a robber did thereafter break into the house via the negligently maintained property, the negligent neighbor was liable for the loss incurred (*i.e.,* he had to "restore to the owner of the house any of his property that he lost").[50]

§ 9.5 Failure to Maintain Property That Damages Another & Damage to Property

[A] Property That Damages Another

Maintenance of irrigation canals was essential to agriculture.[51] Driver and Miles summarize the need for irrigation and, consequently, for laws relating to irrigation as follows:

> In Babylonia rain falls only in the winter — none from June to August.... Consequently, although the rain is of value in the ploughing

---

49. Lipit-Ishtar ¶ 11.

50. *Id. See also* Hammurabi gap ¶ e (same principle); Driver & Miles, Babylonian Laws 170–171; Ellickson & Thorland, *Ancient Land Law*, 71 Chicago-Kent L. Rev. 321, 348 (1995).

51. Christopher J. Eyre, *The Agricultural Cycle, Farming, and Water Management in the Ancient Near East, in* 1 Civilizations of the Ancient Near East 175, 175–177, 180–183 (Jack M. Sasson ed., 1995); Elizabeth C. Stone, *The Development of Cities in Ancient Mesopotamia, in* 1 Civilizations of the Ancient Near East, *supra* ch. 5 note 12, at 235, 239; Roux, Ancient Iraq 24 ("Agriculture...depends almost entirely upon irrigation."); Renger, *Ownership or Possession of Arable Land in Ancient Mesopotamia*, 71 Chicago-Kent L. Rev. 269, 270 (1995) ("Agriculture in the alluvial plain is only possible through artificial irrigation."). *See* Veenker, Legal Procedure 28 (Citing the work of Karl Wittfogel regarding ancient Mesopotamia as "a 'hydraulic society' (i.e. a society whose economy is based upon irrigation [hydro-agriculture] in a flood plain land....) (footnote omitted)." *See also* Ellickson & Thorland, *Ancient Land Law*, 71 Chicago-Kent Law Rev. 321, 329 (1995).

season, the farmer in fact requires some form of irrigation for date-palms, cereal crops and vegetables. * * * * The country there-fore…has always depended for its fertility…almost entirely on perennial irrigation, i.e., irrigation all the year round, and an elaborate system was invented or introduced by the Sumerians or other early dwellers along its two rivers.[52]

Due to the importance of the canals, Hammurabi's Laws imposed liability on persons whose failure to adequately maintain the embankments of the irrigation canals caused flood damage to others.[53] Damage of this nature could have devastating effects: "a moment's carelessness may result not only in leaving crops and cattle dry and parched in one part but also wide-spread floods in another part of a district."[54] As a general rule, a property owner whose lack of maintenance caused damage was required to pay compensatory damages (i.e., "replace the grain whose loss he caused").[55] This general rule does not punish the negligent owner; rather, it merely restores the *status quo ante*. It tries to put the victim back in the position that he would have been in if the negligent conduct had not occurred. It is worthwhile to realize, however, that although this approach compensates the injured party economically (by repaying lost income), it does not require the negligent party to pay the cost of replacing or repairing the land that was damaged. But the law did exact a severe penalty if the owner who caused the damage was unable to supply replacement grain. In that case, the neighbors were permitted to sell him into slavery and to sell his property in order to satisfy the judgment.[56]

---

52. DRIVER & MILES, BABYLONIAN LAWS 150. *Also see* Renger, *Ownership or Possession of Arable Land in Ancient Mesopotamia*, 71 CHICAGO-KENT L. REV. 269, 271 (1995).

53. HAMMURABI ¶ 53. *See also* HAMMURABI ¶¶ 55–56 (similar provisions); Ellickson & Thorland, *Ancient Land Law*, 71 CHICAGO-KENT L. REV. 321, 349 (1995); DRIVER & MILES, BABYLONIAN LAWS 65–68, 152–154; and Westbrook, *Slave and Master*, 70 CHICAGO-KENT LAW REV. 1631 (1995).

54. DRIVER & MILES, BABYLONIAN LAWS 152.

55. HAMMURABI ¶ 53. *See also* HAMMURABI ¶ 55 (similar provisions); and Ellickson & Thorland, *Ancient Land Law*, 71 CHICAGO-KENT L. REV. 321, 349 (1995); DRIVER & MILES, BABYLONIAN LAWS 65–68; Westbrook, *Slave and Master*, 70 CHICAGO-KENT LAW REV. 1631, 1644–45 (1995). *See generally* DRIVER & MILES 151–154 (regarding damages caused by failure to care properly for irrigation); CHRISTOPHER J. EYRE, *The Agricultural Cycle, Farming, and Water Management in the Ancient Near East, in* 1 CIVILIZATIONS OF THE ANCIENT NEAR EAST, *supra* ch. 9 note 51, at 175, 187.

56. HAMMURABI ¶ 54. *See* Westbrook, *Slave and Master*, 70 CHICAGO-KENT L. REV. 1631, 1644 (1995). Driver & Miles comment that, because the nuisance is public, the penalty is severe. DRIVER & MILES, BABYLONIAN LAWS 154. They note that this is somewhat different from the type of injury described in ¶¶ 55–56 in several ways. *Id.*

[B] Damage to Property

Many ancient Mesopotamian laws treat injuries to property as strict liability torts.[57] For example, one of Ur-Nammu's Laws states: "If a man floods(?) another man's field, he shall measure and deliver 720 silas of grain per 100 sars of field."[58] Another text provides that when one person flooded another's field, he had to "replace the grain [*i.e.*, the grain that the water destroyed] according to (the yields of the fields of) his neighbors."[59] This law contemplates using the neighbor's field as a basis for estimating the amount of grain that might have been produced in the field that was destroyed.[60] In this way, the law prohibits a windfall in the event that the area suffered from bad storms or drought.

§ 9.6 Liability for Damage Caused by Oxen[61]

It is clear that oxen were important to the well-being of the economy in ancient Mesopotamia.[62] They were the principal beasts of burden. When an ox caused damage, its owner was not necessarily responsible for compensating the injured party. For example, in Hammurabi's Laws, one law states: "If an ox gores to death a man while it is passing through the streets, that

---

at 153–154. *See* CHRISTOPHER J. EYRE, *The Agricultural Cycle, Farming, and Water Management in the Ancient Near East, in* 1 CIVILIZATIONS OF THE ANCIENT NEAR EAST, *supra* ch. 9 note 51, at 175, 187.

57. *See supra* § 9.1.

58. UR-NAMMU ¶ 31. *See* Ellickson & Thorland, *Ancient Land Law*, 71 CHICAGO-KENT L. REV. 321, 349, n. 153 (1995).

59. SLHF (iv 35–41).

60. *See infra* § 11.2 [H].

61. *See generally* J.J. Finkelstein, *The Goring Ox: Some Historical Perspectives on Deodands, Forfeitures, Wrongful Death and the Western Notion of Sovereignty*, 46 TEMPLE L. Q. 169 (1973); and J.J. Finkelstein, *The Ox That Gored*, TRANSACTIONS OF THE AMERICAN PHILOSHOPHICAL SOCIETY 71/2. Philadelphia: The American Philosophical Society (1981).

62. BRIAN HESSE, *Animal Husbandry and Human Diet in the Ancient Near East, in* 1 CIVILIZATIONS OF THE ANCIENT NEAR EAST 203, 214 (Jack M. Sasson ed., 1995) ("The abundance of cattle remains has been cited as an indirect indication of the significance of intensive agriculture since this usually involves the breaking up of fields with plows."). For more regarding other animals and their relationship to the ancient Mesopotamian economy, *see* Ellickson & Thorland, *Ancient Land Law*, 71 CHICAGO-KENT L. REV. 321, 342 (1995) ("The chief livestock in ancient Mesopotamia were sheep and goats, with cattle and pigs next in importance.").

case has no basis for a claim."[63] According to Finkelstein, this law reflects the concept of contributory negligence in Mesopotamian law: "It was the victim, by his own carelessness, who got in the animal's way, and was gored to death as a result. It is the fact of contributory negligence, then, that frees the owner of the ox of any possible liability, which would otherwise be inexplicable."[64] Similarly, in the Laws of Eshnunna, when an ox gored another ox to death, the owner of the goring ox was required to pay the dead ox's owner one-half of the value of "the living ox" but he also received one-half of the "carcass of the dead ox."[65]

Apparently, the ancient Mesopotamians recognized that oxen were, to a certain degree, uncontrollable, and that when one ox gored another ox to death the two owners needed to share the loss almost equally. But if the goring ox was "a gorer" (*i.e.,* if the ox had a history of goring—so that the owner had actual notice of the ox's dangerous propensity), then the owner had to pay higher damages.[66] This is a sound policy. If an animal owner knows that his animal has caused injuries in the past, the owner has a heightened responsibility to take precautions to reduce the risk that the animal will cause similar injuries in the future. When the town authorities had notified an ox's owner that his ox was a gorer, and told him to restrain the animal, if the ox subsequently gored a man to death, the owner had to pay 30–40 shekels of silver (the amount varied depending on which collection of laws applied).[67]

These laws are quite significant. Here the owner had actual notice of the ox's dangerous propensities and he had received an official warning from the municipality of the known/foreseen danger.[68] Yet even when the animal caused a man's death, the owner's punishment was merely monetary compensation (not capital punishment). The provisions that follow in the text

---

63. HAMMURABI ¶ 250. Driver & Miles maintain that this law contemplates an ox that has broken loose, not one that was being driven. DRIVER & MILES, BABYLONIAN LAWS 442.

64. Finkelstein, *Sex Offenses in Sumerian Laws,* 86 J. OF THE AMERICAN ORIENTAL SOC. 355, 364, n. 30 (1966).

65. ESHNUNNA ¶ 53. *See* JACKSON, ESSAYS, (ch. 5 "The Goring Ox")108, 131–141 (1975).

66. *See supra* § 9.4.

67. ESHNUNNA ¶ 54 (setting damages at 40 shekels). The same rule applied to a vicious dog when authorities had warned the dog owner and the dog bit and killed a man. ESHNUNNA ¶ 56. *See also* DRIVER & MILES, BABYLONIAN LAWS 8; and HAMMURABI ¶ 251 (setting damages at 30 shekels). *See* Good, *Capital Punishment,* 19 STAN. L. REV. 947, 954 (1967).

68. *See* DRIVER & MILES, BABYLONIAN LAWS 171–172.

of both the Laws of Eshnunna and Hammurabi's Laws illustrate again the significance of status[69]: they maintain that, if the victim of the ox's goring was a slave, the compensation was markedly less (15 shekels instead of 40 in the Laws of Eshnunna and 20 shekels instead of 30 in Hammurabi).[70]

§ 9.7 Physician's Liability

A number of provisions in Hammurabi's Laws deal specifically with the liability of doctors who cause injury or death while performing surgical procedures.[71] As is the case with other personal injuries, the laws concerning a physician's liability impose higher damages when the victim was an *awilu* and lower damages when the victim was either a *mushkenu* or slave.[72] One law states that when a doctor's surgery caused blindness or death, his penalty was amputation of a hand.[73] If a slave died as a result of surgery, the doctor had to replace the slave with another "of comparable value."[74] For blinding a slave in surgery, a doctor paid one-half of the slave's value as compensation.[75] It is interesting that Hammurabi's Laws do not tell us what damages were due in cases where a physician set a bone or operated on a ligament unsuccessfully. Driver and Miles propose that these omissions "may possibly be due to the fact that failure in these operations will not usually have had a fatal result and they can be repeated until success is achieved...."[76] If a veterinarian's surgery caused the death of an ox or donkey, the veterinarian was required to compensate the animal's owner with one-quarter of the animal's value.[77]

---

69. *See supra* § 9.2.

70. Eshnunna ¶ 55. *See also* Eshnunna ¶ 57 (analogous provision regarding a vicious dog). *See also* Hammurabi ¶¶ 229–231 (penalties vary for a house builder depending upon whether the victim of a collapsed house was a free man or a slave).

71. *See* Driver & Miles, Babylonian Laws 416–420 (In particular, Driver & Miles present a tabular chart showing a physician's damages for unsuccessful operations. The table is arranged to indicate the differences in compensation that depend on the type of failed operation and the social class of the patient.).

72. *See* Hammurabi ¶¶ 221–223. *See also* Samuel Greengus, *Legal and Social Institutions of Ancient Mesopotamia, in* 1 Civilizations of the Ancient Near East, *supra* ch. 1 note 14 at 469, 476.

73. Hammurabi ¶ 218.

74. Hammurabi ¶ 219.

75. Hammurabi ¶ 220.

76. Driver & Miles, Babylonian Laws 418.

77. Hammurabi ¶ 225. *See* Driver & Miles, Babylonian Laws 420–421.

§ 9.8 Defamation Relating to Sexual Misconduct

In modern tort law, defamatory statements that falsely accuse persons of sexual misconduct are treated as more serious than most other types of ordinary defamation. This may have been the case in ancient Mesopotamia as well. In Ur-Nammu's Laws, when someone accused "the wife of a young man of promiscuity," if the River Ordeal indicated that the accusation was false, the accuser was required to pay 20 shekels of silver.[78] In the Laws of Lipit-Ishtar, when someone falsely accused "another man's virgin daughter" of having "had sexual relations," the compensation paid was 10 shekels.[79]

§ 9.9 Affirmative Defenses to Tort: Assumption of Risk & Contributory Negligence

There are a few laws from the Old Babylonian period that suggest that the ancient Mesopotamians of the eighteenth century B.C. appreciated a legal concept that modern tort law classifies as either assumption of risk or contributory negligence.[80] One particular provision comes from the Laws of Eshnunna,[81] and three are in Hammurabi's Laws.[82] The Eshnunna law states that when one man caused "the death of another member of the *awīlum*-class" "in the course of a brawl," the penalty was to pay 40 shekels of silver.[83] The fact that the death occurred during the course of a brawl is essential. This death is not treated like an intentional homicide. Even as early as the Laws of Ur-Nammu (*c.* 2100 B.C.), the penalty for homicide was death.[84] In the case of a death that occurred in the midst of a brawl, how-

---

78. UR-NAMMU ¶ 14.

79. LIPIT-ISHTAR ¶ 33. *See* Finkelstein, *Sex Offenses in Sumerian Laws*, 86 J. OF THE AMERICAN ORIENTAL SOC. 355, 367, 371 (1966).

80. *See supra* § 2.6 [C] and ch. 9 notes 54–55 and accompanying text.

81. ESHNUNNA ¶ 47A. Possibly ¶ 47 is a similar provision but it is a little less certain than ¶ 47A.

82. HAMMURABI ¶¶ 206–208. DRIVER & MILES, BABYLONIAN LAWS 413 (Driver & Miles point to these laws as illustrations that there was "[a] distinction...between intentional and unintentional homicide or wounding....").

83. ESHNUNNA ¶ 47A.

84. UR-NAMMU ¶ 1.

ever, some of the fault for the death lay with the deceased himself. The word "brawl" implies that both men were to blame for the violence.[85] In modern tort terminology we would say that the dead man either *assumed the risk* of death by taking part in a brawl or that *his fault contributed* to his own injury.

A "brawl" is different from an "attack" in a meaningful way. Because the death occurred in a brawl (and thus the deceased was, therefore, partially responsible for the violence), the killer was not treated as severely as if the death had been completely intentional and involving no fault on the part of the deceased. Similarly, in Hammurabi's Laws, a person who inflicted injuries on another in the course of a brawl was punished less severely than otherwise. For example, when an *awilu* injured another *awilu* in a brawl, the person causing the damage was required to swear an oath stating that he did not strike the other man "intentionally," and he only had to pay the victim's medical expenses (but no punitive damages).[86] Like the provision in the Laws of Eshnunna, Hammurabi's Laws also contain a law that mitigates damages to a payment of 30 shekels when a death occurred in the midst of a brawl between two *awilu*.[87] If the victim was a commoner, the tortfeasor only had to pay 20 shekels.[88]

---

85. *See also* Lafont, *Continuity and Pluralism* 112 (Lafont notes the same concept present in the Covenant Code).

86. HAMMURABI ¶ 206.

87. HAMMURABI ¶ 207.

88. HAMMURABI ¶ 208 ("If he (the victim) is a member of the commoner-class, he shall weigh and deliver 20 shekels of silver.").

CHAPTER 10

Property

§ 10.1 Introduction: Private Property, Agriculture, and Irrigation

Driver and Miles caution us that "it is uncertain whether there is any [ancient Mesopotamian] term equivalent to the English 'property' or 'estate' in the general sense, including all things over which a man may have power of disposition or which will pass at his death."[1] In the most ancient times, the principal god of a community was considered the owner of all of the land, and activities centered around the temple.[2] But by the end of the third millennium, private individuals began owning land as well.[3] It is clear

---

1. Driver & Miles, Babylonian Laws 325.

2. J.N. Postgate, *Royal Ideology and State Administration in Sumer and Akkad, in* 1 Civilizations of the Ancient Near East, *supra* ch. 8 note 5, at 395, 396; Roux, Ancient Iraq 127 ("The city as a whole and its territory were under the protection of a 'national' god who ideally *owned* the city-state (emphasis original)"); Saggs, Babylon 18, 60–61; Dominique Charpin, *The History of Ancient Mesopotamia: An Overview, in* 2 Civilizations of the Ancient Near East, *supra* ch. 1 note 23, at 807, 809 (challenging this belief).

3. Dominique Charpin, *The History of Ancient Mesopotamia: An Overview, in* 2 Civilizations of the Ancient Near East, *supra* ch. 1 note 23, at 807, 809; Norman Yoffee, *The Economy of Ancient Western Asia, in* 3 Civilizations of the Ancient Near East 1387, 1394 (Jack M. Sasson ed., 1995); Ellickson & Thorland, *Ancient Land Law,* 71 Chicago-Kent L. Rev. 321, 337 (1995) ("All commentators agree that, from the earliest periods of ancient Near Eastern history, free family households—even the poorest of them—typically owned their houses and garden plots." (footnotes omitted)); *Id.* at 339 ("The most recent scholarship on Mesopotamia...indicates that private property in fields co-existed with palace and temple property throughout the third millennium."); *Id.* at 353–54. *See* Roux, Ancient Iraq 153; Saggs, Babylon 46, 163–65, 198, 237; Oppenheim, Ancient Mesopotamia 306. *But see* Renger, *Ownership or Possession of Arable Land in Ancient Mesopotamia,* 71 Chicago-Kent L. Rev. 269, 281–284 (1995) (Renger questions whether the documents from the Sargonic period—2334–2154 b.c.—actually support the claim that private individuals owned landed property.).

that the Sumerians appreciated the concept of private ownership of real property and personal property as well.[4] As a practical matter, after the fall of the Ur III Dynasty (2112–2004 B.C.),[5] it became more common for private individuals to own land.[6] By the Old Babylonian period (c. 2000–1600 B.C.), collegia of temple priests, administrators, and the like, jointly owned shares of fields, but each share was considered as held "in private ownership and [the owner] was entitled to sell it, to give it as a dowry, or to leave it to his heirs."[7] In short, as Ellickson and Thorland put it, "there is universal agreement that outright private ownership of agricultural lands was widespread in northern Babylonia by the start of the second millennium (the Old Babylonian period)."[8] Frequently, people used cylinder seals to designate private property as their own.[9] Certainly, by the Old Babylonian period, Mesopotamian law recognized the existence of several classes of property, such as land, the fruits of land, movables, and intangibles.[10]

Agriculture was of primary importance to the economy and society in ancient Mesopotamia.[11] The date palm was the most important crop—

---

4. *See* OPPENHEIM, ANCIENT MESOPOTAMIA 127–28. Regarding private ownership of personal property, *see* I.M. Diakonoff, *Some Remarks on the "Reforms" of Urukagina*, 52 REVUE D'ASSYRIOLOGIE ET D'ARCHÉOLOGIE ORIENTALE 1, 4 (1958) (specifically mentioning livestock owned by wealthy men "of the temple estates...but probably only under the control of the Palace....").

5. DOMINIQUE CHARPIN, *The History of Ancient Mesopotamia: An Overview, in* 2 CIVILIZATIONS OF THE ANCIENT NEAR EAST, *supra* ch. 1 note 23, at 807, 808, 811–12.

6. ROUX, ANCIENT IRAQ 170.

7. HOLLY PITTMAN, *Cylinder Seals and Scarabs in the Ancient Near East, in* 3 CIVILIZATIONS OF THE ANCIENT NEAR EAST 1589, 1589–98, 1592, 1595–96, 1599–1600 (Jack M. Sasson ed., 1995); OPPENHEIM, ANCIENT MESOPOTAMIA 190.

8. Ellickson & Thorland, *Ancient Land Law*, 71 CHICAGO-KENT L. REV. 321, 340 (1995) (footnote omitted). *But see* Renger, *Ownership or Possession of Arable Land in Ancient Mesopotamia*, 71 CHICAGO-KENT L. REV. 269, 295–300 (1995) (Renger argues that most of the arable land during the Old Babylonian period was owned and operated by kings or large estates: "In the Old Babylonian period, private ownership of arable land plays no role, or at least not a measurable role, in the southern part of the alluvial plain of Mesopotamia...." (*Id.* at 295); "Not only was arable land cultivated directly by the palace or other institutional households, but also large portions of the arable land were farmed individually by holders of sustinence or tenancy fields. Privately owned fields, however, are only scarcely attested." (*Id.* at 300.)).

9. SAGGS, BABYLON 26–27. *See also* ROUX, ANCIENT IRAQ 79–80.

10. DRIVER & MILES, BABYLONIAN LAWS 325–328. *See* VEENKER, LEGAL PROCEDURE 15 ("land sale documents...point to private ownership of real estate as well as temple." (footnote omitted)).

11. *See generally* CHRISTOPHER J. EYRE, *The Agricultural Cycle, Farming, and Water Management in the Ancient Near East, in* 1 CIVILIZATIONS OF THE ANCIENT NEAR EAST, *supra* ch. 9 note 51, at 175, 175–189. OPPENHEIM, ANCIENT MESOPOTAMIA 40, 42, 83; SAGGS, BABYLON 44.

analogous in many respects to olives in the Mediterranean.[12] Driver and Miles remark: "The importance of the palm-tree in Babylonian…economy can hardly be over-estimated."[13] The ancient Mesopotamians used dates for making bread, wine, sugar, vinegar, and meal. Palm trees were essential for fuel to burn (*e.g.,* for smiths) and fodder for sheep and cattle. They were really the only domestic source of timber.[14]

Irrigation canals were vital to both agriculture and urban life in Mesopotamia. Thus, central control and constant maintenance were essential.[15] Because the right to use and the obligation to maintain irrigation canals were so important, the Mesopotamians formulated laws governing the use and maintenance of the common irrigation system. There were even "canal police" called *Gugallu.*[16]

§ 10.2 Sale of Land, Prices, Deeds & Recordation of Real Property

As a general rule, once private ownership of real property was recognized, it became possible to sell private property.[17] According to Ellickson

---

12. Francis Joannes, *Private Commerce and Banking in Achaemenid Babylon, in* 3 Civilizations of the Ancient Near East 1475, 1478 (Jack M. Sasson ed., 1995) ("The most profitable crop was the date palm…."); John F. Robertson, *The Social and Economic Organization of Ancient Mesopotamian Temples, in* 1 Civilizations of the Ancient Near East, *supra* ch. 5 note 38, at 443, 446; Oppenheim, Ancient Mesopotamia 313 ("[T]he date palm occupies in Mesopotamia the position of the olive tree around the Mediterranean."). *See also Id.* at 44; Roux, Ancient Iraq 26.

13. Driver & Miles, Babylonian Laws 157.

14. Michael Roaf, *Palaces and Temples in Ancient Mesopotamia, in* 1 Civilizations of the Ancient Near East 423, 424 (Jack M. Sasson ed., 1995) ("[T]he date palm of southern Mesopotamia and poplar and other trees elsewhere provided a source of timber that could be used for roofing…."); Driver & Miles, Babylonian Laws 157.

15. Christopher J. Eyre, *The Agricultural Cycle, Farming, and Water Management in the Ancient Near East, in* 1 Civilizations of the Ancient Near East, *supra* ch. 9 note 41, at 175, 175–177, 180–83; Elizabeth C. Stone, *The Development of Cities in Ancient Mesopotamia, in* 1 Civilizations of the Ancient Near East, *supra* ch. 5 note 12, at 235, 239; Karl W. Butzer, *Environmental Change in the Near East and Human Impact on the Land, in* 1 Civilizations of the Ancient Near East 123, 142–145 (Jack M. Sasson ed., 1995). Oppenheim, Ancient Mesopotamia 41–42, 84–85; Saggs, Babylon 52, 158. *See also* Roux, Ancient Iraq 24. *Cf.* Frank Arnold Hole, *Assessing the Past Through Anthropological Archaeology, in* 4 Civilizations of the Ancient Near East 2715, 2716 (Jack M. Sasson ed., 1995).

16. Saggs, Babylon 158, 236. *See* Ellickson & Thorland, *Ancient Land Law,* 71 Chicago-Kent L. Rev. 321, 375 (1995).

17. *See* Maynard Paul Maidman, *Nuzi: Portrait of an Ancient Mesopotamian*

and Thorland, "The oldest legal documents ever unearthed involve land sales in Mesopotamia. These are pictographic and date from the beginning of the third millennium."[18] A buyer was free to buy any house not encumbered by a service obligation,[19] using as a means of payment "grain, silver, or any other commodity."[20] Some laws established fixed prices for the sale of real estate. For example, one law collection from about 2100 B.C. fixed the price for one sar of land (about 36 square meters) at about 1 shekel of silver.[21] There were "[w]ide variations in real estate prices per unit of area" in the third and second millennia, but in Nuzi during the Old Babylonian period, "fields sold for approximately the value of one year's grain harvest."[22]

There is evidence which suggests that real estate sales required some sort of written documents in order to be considered valid.[23] We have a number of contracts that record the sale of land and houses. Such documents are common beginning in the Ur III period (2112–2004 B.C.). Saggs translates one Old Babylonian text as follows:

> 1 ½ sar (of land) with a house built on it, next to the house of Kununu and next to the house of Irraya, Arad-Zugal has bought from Arad-Nanna. He has paid him 8 ½ shekels of silver as its full price.
>
> Arad-Nanna has taken an oath by the king that he will not in the future say 'it is my house'.
>
> [The names of the witnesses, and the date, follow.][24]

<hr />

Provincial Town, in 2 CIVILIZATIONS OF THE ANCIENT NEAR EAST 931, 944, 946–47 (Jack M. Sasson ed., 1995); Ellickson & Thorland, Ancient Land Law, 71 CHICAGO-KENT L. REV. 321, 376 (1995) ("there is abundant evidence of the sale and leasing of privately owned land in Mesopotamaia." (footnote omitted)).

18. Ellickson & Thorland, Ancient Land Law, 71 CHICAGO-KENT L. REV. 321, 376 (1995).

19. See infra ch. 10 notes 30–35 and accompanying text.

20. HAMMURABI gap ¶c. See Ellickson & Thorland, Ancient Land Law, 71 CHICAGO-KENT L. REV. 321, 376–77 (1995) ("By the latter portion of the third millennium, silver (or some other precious metal) had become the default medium of exchange there." (footnote omitted)).

21. LAWS OF X ¶ r.

22. Ellickson & Thorland, Ancient Land Law, 71 CHICAGO-KENT L. REV. 321, 406–07 (1995).

23. SAGGS, BABYLON 196, 295.

24. Id. at 293–94. See Ellickson & Thorland, Ancient Land Law, 71 CHICAGO-KENT L. REV. 321, 380 (1995) (Using the same example as Saggs, they relate: "A cuneiform land-sale text typically covered only the basics: identity of the parties; barebones land description; price paid; revendication clause; and witnesses." (footnote omitted)).

Once a sale had taken place, it was common for "the clay tablets memorial-
izing land sales . . . [to be] stored together in records offices. . . ."[25]

Certain kinds of property, however, either had restrictions on alienabil-
ity or were entirely inalienable.[26] For example, because of the necessity of
preserving the "patrimonial home base," during the first half of the third
millennium, family members appear to have had some type of veto power
over the "transfer of family land."[27] In addition, a "field, orchard, or house
of a soldier, fisherman, or state tenant" (*i.e.*, the royal grant of land) could
not be sold.[28] If such property were sold, the sale was considered invalid,
and the buyer forfeited the purchase price ("his silver").[29] Furthermore, this
same kind of property — property that a soldier, fisherman, or state tenant
acquired "attached to his service obligation" (*ilkum*) — could not be "assigned in writing to his wife or daughter," nor could it be given "to meet any
outstanding obligation."[30] But a soldier, fisherman, or state tenant *was* permitted to "assign in writing to his wife or daughter" or to pay debts with "a
field, orchard, or house which he himself acquire[d] by purchase."[31]

Special rules also applied to protect the interests of soldiers and fishermen when they were away from home. When a soldier or fisherman was
taken captive abroad, if his property (field and orchard) was transferred to
another in his absence, upon his (the captive's) return, he was entitled to
have his land returned to him.[32] If the captive soldier or fisherman had a
son who "is able to perform the service obligation," then the property was
transferred to him.[33] If the son was too young, one-third of the land was

---

25. Ellickson & Thorland, *Ancient Land Law*, 71 CHICAGO-KENT L. REV. 321, 384
(1995) (Ellickson & Thorland say that this practice dates back to approximately 2500
B.C.).

26. *Id.* at 387–391.

27. *Id.* at 388.

28. HAMMURABI ¶ 36. Ellickson & Thorland, *Ancient Land Law*, 71 CHICAGO-
KENT L. REV. 321, 390–91 (1995); DRIVER & MILES, BABYLONIAN LAWS 112, 123. *See
also* SAGGS, BABYLON 237; ROUX, ANCIENT IRAQ 193–94; OPPENHEIM, ANCIENT
MESOPOTAMIA 46; and, DRIVER & MILES, BABYLONIAN LAWS 123.

29. HAMMURABI ¶ 37. Driver & Miles note that the seller in this instance is actually rewarded, not punished as one might expect. The goal of these provisions is to
discourage purchasers: "he [the seller] gets it [the property] back together with the
purchase money. . . ." DRIVER & MILES, BABYLONIAN LAWS 123.

30. HAMMURABI ¶ 38. This provision is somewhat similar in principle to the story
of the Egyptian Hapdjefai, who segregated the property that was his by virtue of being
a nomarch from his other property. This ability to separate property is a rather sophisticated legal conception.

31. HAMMURABI ¶ 39. *See also* DRIVER & MILES, BABYLONIAN LAWS 124.

32. HAMMURABI ¶ 27. Driver & Miles note that the house is not specifically mentioned in ¶¶ 27–29. DRIVER & MILES, BABYLONIAN LAWS 116.

33. HAMMURABI ¶ 28.

given to the mother, and the mother raised the son.[34] If either a soldier or fisherman abandoned "his field, orchard, or house because of the service obligation" for three years, and someone else took possession and performed the obligation for those three years, the soldier/fisherman lost his rights to the person who took the property and performed the service obligation.[35] This is something like adverse possession but not precisely. Driver and Miles argue that this type of property transfer is different from adverse possession because the new owner actually takes the property under a grant.[36] If the solder/fisherman was gone for only one year, he retained possession and ownership upon his return.[37]

There is, in addition, a very interesting law in Hammurabi's Laws pertaining to situations where a soldier or fisherman was captured "while on a royal campaign." If a merchant bought back the prisoner from his captors, the law provided that the soldier/fisherman would repay the merchant from his own estate if he had sufficient funds. If he did not have sufficient funds, then his city's temple would repay the merchant, unless the temple's funds also were insufficient, in which case, the palace would repay the merchant.[38] However, in no case were the soldier/fisherman's "field, orchard, or house" to "be given for his redemption."[39] This amounted to a kind of social insurance for prisoners of war.

One other law, from the Laws of Eshnunna, created a rule that is somewhat unique regarding the sale of real property. When a man became so poor that he had to sell his house, if the new owner later decided to sell it, the former owner of the house had the legal right to redeem it.[40] This amounts to a right of first refusal for people who had to sell their houses after falling on hard times. Evidence suggests that this type of redemptive right first appeared in the third millennium.[41] Ellickson and Thorland explain that "re-

34. HAMMURABI ¶ 29.
35. HAMMURABI ¶ 30. DRIVER & MILES, BABYLONIAN LAWS 116 (Driver & Miles note that the house is specifically included in ¶¶ 30–31).
36. DRIVER & MILES, BABYLONIAN LAWS 119.
37. HAMMURABI ¶ 31.
38. Driver & Miles emphasize the order of progression on whom the ransom payment falls: 1) captive; 2) temple; 3) royal authorities. DRIVER & MILES, BABYLONIAN LAWS 120.
39. HAMMURABI ¶ 32. DRIVER & MILES, BABYLONIAN LAWS 119–120; Westbrook, *Slave and Master*, 70 CHICAGO-KENT L. REV. 1631, 1652 (1995).
40. ESHNUNNA ¶ 39. *See* RAYMOND WESTBROOK, *Social Justice in the Ancient Near East, in* SOCIAL JUSTICE IN THE ANCIENT WORLD 153.
41. Ellickson & Thorland, *Ancient Land Law*, 71 CHICAGO-KENT L. REV. 321, 400 (1995).

demptive rights were premised on the notion that patrimonial land lost on account of temporary financial distress should be reclaimable."[42]

§ 10.3 Lease of Fields[43]

According to Ellickson and Thorland, "In Mesopotamia, the leasing of both houses and fields was commonplace beginning no later than the middle of the third millennium."[44] A number of laws found in the law collections deal with the rights and obligations of lessors and lessees of fields for cultivation. One such law suggests that a lessee ordinarily paid about one-quarter of his annual crop as rent to the lessor.[45] One provision set a specific rental price for real estate: one shekel of silver was the price to rent "one sar of a roofed-over area."[46] Driver and Miles present evidence of actual texts that show that "a contract under which the owner receives one-third is by far the most common type."[47] When a renter failed to cultivate a field, he had to pay the owner "grain in accordance with his neighbor's yield, and he shall plow and harrow the field which he left fallow and return it to the owner of the field."[48] In essence, these laws required a renter who breached his contract to pay what modern contract law calls expectation damages[49] (the amount of grain that he expected to receive based on the amount produced in his neighbor's field). These laws also imposed an injunction on the breaching party—requiring him to plow the field before returning it to the owner.[50] In Ur-Nammu's Laws, when an owner "gives a

---

42. *Id.*

43. *See generally* OPPENHEIM, ANCIENT MESOPOTAMIA 85–86.

44. Ellickson & Thorland, *Ancient Land Law*, 71 CHICAGO-KENT L. REV. 321, 369 (1995) (footnote omitted). *See generally Id.* at 369–372.

45. This is a provision about someone leasing a field "for cultivation at a rate of one-quarter of the annual crop." SLHF viii 20–21.

46. LAWS OF X ¶ s.

47. DRIVER & MILES, BABYLONIAN LAWS 131.

48. HAMMURABI ¶¶ 42–43.

49. *See infra* § 11.2 [H]. Driver & Miles make this point clear: "The damages are compensatory, not penal, as their object is to put the injured party in as good a position as that in which he would have been if the contract had been performed." DRIVER & MILES, BABYLONIAN LAWS 137 (footnote omitted).

50. Driver & Miles explain the logic of these provisions. According to them, in ¶ 42 the cultivator merely did a poor job, whereas in ¶ 43 he failed to perform at all—he planted nothing. "The offence, therefore, is more serious and the damages correspondingly more severe." DRIVER & MILES, BABYLONIAN LAWS 137. It is the additional task of ploughing—an injunction—that makes the damages more severe: "deep ploughing in order to restore it to good condition." "This is right and logical; for the owner cannot be expected to make good the farmer's deliberate neglect by his own

field to another man to cultivate" and he fails to cultivate it, he must pay "720 silas of grain per 100 sars."[51] In Lipit-Ishtar's Laws, when a man received "fallow land for the purpose of planting an orchard," and failed to do so, "they shall give the fallow land which he neglected to one who is willing to plant the orchard as his share."[52] When a renter negligently failed to cultivate a field for three years, in the fourth year he had to plow it under, return possession to the owner, and pay "3,000 silas of grain per 18 ikus (of field)."[53]

It is always interesting to see how legal systems deal with issues such as impossibility, impracticability, and "acts of god." In contract law, the question often boils down to a question of who will absorb the loss when some unforeseen circumstance makes performance impossible or impracticable. In Hammurabi's Laws, there are several laws that contemplate such situations in relation to the rental of fields for cultivation. These laws tend to apportion loss based on whether the renter had paid his fee prior to the onset of the circumstance that created the impossibility or impracticability. If he had, then he bore the risk;[54] if he had not, then the renter and owner split the loss.[55] But as a practical matter, any payment made before the harvest was probably just a small sum or deposit.[56] According to Driver and Miles, "there is no known case in which the whole rent is paid in advance or before the harvest."[57] Thus, as a general rule, if the renter had paid, that meant that the harvest had already been gathered too; and consequently, in reality, there was very little "risk" that the renter would bear.

---

labour or at his own charges." *Id.* Driver & Miles maintain that, according to actual documents of the time, the owner usually had the responsibility of ploughing when the farmer's contract was finished. *Id.* at 139.

51. UR-NAMMU ¶ 32.

52. LIPIT-ISHTAR ¶ 8.

53. HAMMURABI ¶ 44. DRIVER & MILES, BABYLONIAN LAWS 138–139 (According to Driver & Miles, termination of such a contract was probably not the usual practice. Such contracts were ordinarily renewed from year to year.).

54. This law provides that when a field renter has already paid his rent, the renter bears the risk of loss ("the loss is the cultivator's alone") when "the storm god Adad devastates the field or a flood sweeps away the crops," not the owner. HAMMURABI ¶ 45. *See* Ellickson & Thorland, *Ancient Land Law,* 71 CHICAGO-KENT L. REV. 321, 371–72 (1995); CHRISTOPHER J. EYRE, *The Agricultural Cycle, Farming, and Water Management in the Ancient Near East, in* 1 CIVILIZATIONS OF THE ANCIENT NEAR EAST, *supra* ch. 9 note 51, at 175, 187.

55. This law provides that if the field renter has not yet paid rent "before the catastrophe destroys the field," then the owner and renter "shall divide whatever grain there is remaining in the agreed proportions." HAMMURABI ¶ 46. *See* Ellickson & Thorland, *Ancient Land Law,* 71 CHICAGO-KENT L. REV. 321, 371–72 (1995).

56. DRIVER & MILES, BABYLONIAN LAWS 140.

57. *Id.*

In the case where a tenant paid his annual rent in advance, and then the landlord evicted him "before the expiration of the full term of his lease," the landlord was required to return the tenant's entire rental payment ("forfeit the silver that the tenant gave him").[58] Driver and Miles interpret this law as having been designed "not so much to punish the owner as to protect the occupier."[59] According to Driver and Miles:

> If…the owner breaks the contract and ejects him [*i.e.*, the tenant] before the end of the term, the whole of the rent must be returned to him. It is very unlikely that the owner will incur the risk of this penalty and the occupier is fully protected from eviction by this ingenious provision.[60]

This remedy for breach of a landlord-tenant contract seems punitive. The landlord does not even get to keep a pro rata portion of the rent.

§ 10.4 Gardeners

Somewhat similar to the laws relating to lessors and lessees are the provisions in Hammurabi's Laws concerning gardeners. One such law suggests that there was an established division of fruits when a gardener was responsible for pollinating an owner's date palms: the gardener kept one-third of the yield while the owner took two-thirds.[61] Another law provides that when a landowner entrusted a field to a gardener to plant a date orchard, he was responsible for cultivating it for four years. "[I]n the fifth year, the owner of the orchard and the gardener…divide[d] the yield in equal shares," but the owner got to choose his share first.[62] If the gardener had left a portion of the field uncultivated, that uncultivated portion was included in *his* share of the yield.[63] If, for some reason, a gardener completely failed to cultivate an orchard, he was required to pay an amount equal to "the es-

---

58. HAMMURABI gap ¶ g.
59. DRIVER & MILES, BABYLONIAN LAWS 170.
60. *Id.*
61. HAMMURABI ¶ 64. Driver & Miles say that the most common types of contracts of this nature give the owner one-third of the crop, but that some also give the owner three-fourths and some give him one-half. DRIVER & MILES, BABYLONIAN LAWS 131–132. *See also Id.* at 158, 163–164.
62. HAMMURABI ¶ 60. *See* DRIVER & MILES, BABYLONIAN LAWS 157, 162–163; CHRISTOPHER J. EYRE, *The Agricultural Cycle, Farming, and Water Management in the Ancient Near East, in* 1 CIVILIZATIONS OF THE ANCIENT NEAR EAST, *supra* ch. 9 note 51, at 175, 187.
63. HAMMURABI ¶ 61. *See* DRIVER & MILES, BABYLONIAN LAWS 157, 162–163.

timated yield of the field for the years it is left fallow," using the neighbor's yield as a basis for estimation. In addition, the gardener was required to "perform the required work on the field and return it to the owner...."[64] When a gardener failed to pollinate the date palms in an orchard, causing a decrease in yield, he was required to pay the owner "in accordance with his neighbor's yield."[65]

§ 10.5 Liability of an Owner of Real Property & Trespass

Some laws relate to damage caused on real property (*i.e.*, liability of an owner of real property) and others relate to damage suffered against an owner of land (*i.e.*, trespass). There is one law in Hammurabi's Laws that imposes liability on an owner of real property for damage caused on his property. That law states that when a shepherd takes care of cattle, sheep, or goats for their owner, and keeps them in an enclosure owned by a third party, if either a lion kills an animal or "an epidemic" breaks out, the owner of the enclosure is liable for the loss.[66]

There are several laws that concern trespass on agricultural land. In Hammuarabi's Laws, for example, if a shepherd grazed his sheep on a landowner's property without permission, the shepherd was required to pay an amount of grain, based on the size of the field—"6,000 silas of grain per 18 ikus (of field) to the owner of the field."[67] Another provision states that if a shepherd allowed his sheep to graze in a field "after the termination of pasturing," he had to pay to the owner "18,000 silas of grain per 18 ikus (of field).[68] Presumably this injury was deemed far more severe than merely grazing one's sheep on another's property. This is because the phrase "after termination of pasturing" probably denotes a particular sea-

---

64. HAMMURABI ¶ 62. For more on HAMMURABI ¶¶ 60–63, *see* DRIVER & MILES, BABYLONIAN LAWS 157, 162–163. *See also* Raymond Westbrook, *Cuneiform Law Codes and the Origins of Legislation*, 79 ZEITSCHRIFT FÜR ASSYRIOLOGIE UND VORDERASIATISCHE ARCHÄOLOGIE 201, 209–211 (1989).

65. HAMMURABI ¶ 65. For more about HAMMURABI ¶¶ 64–65, *see* DRIVER & MILES, BABYLONIAN LAWS 158, 163–164. *See also* Raymond Westbrook, *Cuneiform Law Codes and the Origins of Legislation*, 79 ZEITSCHRIFT FÜR ASSYRIOLOGIE UND VORDERASIATISCHE ARCHÄOLOGIE 201, 209–210 (1989).

66. HAMMURABI ¶ 266. The shepherd was required to take an oath claiming that he was not responsible for the damage ("clear himself before the god").

67. HAMMURABI ¶ 57. DRIVER & MILES, BABYLONIAN LAWS 154–155.

68. HAMMURABI ¶ 58.

son; probably a time when crops were in a more advanced stage of development. Thus, damage at that time would be more difficult to rectify.[69] We have a fragment of another law that concerns a situation where a neighbor works "his neighbor's uncultivated plot without his neighbor's permission;" but we really do not know the substance of this law.[70] According to Lipit-Ishtar's Laws, a man who cut down a tree in another's orchard had to pay "20 shekels of silver."[71] If someone cultivated another's field and sued claiming the right to harvest the crop (arguing that the owner neglected his field), the trespasser had to "forfeit his expenses."[72]

§ 10.6 Slaves

We considered some laws relating to slaves in the context of "personal status" in Chapter Five.[73] Nevertheless, many laws concerning slaves have more to do with the "property" aspects of slaves than with slaves as human beings *per se*. Thus, it is necessary here to turn our attention to slave laws that appertain to slaves as property, not people.[74] Ordinarily, private citizens acquired household slaves in one of four ways. A slave could be bought, born in the household to another slave, obtained through warfare, or acquired from debt.[75]

---

69. *See* DRIVER & MILES, BABYLONIAN LAWS 155–157 ("This suggestion…supposes that at some definite time of the year, probably when the corn was in ear, shepherds were required by law to pen their sheep in a fold, possibly at night, so as to prevent them from trespassing on the growing corn." (*Id.* at 156–57)).

70. HAMMURABI gap ¶ d.

71. LIPIT-ISHTAR ¶ 10. *See also* HAMMURABI ¶ 59 (30 shekels payment for cutting down another's date tree); DRIVER & MILES, BABYLONIAN LAWS 160–161 (regarding HAMMURABI ¶ 59). According to Driver & Miles, "The reason for the severe penalty for cutting down trees is their great scarcity and consequently their great value in Babylonia, not only as yielding fruit but also as providing wood and as giving shade." *Id.* at 160 (footnotes omitted).

72. UR-NAMMU ¶ 30. *See* Ellickson & Thorland, *Ancient Land Law*, 71 CHICAGO-KENT L. REV. 321, 343 (1995) ("The earliest of the known codes, the laws of Ur-Namma, provides that a farmer who violates the 'rights' of another by growing a crop on his field forfeits all expenses." (footnote omitted) (the footnote mistakenly cites ¶ 27 instead of ¶ 30)).

73. *See supra* § 5.3.

74. *See* Westbrook, *Slave and Master*, 70 CHICAGO-KENT L. REV. 1631, 1674 (1995) ("The legal systems of the ancient Near East recognized persons as a category of property that might be owned by private individuals.").

75. DRIVER & MILES, BABYLONIAN LAWS 222. According to Driver & Miles:

> The majority of slaves in Babylon belonged to the palace and to the temples, and private persons, except the rich, had few. Slaves were obtained by capture in war and by purchase in markets at home and abroad; the house-

According to Hammurabi's Laws, if someone discovered a fugitive slave, and the slave refused to identify his owner, the finder was required to take the slave to the palace; and the palace was then responsible for returning the slave to his owner.[76] If the finder, instead, kept the slave in his own house, and the slave was later discovered there, the finder was put to death.[77] If the slave escaped from the finder's custody, the finder was not held responsible if he swore "an oath by the god to the owner."[78] The content of this oath is uncertain. The Laws of Lipit-Ishtar provide that when someone harbored a fugitive slave of the same city for one month, the harborer had to "give slave for slave."[79] But if he did not have a slave to give, he had to instead pay 15 shekels of silver.[80] Hammurabi's Laws levy stiffer penalties. A person received the death penalty for either assisting a slave in his escape "through the main city-gate"[81] or for harboring a slave in one's house.[82] Westbrook notes, however, that Mesopotamian law also provided a carrot as well as a stick: "By the same token, one who brought back a fugitive slave was entitled to a reward from the slave's master, set by the law codes at between two and six shekels of silver."[83]

The civil penalty under the Laws of Eshnunna for "deflowering" someone else's female slave was 20 shekels of silver.[84] Under Ur-Nammu's Laws,

---

slaves were the children of slaves. A large number, too, were Babylonians by birth who had by reason of poverty sold themselves or been sold by their fathers or had been seized by creditors.

Id. at 222. See SAMUEL GREENGUS, Legal and Social Institutions of Ancient Mesopotamia, in 1 CIVILIZATIONS OF THE ANCIENT NEAR EAST, supra ch. 1 note 14 at 469, 477–78. OPPENHEIM, ANCIENT MESOPOTAMIA 75.

76. HAMMURABI ¶ 18. DRIVER & MILES, BABYLONIAN LAWS 105–108.

77. HAMMURABI ¶ 19. DRIVER & MILES, BABYLONIAN LAWS 107.

78. HAMMURABI ¶ 20. DRIVER & MILES, BABYLONIAN LAWS 107.

79. LIPIT-ISHTAR ¶ 12. See Westbrook, Slave and Master, 70 CHICAGO-KENT L. REV. 1631, 1671 (1995).

80. LIPIT-ISHTAR ¶ 13. See Westbrook, Slave and Master, 70 CHICAGO-KENT L. REV. 1631, 1671 (1995).

81. HAMMURABI ¶ 15. See DRIVER & MILES, BABYLONIAN LAWS 105–108; Westbrook, Slave and Master, 70 CHICAGO-KENT L. REV. 1631, 1671 (1995).

82. HAMMURABI ¶ 16. See also DRIVER & MILES, BABYLONIAN LAWS 105–108; Westbrook, Slave and Master, 70 CHICAGO-KENT L. REV. 1631, 1671 (1995); and, Good, Capital Punishment 19 STAN. L. REV. 947, 952 (1967).

83. Westbrook, Slave and Master, 70 CHICAGO-KENT L. REV. 1631, 1672 (1995) (citing UR-NAMMU ¶ 14, LIPIT-ISHTAR ¶¶ 22–23, and HAMMURABI ¶ 17). In Hammurabi's Laws, when someone returned a fugitive slave, the reward was 2 shekels of silver. HAMMURABI ¶ 17. DRIVER & MILES, BABYLONIAN LAWS 107. One of Ur-Nammu's Laws also established a fixed reward for someone who returned a runaway slave to his master. UR-NAMMU ¶ 17.

84. ESHNUNNA ¶ 31. See Finkelstein, Sex Offenses in Sumerian Laws, 86 J. OF THE AMERICAN ORIENTAL SOC. 355, 356 (1966) ("[T]he relatively high penalty imposed

the same offense carried a five-shekel payment.[85] In an ancient document from Nippur, we discover that the penalty for this offense could be quite steep: "The assembly of Nippur addressed (the litigants): 'Because he deflowered the slave girl without (her) owner('s knowledge), Lugal-melam is to pay ½ mina of silver [*i.e.,* 30 shekels] to Kuguzana her owner'...."[86] The slave's owner retained the deflowered slave.

In Hammurabi's Laws, when an *awilu* struck a female slave owned by another *awilu* and thereby caused her to miscarry, the striker had to pay 2 shekels of silver.[87] If the female slave died, he had to pay the owner 20 shekels.[88] This is somewhat analogous to the modern concept called trespass to chattels.[89] Fundamentally, when someone damages another's property, the civil remedy is payment equal to the loss in value of the damaged property.[90]

Westbrook relates that "[s]laves were treated as ordinary chattels and could be sold, pledged, hired, given as gifts, inherited, and forfeited."[91] Nevertheless, there is evidence suggesting that debt-slaves and famine slaves[92] (who ordinarily could gain their freedom by payment of money) were not freely alienable as was the case with chattel slaves.[93] Similarly, although slaves were, technically speaking, property, only chattel-slaves could be

---

on the attacker must be construed as at least a partial compensation to the girl's master for the reduction in her value should her master have contemplated selling her or giving her away in marriage."). *See also Id.* at 369.

85. UR-NAMMU ¶ 8.

86. Finkelstein, *Sex Offenses in Sumerian Laws*, 86 J. OF THE AMERICAN ORIENTAL SOC. 355, 359 (1966).

87. HAMMURABI ¶ 213.

88. HAMMURABI ¶ 214.

89. *See generally* W. PROSSER & W. KEETON, THE LAW OF TORTS 85–88, § 14 (5th ed. 1984).

90. *See* Eichler, *Literary Structure* at 80 (citing JJ. Finkelstein, *Sex Offenses in Sumerian Laws*, 86 JAOS 360 (1966)). Finkelstein summarizes the issue in the context of the rape of a slave girl as follows:

> From the juridical point of view it may be worth mentioning that the trial does not discuss the question of whether the slave-girl was raped or a willing partner in the offence. This is unquestionably to be explained by the fact that in the eyes of Mesopotamian law, consent in such cases is immaterial; the slave-girl is not considered a legal person. Hence, her sexual violation, whether by rape, seduction, or even by her own solicitation, is exclusively considered as a tortious invasion against her owner, for which he may seek redress, if the act had been done without *his* consent or knowledge.

Finkelstein, *Sex Offenses in Sumerian Laws*, 86 J. OF THE AMERICAN ORIENTAL SOC. 355, 360 (1966).

91. Westbrook, *Slave and Master*, 70 CHICAGO-KENT L. REV. 1631, 1660 (1995).

92. *See supra* § 5.3.

93. Westbrook, *Slave and Master*, 70 CHICAGO-KENT L. REV. 1631, 1662 (1995).

punished by physical maltreatment—debt-slaves and other "pledges" could not.[94]

Hammurabi's Laws appear to grant an implied warranty of title for a slave buyer: "If a man purchases a slave or slave woman and then claims arise, his seller shall satisfy the claims."[95] Actual contracts from the Old Babylonian period show that this provision provided assurance to the buyer that the seller had good title to the slave to transfer to the buyer.[96] Ancient slave-sale contracts contain "[a]s many as fifteen different warranties...although almost never in the same document."[97] Some of these express warranties stated that the slave would not escape, that the slave would not be delinquent, that the slave was not actually free, and that the slave would not die during the first 100 days.[98]

When a buyer purchased a stolen slave abroad, his rights and also the original owner's rights depended upon whether the slave himself was a native of the country where the transaction occurred. If the slave was a native, then the original owner was entitled to reclaim the stolen slave at no cost. The defrauded buyer took the loss.[99] But if the stolen slave was from another country, then the owner had to pay the buyer his purchase price in order to redeem his slave.[100] Presumably, the law assumes that a buyer should be more suspicious and cautious when a seller offers native slaves for sale. Perhaps native slaves would be easier for a thief to secure; whereas foreign slaves would have to have been transported a distance.

If a slave falsely alleged that his owner was not his owner, the owner was entitled to bring charges against the slave, with the penalty of having an ear cut off.[101] This law suggests that, absent such a denial, a master did not have carte blanche to maim a slave.[102] Documents from Nuzi report that a slave

---

94. *Id.* at 1666.

95. HAMMURABI ¶ 279.

96. DRIVER & MILES, BABYLONIAN LAWS 479. Westbrook and Wilcke, *Liability of an Innocent Purchaser of Stolen Goods*, 25 ARCHIV FÜR ORIENTFORSCHUNG 111, 118 (1974–1977).

97. Westbrook, *Slave and Master*, 70 CHICAGO-KENT L. REV. 1631, 1663 (1995).

98. *Id.* at 1663–64.

99. HAMMURABI ¶ 280. *See* DRIVER & MILES, BABYLONIAN LAWS 482–487 (Driver & Miles interpret the slave being a "native" as synonymous with being a Babylonian, and therefore take a different tack to interpretation) and Westbrook, *Slave and Master*, 70 CHICAGO-KENT L. REV. 1631, 1664–65 (1995) (same).

100. HAMMURABI ¶ 281.

101. HAMMURABI ¶ 282. According to Driver & Miles, this "is the only case in the Laws which the aggrieved party is said himself to inflict the penalty of mutilation." DRIVER & MILES, BABYLONIAN LAWS 489 (footnote omitted).

102. Westbrook, *Slave and Master*, 70 CHICAGO-KENT L. REV. 1631, 1667 (1995).

could be punished for this same transgression by blinding.[103] In Ur-Nammu's Laws, a slave woman was punished by having her mouth washed out with a litre of salt if she cursed "someone acting with the authority of her mistress."[104]

§ 10.7 Miscellaneous

[A] Acquisition of Property Through Paying Taxes

In Lipit-Ishtar's Laws, if a property owner defaulted on his property taxes, and someone else began paying the property taxes and continued to do so for three years, the person who assumed the tax burden became rightful owner instead of the defaulter.[105]

[B] Adjacent Property Owners

There are a few provisions in the law collections that deal with the rights and obligations of adjacent property owners. One such law suggests that adjacent property owners shared responsibility for the maintenance of a common wall.[106] We have another law that concerns adjacent property owners who contract — one owner agreeing not to build a house and not to place beams on their common wall.[107] Another provision states that an adjacent property owner who rebuilt a common wall "by himself" was entitled to payment from the adjacent property owner "for the maintenance expenses for the common wall" (it does say how much — one and a half shekels — but we do not know what proportion that amount represents).[108]

[C] Ancestral Property

According to Saggs, an ancient letter suggests that a royal ordinance of Rim-Sin (1822–1763 B.C) provided that "a son was able to reclaim landed

---

103. *Id.*
104. Ur-Nammu ¶ 25.
105. Lipit Ishtar ¶ 18.
106. SLHF (iii 18–19). *See* Ellickson & Thorland, *Ancient Land Law*, 71 Chicago-Kent L. Rev. 321, 348 (1995).
107. SLHF (iii 32–38). *See also* Saggs, Babylon 176 ("Often two adjacent houses would have a common wall, and in some cases contracts are known confirming to both neighbors the right to lay joists on the wall.").
108. SLHF (iii 26–31).

property sold by his father. There is some evidence suggesting that at an early period the original owners of land, or their families, had the right (in certain circumstances) of resuming ancestral land, and the ordinance of Rim-Sin may have been enforcing a tradition falling into desuetude."[109]

[D] Restrictive Covenants

We know of one type of property sale that could occur with a restrictive covenant. Once bought, it is possible that a female slave could be used as a concubine. However, occasionally a seller sold a female slave with a restrictive covenant attached requiring that she would not be used in this manner; but rather would be married either to another slave or to a freeman.[110]

[F] "Ancient Kudurrus" & Kudurrus

As early as 3000 B.C., the Mesopotamians recorded the size of fields on large stone documents (*e.g.*, tablets, plaques, and stelae).[111] The practice of using large stones to memorialize information about tracts of land (including the acreage and various transactions involving the transfer of ownership) continued off and on throughout the second millennium until about 2250 B.C.[112] Modern scholars refer to these monuments as "ancient *kudurrus*."[113] About sixty such ancient *kudurrus* have been discovered and studied. They appear to come from both northern and southern Mesopotamia and relate to tracts of land that are both large and small—some as large as 1,600 acres and as small as 15 acres.[114]

It is not until after the time of Hammurabi that we find the use of *kudurrus*, or boundary stones, to indicate the demarcation of agricultural lands.[115] Ellickson and Thorland describe them as follows:

---

109. SAGGS, BABYLON 221. *See* DOMINIQUE CHARPIN, *The History of Ancient Mesopotamia: An Overview, in* 2 CIVILIZATIONS OF THE ANCIENT NEAR EAST, *supra* ch. 1 note 23, at 807, 815, for the date of Rim-Sin.

110. SAGGS, BABYLON 170.

111. *See generally* Renger, *Ownership or Possession of Arable Land in Ancient Mesopotamia*, 71 CHICAGO-KENT L. REV. 269, 273–278 (1995).

112. *Id.* at 273.

113. *Id.* ("Because of the similarities in form (written on stone) and in content (dealing with fields) that they share with land grant documents of the second half of the second millennium B.C. (called *kudurru* "boundary stone" in Akkadian), they have been labeled *ancient kudurrus* by I.J. Gelb....").

114. *Id.* at 273–276.

115. DOMINIQUE CHARPIN, *The History of Ancient Mesopotamia: An Overview, in* 2 CIVILIZATIONS OF THE ANCIENT NEAR EAST, *supra* ch. 1 note 23, at 807, 819; WAL-

Small stelae, called *kudurrus* in Akkadian, were prepared to memorialize royal land grants. The original stone was deposited in a temple, where it would be accessible for public viewing, and a clay copy
was delivered to the grantee. A *kudurrum* described the land being
granted and listed tenurial obligations due. The text also included a
list of witnesses and elaborate curses to deter tampering with both
the stela and the grantee's interest.[116]

We have over eighty of these pillar-shaped stone boundary markers. Most
date from roughly 1400–650 B.C., but only a fraction can be dated with any
measure of certainty. As a general rule, the *kudurrus* were set up in circumstances where the king granted land; thus, they serve to publicize the royal
grant.[117]

---

ter Sommerfeld, *The Kassites of Ancient Mesopotamia: Origins, Politics, and Culture,*
in 2 Civilizations of the Ancient Near East, *supra* ch. 1 note 2, at 917, 920–22;
Oppenheim, Ancient Mesopotamia 123.

116. Ellickson & Thorland, *Ancient Land Law,* 71 Chicago-Kent L. Rev. 321,
385, n. 369 (1995).

117. Walter Sommerfeld, *The Kassites of Ancient Mesopotamia: Origins, Politics,
and Culture, in* 2 Civilizations of the Ancient Near East, *supra* ch. 1 note 2, at
917, 920–22; Oppenheim, Ancient Mesopotamia 234, 286.

CHAPTER 11

Trade, Contracts, & Business Law

§ 11.1 Trade

[A] Early Foreign Trade[1]

The palaces and temples conducted almost all foreign trade during the earliest periods of Mesopotamian history.[2] It was not until Mesopotamian civilization was in its more mature stages (*i.e.,* certainly by the Old Babylonian period) that private individuals began pursuing commercial interests abroad.[3] Mesopotamia was well-known particularly for its overland trade.[4] The earliest foreign trade — at least on a modest scale — had certainly begun by the Neolithic period (*c.* 7000 B.C.) at Jarmo in Northern Iraq.[5] Presumably, the earliest trading was conducted by simple barter.[6] Evidence in the form of certain semi-precious stones and seashells reveals that, in the two millennia following Jarmo, Mesopotamian trade continued to expand slowly.[7]

---

1. Roux suggests that the unique geography of Mesopotamia significantly influenced trade routes. Roux, Ancient Iraq 19.
2. Samuel Greengus, *Legal and Social Institutions of Ancient Mesopotamia, in* 1 Civilizations of the Ancient Near East, *supra* ch. 1 note 14 at 469, 481.
3. *Id.*
4. *See generally* Michael C. Astour, *Overland Trade Routes in Ancient Western Asia, in* 2 Civilizations of the Ancient Near East 1401, 1401–1420 (Jack M. Sasson ed., 1995). Oppenheim, Ancient Mesopotamia 90.
5. Saggs, Babylon 9, 269. Roux, Ancient Iraq 55 (Roux posits early commerce occurring in the paleolithic era: "They [*i.e.,* "Palaeolithic men of Iraq"] also had commercial intercourse with the Anatolian plateau and the Iranian highlands.").
6. Saggs, Babylon 273.
7. Norman Yoffee, *The Economy of Ancient Western Asia, in* 3 Civilizations of the Ancient Near East, *supra* ch. 10 note 3, at 1387, 1391; Saggs, Babylon 11, 269–70. *See also* Roux, Ancient Iraq 64.

In the Ubaid period (*c.* 4500–4000 B.C.) the Mesopotamians imported lumber for temples. Apparently, they moved timber overland from Syria to Carchemish and then transported it downriver on the Euphrates.[8] Archaeologists have discovered cylinder seals in Egypt that date from the last centuries of the fourth millennium B.C., the Uruk period (*c.* 3500–3100 B.C.) and the Jemdat Nasr period (*c.* 3100–3000 B.C.).[9] This is significant because it was in Mesopotamia that cylinder seals were first developed. Consequently, the presence of cylinder seals in Egypt indicates cultural exchange between the peoples of Mesopotamia and Egypt.[10] Generally speaking, the Jemdat Nasr period was a period during which the Mesopotamians extended the reach of their trading into many directions.[11] Evidence from pottery and cylinder seals suggests that some degree of trade between Mesopotamia and the Aegean islands existed in the fourth millennium.[12] Early in the third millennium B.C., the Mesopotamians also traded with Egypt and Somaliland.[13]

We know that in addition to domestic business activity, the ancient Mesopotamians conducted extensive foreign trade. Even in the Early Dynastic period (*c.* 2900–2350 B.C.),[14] they traded domestic grain for precious stones and timber from foreigners.[15] Because Mesopotamia had virtually no timber, stones, or metal, the Sumerians were forced to establish foreign trade routes early in their history. Perhaps as early as 2700 B.C., caravans traveled to the mountains of Iran carrying grain (barley) which they exchanged for lapis lazuli and other stones.[16] Both art and artifacts show that the Mesopotamians traded with the Indus Valley in the third millennium B.C.[17] Because they carried on extensive trading from a very early period in

---

8. SAGGS, BABYLON 271; ROUX, ANCIENT IRAQ 30, 73.

9. *See* ROUX, ANCIENT IRAQ 61 for dates. Regarding the cultural exchange between Mesopotamia and Egypt during this period, *see Id.* at 83–84.

10. SAGGS, BABYLON 27.

11. Historians date the Jemdat Nasr period at roughly 3100–3000 B.C. ROUX, ANCIENT IRAQ 61, 76. Regarding the advances in technology and industry during this period *see Id.* at 75–85. *See also* SAGGS, BABYLON 27, 66, 276.

12. SAGGS, BABYLON 277–78.

13. *Id.* at 271–72.

14. DOMINIQUE CHARPIN, *The History of Ancient Mesopotamia: An Overview, in* 2 CIVILIZATIONS OF THE ANCIENT NEAR EAST, *supra* ch. 1 note 23, at 807, 808.

15. SAGGS, BABYLON 40. *See also* ROUX, ANCIENT IRAQ 135.

16. MICHAEL C. ASTOUR, *Overland Trade Routes in Ancient Western Asia, in* 2 CIVILIZATIONS OF THE ANCIENT NEAR EAST, *supra* ch. 11 note 4 at 1401, 1403–04; SAGGS, BABYLON 166. *See also* ROUX, ANCIENT IRAQ 117 (mentioning the commercial travails of Enmerkar).

17. DANIEL T. POTTS, *Distant Shores: Ancient Near Eastern Trade with South Asia and Northeast Africa, in* 3 CIVILIZATIONS OF THE ANCIENT NEAR EAST 1451, 1456–59

their history, the ancient Mesopotamians needed contract rules and a Law Merchant.[18]

[B] Foreign & Domestic Trade During the Time of the Great Law Collections[19]

A significant amount of foreign trade during the period of the great law collections (*i.e.,* from 2300–1600 B.C.) consisted of trading textiles for metal, stone, timber, spice, and perfume.[20] For the most part, the palaces and temples used laborers to weave the textiles that they exported in exchange for foreign goods.[21] Listed below, in chronological order, are some of the more prominent places where Mesopotamian traders ventured and some of the goods that they traded:

- 2334–2279 B.C. (Sargon): Kanesh (a city just under 200 miles south of the Black Sea; approximately 500 miles from Assur by donkey caravan with about 200 donkeys) (tin and textiles exchanged for silver and gold).[22]

(Jack M. Sasson ed., 1995); SAGGS, BABYLON 33. *See also* ROUX, ANCIENT IRAQ 153; A.L. Oppenheim, *The Seafaring Merchants of Ur*, 74 J. OF THE AMERICAN ORIENTAL SOC. 6, 12 (1954).

18. *See e.g.,* KLAAS R. VEENHOF, *Kanesh: An Assyrian Colony in Anatolia, in* 2 CIVILIZATIONS OF THE ANCIENT NEAR EAST 859, 866 (Jack M. Sasson ed., 1995). *See also* A.L. Oppenheim, *The Seafaring Merchants of Ur*, 74 J. OF THE AMERICAN ORIENTAL SOC. 6, 12 (1954) (Describing a letter from one merchant to another reminding him of the need "to adhere to certain ethical and social standards in business transactions.").

19. *See generally* DANIEL T. POTTS, *Distant Shores: Ancient Near Eastern Trade with South Asia and Northeast Africa, in* 3 CIVILIZATIONS OF THE ANCIENT NEAR EAST, *supra* ch. 11 note 17, at 1451, 1451–1463; MICHAEL C. ASTOUR, *Overland Trade Routes in Ancient Western Asia, in* 2 CIVILIZATIONS OF THE ANCIENT NEAR EAST, *supra* ch. 11 note 4, at 1401, 1408–1414; and, NORMAN YOFFEE, *The Economy of Ancient Western Asia, in* 3 CIVILIZATIONS OF THE ANCIENT NEAR EAST, *supra* ch. 10 note 3, at 1387, 1392–1394.

20. OPPENHEIM, ANCIENT MESOPOTAMIA 63. *See also* A.L. Oppenheim, *The Seafaring Merchants of Ur*, 74 J. OF THE AMERICAN ORIENTAL SOC. 6, 13 (1954).

21. SAMUEL GREENGUS, *Legal and Social Institutions of Ancient Mesopotamia, in* 1 CIVILIZATIONS OF THE ANCIENT NEAR EAST, *supra* ch. 1 note 14 at 469, 481; OPPENHEIM, ANCIENT MESOPOTAMIA 90–91.

22. NORMAN YOFFEE, *The Economy of Ancient Western Asia, in* 3 CIVILIZATIONS OF THE ANCIENT NEAR EAST, *supra* ch. 10 note 3, at 1387, 1392–1393; MICHAEL C. ASTOUR, *Overland Trade Routes in Ancient Western Asia, in* 2 CIVILIZATIONS OF THE ANCIENT NEAR EAST, *supra* ch. 11 note 4, at 1401, 1406–1407; and, KLAAS R. VEENHOF, *Kanesh: An Assyrian Colony in Anatolia, in* 2 CIVILIZATIONS OF THE ANCIENT NEAR EAST, *supra* ch. 11 note 18, at 859, 862–64; SAGGS, BABYLON 50, 69. These dates for Sargon are those given by Roux. ROUX, ANCIENT IRAQ 148.

- 2254–2218 B.C. (Naram-Sin): India, Cyprus, Northern Syria (elephants, apes, assorted beasts, timber).[23]
- 2141–2122 B.C. (Gudea): Magan (copper and diorite), Gubi, Tilmun, Lebanon, Kimash (a city in the mountains of western Iran), Hahu (in Asia Minor) (timber, stone, bitumen, gypsum, diorite, copper).[24]
- 2112–2095 B.C. (Ur-Nammu): Magan (copper, diorite).[25]
- 2017–1985 B.C. (Ishbi-Irra): Anatolia, Asia Minor.[26]
- 1900s B.C.: Anatolia, Asia Minor.[27]
- 1900 B.C.: Tilmun (copper, timber).[28]
- 1800 B.C. (Mari Texts): Persian Gulf, Aleppo, Orontes Valley.[29]

The Mesopotamians imported a wide variety of goods from abroad. Among the products imported were metals, timber, precious stones, spices, perfumes, wine, beads, ivory, onions, and rare animals.[30] We also know that the Mesopotamians imported wool, hair, and leather in exchange for tex-

---

23. MICHAEL C. ASTOUR, *Overland Trade Routes in Ancient Western Asia, in* 2 CIVILIZATIONS OF THE ANCIENT NEAR EAST, *supra* ch. 11 note 4, at 1401, 1407; DANIEL T. POTTS, *Distant Shores: Ancient Near Eastern Trade with South Asia and Northeast Africa, in* 3 CIVILIZATIONS OF THE ANCIENT NEAR EAST, *supra* ch. 11 note 17, at 1451, 1456–1459; SAGGS, BABYLON 51–52; ROUX, ANCIENT IRAQ 32. *See also* A.L. Oppenheim, *The Seafaring Merchants of Ur*, 74 J. OF THE AMERICAN ORIENTAL SOC. 6, 12 (1954).

24. MICHAEL C. ASTOUR, *Overland Trade Routes in Ancient Western Asia, in* 2 CIVILIZATIONS OF THE ANCIENT NEAR EAST, *supra* ch. 11 note 4, at 1401, 1408; DANIEL T. POTTS, *Distant Shores: Ancient Near Eastern Trade with South Asia and Northeast Africa, in* 3 CIVILIZATIONS OF THE ANCIENT NEAR EAST, *supra* ch. 11 note 17, at 1451, 1454–1456; SAGGS, BABYLON 54. Regarding bitumen specifically, Roux says: "There is even some evidence that, at least during certain periods in their history, they exported it." ROUX, ANCIENT IRAQ 30 (footnote omitted). *See also Id.* at 160.

25. DANIEL T. POTTS, *Distant Shores: Ancient Near Eastern Trade with South Asia and Northeast Africa, in* 3 CIVILIZATIONS OF THE ANCIENT NEAR EAST, *supra* ch. 11 note 17, at 1451, 1456; SAGGS, BABYLON 56. *See also* ROUX, ANCIENT IRAQ 159.

26. SAGGS, BABYLON 62; OPPENHEIM, ANCIENT MESOPOTAMIA 164.

27. SAGGS, BABYLON 68.

28. DANIEL T. POTTS, *Distant Shores: Ancient Near Eastern Trade with South Asia and Northeast Africa, in* 3 CIVILIZATIONS OF THE ANCIENT NEAR EAST, *supra* ch. 11 note 17, at 1451, 1453–54, 1455; SAGGS, BABYLON 274. *See also* A.L. Oppenheim, *The Seafaring Merchants of Ur*, 74 J. OF THE AMERICAN ORIENTAL SOC. 6–7 (1954).

29. MICHAEL C. ASTOUR, *Overland Trade Routes in Ancient Western Asia, in* 2 CIVILIZATIONS OF THE ANCIENT NEAR EAST, *supra* ch. 11 note 4, at 1401, 1413–1414; OPPENHEIM, ANCIENT MESOPOTAMIA 92.

30. NORMAN YOFFEE, *The Economy of Ancient Western Asia, in* 3 CIVILIZATIONS OF THE ANCIENT NEAR EAST, *supra* ch. 10 note 3, at 1387, 1392–1394; DANIEL T. POTTS, *Distant Shores: Ancient Near Eastern Trade with South Asia and Northeast Africa, in* 3 CIVILIZATIONS OF THE ANCIENT NEAR EAST, *supra* ch. 11 note 17, at 1451, 1453–14596; OPPENHEIM, ANCIENT MESOPOTAMIA 117. *See also* A.L. Oppenheim, *The Seafaring Merchants of Ur*, 74 J. OF THE AMERICAN ORIENTAL SOC. 6, 13 (1954).

tiles produced by workshops in the great temple and palace organizations.[31] It is likely that the government controlled the production and export of metals that were used to produce weapons and armor for use by armies.[32]

The seas and rivers provided the principal media of transport for foreign trade.[33] As Oppenheim aptly notes in his article "The Seafaring Merchants of Ur,"[34] "Oversea trade with its enormous returns...places the merchant traveling by boat in a very favorable position compared to that of his colleague who follows the caravan routes."[35] Ur served as the principal seaport for all of Mesopotamia.[36] They traded by sea with Eastern lands called Magan and Meluhha.[37] Copper ore, ivory, and precious stones were imported through the Persian Gulf from places that were either near or beyond Oman.[38] In addition to maritime trade, the Mesopotamians developed "several well-traveled roads [that] supported a process of continuous give and take...."[39] There is evidence to suggest that, when merchants passed through foreign lands, the custom was for them to pay certain fees to the local officials. The fees, then, entitled them to use the wells in the vicinity and also bought the protection of the local ruler.[40]

---

31. SAMUEL GREENGUS, *Legal and Social Institutions of Ancient Mesopotamia, in* 1 CIVILIZATIONS OF THE ANCIENT NEAR EAST, *supra* ch. 1 note 14 at 469, 481; OPPENHEIM, ANCIENT MESOPOTAMIA 83–84. *See also* A.L. Oppenheim, *The Seafaring Merchants of Ur*, 74 J. OF THE AMERICAN ORIENTAL SOC. 6, 13 (1954).

32. SAGGS, BABYLON 280–81.

33. *See generally* GEORGE F. BASS, *Sea and River Craft in the Ancient Near East, in* 3 CIVILIZATIONS OF THE ANCIENT NEAR EAST 1421, 1421–22 (Jack M. Sasson ed., 1995), 1425; MICHAEL C. ASTOUR, *Overland Trade Routes in Ancient Western Asia, in* 2 CIVILIZATIONS OF THE ANCIENT NEAR EAST, *supra* ch. 11 note 4, at 1401, 1403.

34. A.L. Oppenheim, *The Seafaring Merchants of Ur*, 74 J. OF THE AMERICAN ORIENTAL SOC. 6 (1954).

35. *Id.* at 6, 9.

36. SAGGS, BABYLON 63. *See also* A.L. Oppenheim, *The Seafaring Merchants of Ur*, 74 J. OF THE AMERICAN ORIENTAL SOC. 6 (1954).

37. DANIEL T. POTTS, *Distant Shores: Ancient Near Eastern Trade with South Asia and Northeast Africa, in* 3 CIVILIZATIONS OF THE ANCIENT NEAR EAST, *supra* ch. 11, note 17, at 1451, 1451–1463; GEORGE F. BASS, *Sea and River Craft in the Ancient Near East, in* 3 CIVILIZATIONS OF THE ANCIENT NEAR EAST, *supra* ch. 11 note 33, at 1421, 1425. *See* ROUX, ANCIENT IRAQ 30. Roux suggests that Meluhha was, perhaps, the Indus Valley: "Proto-Indian seals, vases and ornaments found in Iraq testify to commercial relations with the Indus valley (perhaps the Meluhha of our texts)...." ROUX, ANCIENT IRAQ 153. *See also supra* ch. 11 notes 24–25.

38. OPPENHEIM, ANCIENT MESOPOTAMIA, 36, 63–64. *See also* A.L. Oppenheim, *The Seafaring Merchants of Ur*, 74 J. OF THE AMERICAN ORIENTAL SOC. 6 (1954).

39. OPPENHEIM, ANCIENT MESOPOTAMIA 37. *See generally* MICHAEL C. ASTOUR, *Overland Trade Routes in Ancient Western Asia, in* 2 CIVILIZATIONS OF THE ANCIENT NEAR EAST, *supra* ch. 11 note 4, at 1401, 1401–1420.

40. NORMAN YOFFEE, *The Economy of Ancient Western Asia, in* 3 CIVILIZATIONS OF THE ANCIENT NEAR EAST, *supra* ch. 10 note 3, at 1387, 1393; SAGGS, BABYLON 279. *See*

In the last century of the third millennium B.C. (*i.e.*, the Ur III period, *c.* 2112–2004 B.C.),[41] Mesopotamians developed rather extensive trade routes.[42] The reign of Hammurabi saw "an enlargement of the political horizon, which now stretched effectively from Telmun and Susa to Anatolia and the littoral of the Mediterranean, thus provoking and favoring the exchange of goods and ideas throughout the entire Near East."[43] The volume of trade decreased dramatically in the centuries after Hammurabi.[44]

Hundreds of years later, in the first millennium B.C., there is ample evidence for trade between Sippar, Babylon, and Uruk with Greece and the Mediterranean.[45] The Assyrians in the first millennium admitted proudly that they borrowed and adapted foreign arts and technologies. Texts specifically mention metallurgy, architecture, and glazes. When they conquered foreign lands, they brought back Egyptian prisoners of war who were skilled bakers, brewers, shipwrights, cartwrights, veterinarians, and dream interpreters.[46] In the final centuries of the first millennium B.C., it appears that the Arabs used the same trade routes first established by the Mesopotamians from southern Babylonia to the Persian Gulf.[47]

Most domestic trade within Mesopotamia proper was conducted by boats on the Tigris and Euphrates.[48] The canals that were maintained provided a network of travel, making commerce throughout Mesopotamia more extensive.[49] Merchants transported goods such as wine, building materials, metal, wool, and the like.[50]

---

also SAMUEL GREENGUS, *Legal and Social Institutions of Ancient Mesopotamia, in* 1 CIVILIZATIONS OF THE ANCIENT NEAR EAST, *supra* ch 1 note 14 at 469, 483.

41. The Ur III period was one of the grand periods in ancient Mesopotamian history. Its founder was Ur-Nammu. Ur-Nammu, of course, was responsible for a significant law collection. *See supra* § 2.3. *See* ROUX, ANCIENT IRAQ 154–155.

42. MICHAEL C. ASTOUR, *Overland Trade Routes in Ancient Western Asia, in* 2 CIVILIZATIONS OF THE ANCIENT NEAR EAST, *supra* ch. 11 note 4, at 1401, 1401–1420; DANIEL T. POTTS, *Distant Shores: Ancient Near Eastern Trade with South Asia and Northeast Africa, in* 3 CIVILIZATIONS OF THE ANCIENT NEAR EAST, *supra* ch. 11 note 17, at 1451, 1451–1463; OPPENHEIM, ANCIENT MESOPOTAMIA 155, 277.

43. OPPENHEIM, ANCIENT MESOPOTAMIA 155.

44. *Id.* at 64.

45. *Id.* at 65.

46. *Id.* at 66–67.

47. *Id.* at 61.

48. GEORGE F. BASS, *Sea and River Craft in the Ancient Near East, in* 3 CIVILIZATIONS OF THE ANCIENT NEAR EAST, *supra* ch. 11 note 33, at 1421, 1421–22; SAGGS, BABYLON 44.

49. SAGGS, BABYLON 56, 166–67.

50. *Id.* at 279, 292.

[C] The Market & Merchants

It was not common for Mesopotamian cities to have a market like the Athenian Agora. Such an institution does not appear in Mesopotamia until the second half of the first millennium.[51] The harbor area—which was called the *kar* in Sumerian and *karu* or *kārum* in Akkadian—seems to have been the hub for commercial activity in most Mesopotamian towns.[52] According to Oppenheim:

> The *karum* had administrative independence and also a separate legal status important for the citizens transacting business there. In the *karum* lived the foreign traders; there they had their stores and were provided for by the tavernkeeper of the *karum*.[53]

The merchants of the Old Babylonian period were called *tamkarūm*.[54] The word *tamkarūm* also refers to several different types of commercial professions. For example, slave traders, sea merchants, overland traders, brokers, merchant bankers, money lenders, and even some government agents were all referred to as *tamkarūm*.[55]

[D] Spread of Cuneiform & Link to Trade & Culture

Pretty clearly, there was no concept operating in ancient Mesopotamia akin to the patent or trade secret laws that we have in modern legal systems. Everyone simply copied everybody else. Advances in technology spread fur-

---

51. OPPENHEIM, ANCIENT MESOPOTAMIA 129.

52. KLAAS R. VEENHOF, *Kanesh: An Assyrian Colony in Anatolia, in* 2 CIVILIZA-TIONS OF THE ANCIENT NEAR EAST, *supra* ch. 11 note 18, at 859, 866–674. The rich developed a highly organized trade. Thus, it stands to reason that many early laws reflected commercial interests. OPPENHEIM, ANCIENT MESOPOTAMIA 114, 116. *See also* A.L. Oppenheim, *The Seafaring Merchants of Ur*, 74 J. OF THE AMERICAN ORIENTAL SOC. 6, 12 (1954).

53. OPPENHEIM, ANCIENT MESOPOTAMIA 116.

54. SAMUEL GREENGUS, *Legal and Social Institutions of Ancient Mesopotamia, in* 1 CIVILIZATIONS OF THE ANCIENT NEAR EAST, *supra* ch. 1 note 14 at 469, 482.

55. SAGGS, BABYLON 287 ("In the Old Babylonian period trade was largely the concern of a class known as *tamkaru* (singular *tamkarūm*); this term is commonly translated 'merchant', though, as is pointed out by the Dutch scholar W.F. Leemans, the word connotes rather more than this, since the *tamkarūm* in his various activities might be not only a merchant travelling in goods himself, but also a broker, a merchant banker, a money lender, or—one might add—a government agent."). *See also Id.* at 288–89. OPPENHEIM, ANCIENT MESOPOTAMIA 92. *See also* DRIVER & MILES, BABYLONIAN LAWS 120; RAYMOND WESTBROOK, *Social Justice in the Ancient Near East, in* SOCIAL JUSTICE IN THE ANCIENT WORLD 156.

ther and faster than religious concepts and languages. Thus, technical innovations offer physical evidence of the spread of culture and commerce.[56] Obviously, extensive foreign trade resulted in improved living conditions in Mesopotamia while simultaneously spreading Mesopotamian culture abroad.[57] The spread of cuneiform writing and the proliferation of scribes trained in the cuneiform tradition spread legal customs and procedures as well.[58] Writing and law made their way along trade routes side by side with timber, metals, and stone.[59] For example, scribes kept bureaucratic accounts, international agreements, royal transactions, and contracts. Texts such as these have been discovered in Alalakh, Ugarit, and Nuzi.[60]

§ 11.2 Contract Law[61]

[A] Introduction

Driver and Miles remark that, in the Old Babylonian period, "[t]he law of contract is simple and well developed...."[62] Nevertheless, they characterize "[t]he absence... of any rules regulating the general law of sale" as "perhaps the most striking omission" in Hammurabi's Laws.[63] A significant per-

---

56. ANN C. GUNTER, *Material, Technology, and Techniques in Artistic Production, in* 3 CIVILIZATIONS OF THE ANCIENT NEAR EAST, *supra* ch. 8 note 29, at 1539, 1540–43; OPPENHEIM, ANCIENT MESOPOTAMIA 311.

57. ANN C. GUNTER, *Material, Technology, and Techniques in Artistic Production, in* 3 CIVILIZATIONS OF THE ANCIENT NEAR EAST, *supra* ch. 8 note 29, at 1539, 1541–42; OPPENHEIM, ANCIENT MESOPOTAMIA 91.

58. HERMAN VANSTIPHOUT, *Memory and Literacy in Ancient Western Asia, in* 4 CIVILIZATIONS OF THE ANCIENT NEAR EAST 2181, 2186 (Jack M. Sasson ed., 1995); JEREMY A. BLACK AND W. J. TAIT, *Archives and Libraries in the Ancient Near East, in* 4 CIVILIZATIONS OF THE ANCIENT NEAR EAST 2197, 2205 (Jack M. Sasson, ed., 1995). *See also* LAURIE E. PEARCE, *The Scribes and Scholars of Ancient Mesopotamia, in* 4 CIVILIZATIONS OF THE ANCIENT NEAR EAST, *supra* ch. 5 note 31, at 2265, 2270–71, 2273.

59. CYRUS H. GORDON, *Recovering Canaan and Ancient Israel, in* 4 CIVILIZATIONS OF THE ANCIENT NEAR EAST 2779, 2786 (Jack M. Sasson ed., 1995); OPPENHEIM, ANCIENT MESOPOTAMIA 69–70. For more about the commercial relationship between Mesopotamia and Syria, *see* ROUX, ANCIENT IRAQ 84.

60. OPPENHEIM, ANCIENT MESOPOTAMIA 70–72.

61. Norman Yoffee contends that "litigations usually arise from the noncompliance or nonperformance of contractual situations or preexisting obligations. In short, contracts are the stuff from which court cases are produced...." Yoffee, *Context and Authority* 98.

62. DRIVER & MILES, BABYLONIAN LAWS 57.

63. *Id.* at 479.

centage of all extant cuneiform texts are records of business transactions.[64] Roux notes that Mesopotamian contracts "tell us that private persons of all ranks could freely sell, exchange, donate, or let out houses, fields, gardens, fishery ponds, livestock and slaves...."[65]

The Akkadian term for "contract" in a general sense is *riksātum*.[66] The word *riksātum* was used to denote transactions involving the sale of goods, deposit, hiring for services, agency, trust, and marriage.[67] According to Westbrook, "Throughout Mesopotamian sale law...ownership passed with full payment of the price...."[68]

[B] Formalities: Seals, Witnesses, Oaths, & Clay Envelopes

When parties make a contemporaneous swap or an exchange of goods, they usually do not bother to memorialize such an exchange in writing.[69] On the other hand, when parties contemplate an exchange that involves future performance, it is more common to reduce those agreements to writing. The Sumerians were fond of recording their buying and selling on cuneiform tablets.[70] Various laws in the Mesopotamian law collections seem to have required a seal or imposed a penalty if a merchant failed to use a sealed document.[71] Apparently, many contracts were considered invalid unless there were witnesses present[72] and their names were inscribed at the end of the text.[73] Occasionally, parties took oaths when making a

64. JEREMY A. BLACK AND W. J. TAIT, *Archives and Libraries in the Ancient Near East, in* 4 CIVILIZATIONS OF THE ANCIENT NEAR EAST, *supra* ch. 11 note 58, at 2197, 2202–03; SAGGS, BABYLON 196.

65. ROUX, ANCIENT IRAQ 129.

66. Greengus, *The Old Babylonian Marriage Contract*, 89 J. OF THE AMERICAN ORIENTAL SOC. 505, 513–14 (1969).

67. *Id.* at 505, 513.

68. Westbrook, *Slave and Master*, 70 Chicago-Kent L. Rev. 1631, at 1662 (1995).

69. *See generally* DANIEL C. SNELL, *Methods of Exchange and Coinage in Ancient Western Asia, in* 3 CIVILIZATIONS OF THE ANCIENT NEAR EAST 1487, 1487–88 (Jack M. Sasson ed., 1995).

70. OPPENHEIM, ANCIENT MESOPOTAMIA 276; SAGGS, BABYLON 22.

71. *See e.g.*, HAMMURABI gap ¶ m; SLHF (ii 34–36).

72. Lafont makes the point that requiring formalism or symbolism when making a contract "helps the witnesses to remember the agreement of the parties." Lafont, *Continuity and Pluralism* 105.

73. OPPENHEIM, ANCIENT MESOPOTAMIA 281. *See* WESTBROOK, OLD BABYLONIAN MARRIAGE LAW 6.

contract.[74] Thus, the two most common legal requirements for valid contracts in ancient Mesopotamia appear to have been: 1) the presence of witnesses; and, 2) a written document recording the obligations of the parties.[75]

Mesopotamian contract law did not require any one specific formula necessary for validity. Instead, contracts—sales contracts in particular—appear in a wide variety of forms. One scholar extols this diversity as a virtue, "testifying to the richness and the variety of oriental law on this topic."[76] Nevertheless, during certain periods, many contracts contained common elements and patterns. Renger summarizes sales contracts at the end of the second millennium as follows:

> [S]ale contracts from the time of the Third Dynasty of Ur display the following elements—some of them obligatory, others not. In addition to an operative section, which contains the object of the transaction with its physical and legal description, its equivalent (price), the names of buyer(s), and seller(s), and the operative verbs for buying and for taking into possession, the documents continue with a great number of additional clauses recording the complete payment of the price, the completion of the deed, the symbolic act of having the slave, the object of the sale, pass over the pestle, and the delivery of the object. In addition, one finds no-contest, eviction, and delinquency clauses that were confirmed by an oath. Furthermore, the documents can name a guarantor, a weigher of silver (i.e., of the purchase price), an authorizing official of the palace, and the scribe who wrote the document. The document must name the witnesses in whose presence the deed was concluded and an oath was taken. Also mentioned are the location of the transaction and the date when the document was written. The document is sealed by those relinquishing a right.[77]

Instead of a signature, Mesopotamian contracts required that the parties who undertook the contractual obligations make a mark in the soft clay of the document. The most common methods of making such a mark to indi-

---

74. SAGGS, BABYLON 63. Lafont suggests that oaths were more commonly required for contracts in the south. Lafont, *Continuity and Pluralism* 105.

75. SAGGS, BABYLON 291.

76. Lafont, *Continuity and Pluralism* 107 (footnote omitted).

77. Renger, *Ownership or Possession of Arable Land in Ancient Mesopotamia*, 71 CHICAGO-KENT L. REV. 269, 286 (1995) (citing the work of Steinkeller, SALE DOCUMENTS OF THE UR-III PERIOD, Stuttgart, 1989).

cate that the party was present and therefore consented to the obligation were: 1) with a cylinder seal; 2) with a seal ring; and, 3) with the hem of a garment.[78]

One unique practice—especially prevalent during and after the Ur III period (2112–2004 B.C.)—was to encase the original cuneiform tablet in a clay envelope. A duplicate copy of the contract was written on the outside of the clay envelope itself.[79] In the event of a subsequent dispute about the agreement, the tablet on the inside was consulted and treated as the controlling document. This duplicate text was intended to deter any attempts to alter the wording of the contract in the envelope's text.[80]

[C] Capacity to Contract

We know very little about the laws concerning an individual's capacity to enter into contracts. A woman could enter into a binding agreement with her husband promising that his creditors would not be permitted to take her as a "debt-hostage."[81] Women could also own and sell property.[82] Before a man could legally be given credit, he had to have either "received his inheritance share [from his father] or a slave."[83] Hammurabi's Laws imposed a restriction on a person's ability to contract freely in at least one situation. If a child died while in a wet nurse's care, she was not permitted to contract to care for another child without the permission of the dead child's parents.[84] The penalty for violating this provision was to have her breast cut off.

---

78. Holly Pittman, *Cylinder Seals and Scarabs in the Ancient Near East, in* Civilizations of the Ancient Near East, *supra* ch. 10 note 7, at 1589, 1599–1600; Oppenheim, Ancient Mesopotamia 281–82.

79. Westbrook, Old Babylonian Marriage Law 6; Holly Pittman, *Cylinder Seals and Scarabs in the Ancient Near East, in* Civilizations of the Ancient Near East, *supra* ch. 10 note 7, at 1589, 1599; Renger, *Ownership or Possession of Arable Land in Ancient Mesopotamia,* 71 Chicago-Kent L. Rev. 269, 294 (1995).

80. Holly Pittman, *Cylinder Seals and Scarabs in the Ancient Near East, in* Civilizations of the Ancient Near East, *supra* ch. 10 note 7, at 1589, 1599; Saggs, Babylon 291; Oppenheim, Ancient Mesopotamia 282.

81. Hammurabi ¶ 151. *See* Driver & Miles, Babylonian Laws 230–233; Westbrook, Old Babylonian Marriage Law 50–51.

82. Hammurabi ¶¶ 39–40. Maynard Paul Maidman, *Nuzi: Portrait of an Ancient Mesopotamian Provincial Town, in* 2 Civilizations of the Ancient Near East, *supra* ch. 10 note 17, at 931, 944–45.

83. Eshnunna ¶ 16.

84. Hammurabi ¶ 194. *See* Driver & Miles, Babylonian Laws 405–406.

[D] Contracts Void Due to Public Policy

A community generally considers certain types of transactions void when the community, as a whole, believes that such transactions violate public policy. For example, in modern America, a contract to build a counterfeiting machine is void because it violates public policy. In ancient Mesopotamia, there were a few laws that prohibited specific kinds of contracts in this manner. For example, a contract to purchase "a field, orchard, or house" from a "soldier, fisherman, or state tenant" was void. The seller was entitled to reclaim his real property and the buyer forfeited his payment.[85] A contract to purchase from a soldier livestock that the king had given him was also void.[86] Thus, as a general rule, property given by the king to servicemen was deemed inalienable. Driver and Miles interpret this kind of paternalism as a positive thing: "the prohibition of sale or exchange is clearly a protection of the tenant against his creditors to prevent him from being reduced to penury, which would be contrary to public policy."[87] One of the Laws of Eshnunna prohibited merchants and women innkeepers from accepting "silver, grain, wool, oil, or anything else from a male or female slave."[88] Thus, these contracts with slaves were also void due to public policy.

[E] Bailment Contracts

We have a fair amount of information about bailment contracts in ancient Mesopotamia.[89] A bailment usually occurs when an owner of personal property (the bailor) temporarily transfers possession of his property to another person (bailee). For example, if I loan my hoe or saw to my neighbor, I am the bailor and he is the bailee. It is considered a bailment whether or not I charge a fee for the loan of the implement. According to Hammurabi's Laws, in order to have a valid bailment contract (at least a

---

85. HAMMURABI ¶ 41. *See also* DRIVER & MILES, BABYLONIAN LAWS 125–126.

86. HAMMURABI ¶ 35. According to Driver & Miles, "anyone who buys it loses his money." DRIVER & MILES, BABYLONIAN LAWS 123.

87. DRIVER & MILES, BABYLONIAN LAWS 126.

88. ESHNUNNA ¶ 15.

89. One must be cautious about applying the modern concept of bailment to ancient law collections. Jackson has pointed out this problem clearly. JACKSON, ESSAYS (ch. 3 "Principles and Cases: The Theft Laws of Hammurabi") 70 (1975) ("It is the anachronistic search for principles which insists on finding common ground between these cases, by subsuming them all beneath the common concept of 'bailee'. But the Laws of Hammurabi have no word for 'bailee'. Such a general conception is entirely absent.").

bailment for the benefit of the bailor), the agreement had to be in writing, and the objects that were to be bailed had to be shown to witnesses.[90]

Both the Laws of Lipit-Ishtar and Hammurabi's Laws provide that when a renter broke a rented ox's horn or tail, the renter had to pay one-quarter of the ox's value (in silver) as compensation to the ox's owner.[91] Both Hammurabi's Laws and a student tablet of laws from about 1800 B.C. fixed an oxen renter's damages at one-quarter of the animal's value when he (the renter) severed the ox's hoof tendon.[92] Lipit-Ishtar's Laws established damages for the same offense at one-third of the ox's value,[93] and they also state that if the renter were to destroy the animal's eye, he had to pay in silver one-half of its value.[94]

Hammurabi's Laws recognize the need to consider fault and negligence when deciding whether a bailee should be liable for the loss of a bailed draft or other domestic animal.[95] For example, as a general rule, a bailee of an ox or donkey was not liable to the owner/bailor for loss in the event that a lion killed the animal either "in the open country" or while it was yoked.[96] Presumably, the bailee in this situation could not be responsible for a loss caused by the attack of a wild animal.[97] By the same token, if any other "act of god" caused the ox's death, the bailee was not held responsible.[98] On the other hand, if a bailor caused the death of a rented animal "either by negligence or by physical abuse," he was legally bound to replace the animal with another of comparable value.[99] Such negligence apparently included situations where a rented ox was just plain lost.[100]

---

90. HAMMURABI ¶¶ 121–123 (There was, in essence, a complete statute of frauds defense for bailment for the benefit of the bailor). *See* DRIVER & MILES, BABYLONIAN LAWS 233–237.

91. LIPIT-ISHTAR ¶¶ 36–37; HAMMURABI ¶ 248. Another set of student-copied laws provided that when a renter cut off an ox's horn, he had to pay one-third of its value. RENTED OXEN ¶ 2. The same student tablet contains a provision specifying damages when the renter cuts off the ox's tail, but the text is too damaged for us to determine what the payment was for such an injury. RENTED OXEN ¶ 4.

92. HAMMURABI ¶ 248; RENTED OXEN ¶ 3.

93. LIPIT-ISHTAR ¶ 34.

94. LIPIT-ISHTAR ¶ 35; RENTED OXEN ¶ 1 (same); HAMMURABI ¶ 247 (same).

95. *See supra* § 9.1.

96. HAMMURABI ¶ 244; SLHF (vi 32–36). DRIVER & MILES, BABYLONIAN LAWS 438.

97. For other similar provisions in ancient Mesopotamian collections, *see* RENTED OXEN ¶¶ 7–8; SLEX ¶ 9'; SLHF (vi 16–22).

98. HAMMURABI ¶ 249. DRIVER & MILES, BABYLONIAN LAWS 438.

99. HAMMURABI ¶ 245, *see also* HAMMURABI ¶ 263. Compensation of this sort seems comparable to tort compensation in contemporary America where returning the plaintiff to the *status quo ante* is the general goal. *See also* DRIVER & MILES, BABYLONIAN LAWS 438, 455–456, 461, 464.

100. SLEX ¶ 10'.

These rules could create interesting problems of proof. For example, if a renter lost his rented ox, it would be to his advantage to try to prove that a lion had attacked and killed the ox.[101] Also, when a rented ox died "while crossing a river," the general rule was that the renter was liable to the owner for the full value of the ox.[102] Arguably, the renter should be responsible for deciding when and where to cross a river. That is, perhaps, why Mesopotamian law considered the renter at fault in this situation. Similarly, a bailee, under Hammurabi's Laws, had to replace the animal if he caused damage so severe that it was rendered virtually useless (*i.e.,* broke its leg or cut its neck tendon).[103]

When the renter of a boat agreed to follow a certain route, if he breached his contract and failed to follow that route, and if the boat sank, he had to both replace the boat and pay the cost ("in grain") of the rental.[104] A boat renter had to pay as much as one-half the boat's value if he caused certain kinds of damage to it.[105] Hammurabi's Laws provided that a boatman who rented a boat and negligently caused it "to sink or to become lost," had to "replace the boat for the owner of the boat."[106] If the boatman was able to raise the boat, he only had to pay the owner one-half of its value.[107]

In Hammurabi's Laws, a bailee of grain appears to have been strictly liable to his bailor and, in the event of any loss, was required to pay double the amount of grain that was stored.[108] This was the law even in situations

---

101. *See* DRIVER & MILES, BABYLONIAN LAWS 239 ("[P]roof of killing by a lion can be given by material and circumstantial evidence, but this cannot be done where the cause of death is the act of God.").

102. RENTED OXEN ¶ 6; SLHF (vi 23–31).

103. HAMMURABI ¶ 246.

104. LIPIT ISHTAR ¶ 5; SLHF (iv 42–v 11). A student exercise tablet of laws provides that "until he restores the boat" the renter in this situation "shall measure and deliver one-half of its hire in grain to its owner." SLEX ¶ 3'.

105. SLHF (v 12–20).

106. HAMMURABI ¶ 236–237; *see also* LIPIT-ISHTAR ¶ 4, ESHNUNNA ¶ 5 (*see* DRIVER & MILES, BABYLONIAN LAWS 8). For a general discussion of this issue, the parties involved, and the liabilities, *see* DRIVER & MILES, BABYLONIAN LAWS 430–431, 461 (concept of negligence).

107. HAMMURABI ¶ 238.

108. HAMMURABI ¶ 120. *See* DRIVER & MILES, BABYLONIAN LAWS 233–236. *See also* HAMMURABI ¶ 124 ("If a man gives silver, gold, or anything else before witnesses to another man for safekeeping and he [*i.e.,* the bailee] denies it, they shall charge and convict that man, and he shall give twofold that which he denied."). *See* DRIVER & MILES, BABYLONIAN LAWS 237–239 ("Presumably this means that he must return the article deposited and its value or must pay double its value if he does not produce the

where "[t]he contract was merely a gratuitous deposit with a friend for safe custody."[109] Under the Laws of Eshnunna, when a bailee lost bailed goods "without evidence that the house ha[d] been broken into," the bailee had to replace the bailor's goods.[110] But he did not have to replace bailed goods if they were stolen, so long as some of his property also had been stolen along with the bailed goods.[111] Hammurabi's Laws changed this rule. According to Hammurabi, even if some of the bailee's goods had been stolen along with the bailor's, the bailee was still liable to the bailor for the loss of the bailed goods: "the householder who was careless shall make restitution and shall restore to the owner of the property that which was given to him for safekeeping and which he allowed to be lost...."[112]

[F] Contracts on an International Scale: Treaties

It would be difficult to say that the ancient Mesopotamians developed "international law" on any kind of broad scale or in a complex manner.[113] Instead, most international law in ancient Mesopotamia was limited to treaties and alliances between or among states.[114] Thus, in many respects, it is suitable to consider these international agreements in the context of general contract law. The Mesopotamians believed that the gods gave mankind international law: a concept of treaties and alliances and the treatment of nations defeated in war.[115] In order to make treaties and alliances binding, leaders had to swear oaths in the presence of the gods.[116] Even in the Early Dynastic period (*c.* 2900–2350 B.C.), governments accepted "[c]ertain

article itself." (*Id.* at 239) "The main problem, however, is whether the liability of the depositee, who receives no reward for his trouble, is based on negligence...or whether he warrants the safe custody and is liable for loss of the deposit without proof of negligence." (*Id.*)).

109. DRIVER & MILES, BABYLONIAN LAWS 236.
110. ESHNUNNA ¶ 36.
111. ESHNUNNA ¶ 37. The bailee did, in addition, have to take an oath stating that he had not defrauded the bailor.
112. HAMMURABI ¶ 125. Driver & Miles conclude: "The circumstance that he has lost some of his own property...must have been stated in order to prove that he has not himself stolen the deposit." DRIVER & MILES, BABYLONIAN LAWS 239. *See also Id.* at 461 (regarding the concept of negligence).
113. SAMUEL GREENGUS, *Legal and Social Institutions of Ancient Mesopotamia, in* 1 CIVILIZATIONS OF THE ANCIENT NEAR EAST, *supra* ch. 1 note 14 at 469, 482–83.
114. *Id.*
115. *Id.*
116. *Id.* at 482; SAGGS, BABYLON 222.

codes of conduct in inter-state relations."[117] According to Greengus, "the earliest [treaty] example comes from Ebla during the third millennium."[118]

Beginning with the Sumerians and then intermittently throughout Mesopotamian history, warring states terminated hostilities by means of formal peace treaties.[119] Oppenheim describes early Mesopotamian treaties as follows:

> The Sumerian Stela of the Vultures, which proclaims the new boundaries established by the victorious Ennatum of the city of Lagaš and the ruler of Umma, is an isolated instance. A treaty written in Old Elamite and mentioning Naram-Sin of Akkad cannot be understood. Yet, there are allusions to international treaties in the texts from Mari, and such an agreement has been found in the old layers of Alalakh. Of the several peace treaties concluded between Assyria and Babylonia during their protracted conflicts, we have only one, and that in a fragmentary state: between Šamši-Adad V (823–811 B.C.) and Marduk-zakir-šumi (854–819 B.C.).[120]

A significant portion of what we know about international agreements comes from letters written at Mari at the beginning of the second millennium B.C. (*i.e.,* before the reign of Hammurabi).[121] For example, we learn of states forging alliances by means of treaties. In order to formalize those treaties, leaders took oaths and performed other rituals or symbolic acts, such as "the touching the throat."[122] According to Greengus, "[t]reaties were essentially formal covenants or agreements between monarchs, solemnly undertaken by means of sworn oaths and symbolic rites."[123] Saggs describes these international accords as follows:

> Each of the coalitions... was headed by a suzerain, who would expect his vassals to accommodate their foreign policy to his, to re-

---

117. SAGGS, BABYLON 223.

118. SAMUEL GREENGUS, *Legal and Social Institutions of Ancient Mesopotamia, in* 1 CIVILIZATIONS OF THE ANCIENT NEAR EAST, *supra* ch. 1 note 14 at 469, 482.

119. OPPENHEIM, ANCIENT MESOPOTAMIA 284.

120. *Id.* (footnotes omitted). For mention of later Assyrian treaties, *see Id.* at 285.

121. DOMINIQUE CHARPIN, *The History of Ancient Mesopotamia: An Overview, in* 2 CIVILIZATIONS OF THE ANCIENT NEAR EAST, *supra* ch. 1 note 23, at 807, 816; JACK M. SASSON, *King Hammurabi of Babylon, in* 2 CIVILIZATIONS OF THE ANCIENT NEAR EAST, *supra* ch. 1 note 38, at 901, 909–911; SAGGS, BABYLON 223.

122. SAMUEL GREENGUS, *Legal and Social Institutions of Ancient Mesopotamia, in* 1 CIVILIZATIONS OF THE ANCIENT NEAR EAST, *supra* ch. 1 note 14 at 469, 482; SAGGS, BABYLON 224.

123. SAMUEL GREENGUS, *Legal and Social Institutions of Ancient Mesopotamia, in* 1 CIVILIZATIONS OF THE ANCIENT NEAR EAST, *supra* ch. 1 note 14 at 469, 482.

frain from having diplomatic relations with his enemies, and also to give him military support in the event of war. Thus we find Shamshi-Adad of Assyria ordering Yasmah-Adad, who was sub-king of Mari as well as Shamshi-Adad's son, to put himself and his troops and staff at Shamshi-Adad's disposal...."[124]

Leaders often cemented alliances by arranging a marriage between members of the royal families.[125] Furthermore, when states were about to negotiate regarding the potentiality of becoming allies, they occasionally exchanged hostages to ensure that the discussions would be conducted in good faith. We know of one instance when negotiations failed and the hostages were executed.[126] Ordinarily, when states negotiated a treaty, they agreed not only to a military alliance, but also to extradite criminals and permit free trade and transportation.[127] When a ruler wished to send a diplomatic gift to another ruler, he employed traders called *ša mandatti*. They were usually protected by treaty.[128]

[G] Miscellaneous Contract Rules

[1] Implied Warranties

Hammurabi's Laws contain two implied warranties that establish fixed lengths of time for the performance of a product or service. One such law imposed an implied one-year warranty on a boatman's caulking services. Under the terms of the implied warranty, a boatman whose caulking proved to be defective within one year's time had to do the work over again at his own expense.[129] The other implied warranty related to the sale of

---

124. SAGGS, BABYLON 225.

125. SAMUEL GREENGUS, *Legal and Social Institutions of Ancient Mesopotamia, in* 1 CIVILIZATIONS OF THE ANCIENT NEAR EAST, *supra* ch. 1 note 14 at 469, 483; SAGGS, BABYLON 227.

126. SAGGS, BABYLON 226.

127. SAMUEL GREENGUS, *Legal and Social Institutions of Ancient Mesopotamia, in* 1 CIVILIZATIONS OF THE ANCIENT NEAR EAST, *supra* ch. 1 note 14 at 469, 482–83; SAGGS, BABYLON 227, 231; OPPENHEIM, ANCIENT MESOPOTAMIA 146, 161.

128. OPPENHEIM, ANCIENT MESOPOTAMIA 93. *See also* SAMUEL GREENGUS, *Legal and Social Institutions of Ancient Mesopotamia, in* 1 CIVILIZATIONS OF THE ANCIENT NEAR EAST, *supra* ch. 1 note 14 at 469, 483.

129. HAMMURABI ¶ 235. GEORGE F. BASS, *Sea and River Craft in the Ancient Near East, in* 3 CIVILIZATIONS OF THE ANCIENT NEAR EAST, *supra* ch. 11 note 33, at 1421, 1421. Driver & Miles relate that this caulking process "was the final operation in the construction of a ship...." DRIVER & MILES, BABYLONIAN LAWS 428. Driver & Miles also note the similarity between the remedy afforded in this provision for poor workmanship and that of a builder in HAMMURABI ¶¶ 232–233. *Id.* at 428–429.

slaves. If a slave exhibited signs of epilepsy within one month after being sold, the buyer was entitled to revoke acceptance of the slave and the seller was required to return the purchase price to the buyer.[130] This was one area where Hammurabi's Laws may have had a normative effect on subsequent legal practice. In the period after the promulgation of Hammurabi's Laws, many slave contracts began including an express warranty of this kind.[131]

[2] Order of Performance & Time for Payment

In many contracts the general presumption is that the buyer or bailee will pay the seller or bailor at the time that the seller or bailor transfers possession of the subject property. However, there are certain types of contracts where a buyer's or bailee's performance (*i.e.*, payment) is delayed. For example, when a boatman rented a boat for a period of one year, the presumption was that the boatman would pay the owner/bailor his fee "in grain" at the end of the year.[132] This practical rule permitted a boatman to acquire sufficient grain during the course of the rental period. It would have been impractical to require a boat bailee to pay rental in advance (since it was by using the boat that the renter would acquire enough money to pay the rent). Other types of loans also operated on the assumption that the person receiving the loan would pay later: "after the coming harvest-time or till the conclusion of the trading journey in connection with which it had been made."[133]

[3] Consignment

There was a special law in Hammurabi's Laws that dealt with consignment contracts. If a consignee failed to deliver goods for his consignor as promised, the consignee was liable to his consignor for five times the amount of property that had been consigned to him.[134]

[4] Excuses for Non-Performance of a Contract: Contracts Voidable Due to Impossibility or Impracticability

Ordinarily a person who rented a field for cultivation owed the owner a percentage of his yield. If, however, the renter was unable to pay because

---

130. HAMMURABI ¶ 278. *See* DRIVER & MILES, BABYLONIAN LAWS 429 (also pointing out that a slave was guaranteed not to flee for three days (HAMMURABI ¶ 278)). *See also Id.* at 479.

131. DRIVER & MILES, BABYLONIAN LAWS 479.

132. SLHF (v 37–44).

133. SAGGS, BABYLON 290.

134. HAMMURABI ¶ 112.

storms, flooding, or drought had ruined his crops, he was excused from payment for that year ("in that year he will not repay grain to his creditor").[135] This law recognized a principle that modern contract law considers an excuse. In modern law we would say that the renter did not have to pay because his performance is either "impossible" or "impractical" due to an unforseen change in circumstances.[136]

[H] Remedies for Breach of Contract

The ancient Mesopotamian law collections contain several provisions that establish damages for breach of contract. Taken as a whole, these provisions tend to give either: 1) expectation damages (*i.e.,* damages intended to put the non-breaching party into the economic position that he would have been in if the breaching party had performed instead of breaching) plus consequential damages (damages that result from the breach and that were reasonably foreseeable at the time of making the contract); or 2) damages that impose penalties for breach of contract and which can have the *in terrorem* effect of deterring breach and coercing performance thereby. There is also one provision relating to breach of contract to marry that seems to liquidate damages—that is, the measure of damages may reflect a reasonable estimate of what expectation loss would be *ex ante*.

One example of expectation damages can be found in a law of Hammurabi's relating to a gardener who fails to pollinate the date palms in an orchard, causing a decrease in yield. In this provision, the gardener who breached his contract to pollinate the orchard was required to pay the owner "in accordance with his neighbor's yield."[137] In terms of contract damages, this law is instructive. The gardener who breached his contract by failing to pollinate the date palms was required to pay the difference between that which he promised (*i.e.,* pollinated crops that bear fruit) *versus* that which he delivered (*i.e.,* unpollinated, failing crops). The neighbor's yield is used simply as a tool for establishing a reasonable expectation for the yield that the gardener could have achieved if he had kept his bargain

---

135. HAMMURABI ¶ 48. *See* DRIVER & MILES, BABYLONIAN LAWS 141–145. According to Driver & Miles, "The debtor remains liable to repay the capital sum lent but is excused payment of the interest of that year and no more; the other terms of the contract remain in force." *Id.* at 145. *See also* HAMMURABI ¶¶ 55–56 (cases where floods destroy crops).

136. *See* SAGGS, BABYLON 293 (Saggs cites an Old Babylonian document wherein a party pleaded bad wheather as an excuse for delay).

137. HAMMURABI ¶ 65. *See also* DRIVER & MILES, BABYLONIAN LAWS 158, 163–164

(*i.e.*, an analogue for comparison).[138] Driver and Miles explain that "an esti-mate must be made of the amount which he would have paid if he had car-ried out his contract and raised a crop."[139] They conclude, then, that "[t]he precise quantity which he must pay as damages will depend on the size of his farm and will be determined on the assumption that he has grown as many bushels to the acre as his neighbours." [140]

Another of Hammurabi's Laws regarding a breach by a building con-tractor also illustrates expectation damages. When a building contractor built a house but failed to "make it conform to specifications so that a wall then buckles...," the builder was required to repair the wall at his own cost.[141] This remedy provides for expectation damages because, by forcing the builder to repair the wall, the law requires him to put the non-breach-ing party (the homeowner) in as good a position as he would have been in had the builder fully performed. The contractor was also responsible for consequential damages — such as damage to property caused by the build-ing's collapse.[142] The builder was required to replace whatever property was destroyed in the collapse.[143] Thus, a contractor's damages could include consequential damages plus an injunction (*i.e.*, replacement) to achieve the expectation damages.

The *Sumerian Law Handbook of Forms* (c. 1700 b.c.) contains another law that provides for consequential damages. As was noted above, a boat bailee was required both to replace the boat and to pay the rental fee if the boat sank as a result of his failure to follow the route agreed to in the bail-ment contract.[144] The loss of the boat itself was a foreseeable consequence of the renter's breach.

Several provisions in the Mesopotamian law collections establish penal-ties for breach of contract. Edwin Good observes that "[t]he severe penal-ties for breach of contract reflect a supposition that society functions best when its members speak and act with integrity."[145] One of Hammurabi's Laws provides for a harsh penalty in the event that a tenant-farmer was un-

---

138. Driver & Miles note that a number of provisions (*e.g.,* Hammurabi ¶¶ 42, 43, 55, 62, 65) use the neighbor's yield as a measure of damages. Driver & Miles, Babylonian Laws 135–136. *See also* Raymond Westbrook, *Cuneiform Law Codes and the Origins of Legislation,* 79 Zeitschrift für Assyriologie und Vorderasiatis-che Archäologie 201, 209–210, and n. 36 (1989).
139. Driver & Miles, Babylonian Laws 136.
140. *Id.*
141. Hammurabi ¶ 233. *See* Driver & Miles, Babylonian Laws 426.
142. Hammurabi ¶ 232. *See* Driver & Miles, Babylonian Laws 426.
143. Hammurabi ¶ 232.
144. SLHF (iv 42–v 11). *See supra* ch. 11 note 104 and accompanying text.
145. Good, *Capital Punishment,* 19 Stan. L. Rev. 947, 975 (1967).

able to "satisfy his obligation" to the field's owner: the insolvent contract breacher was "dragged around through that field by the cattle."[146] Jurisprudentially speaking, it is interesting to see a legal system employing physical punishment as a substitute for money damages when a person was unable to pay the compensation required. To a certain degree, modern criminal statutes that provide bail for persons in jail have the same effect. If someone is unable to pay bail, he must remain incarcerated.

One of the Laws of Eshnunna imposes damages for breach of contract that amount to ten times the contract sum.[147] That law provides that when a workman received one shekel as payment in advance to work as a harvester, if he breached his contract by failing to harvest, then he was required to pay 10 shekels to the man for whom he was supposed to have performed the work.[148] This measure of damages appears punitive and designed to try to coerce the laborer into performing (to avoid having to pay damages by a factor of ten). Presumably, it would cost the landowner less than 10 shekels for every one (*i.e.*, every one shekel that he was paying the original worker) to replace the workman with a substitute laborer.[149]

The laws dealing with breach of promise to marry may have been designed to liquidate damages in an amount which estimates the actual loss that might reasonably occur. Once a man promised to marry a particular woman and brought marriage gifts to her father, if he then changed his mind in favor of another woman, he forfeited the marriage gifts to the woman's father.[150] If, on the other hand, it was the bride's father who changed his mind (not the groom), then the bride's father had to pay the groom twice the value of the marriage gifts that he had brought ("twofold everything that had been brought to him").[151]

---

146. Hammurabi ¶ 256. *See* Driver & Miles, Babylonian Laws 448.

147. Eshnunna ¶ 9.

148. *Id.*

149. There is, in addition, a curious law in Hammurabi's Laws that also appears to impose a penalty of sorts—but not really for breach *per se*. That law applies to situations where a seller dies: "If the seller should die, the buyer shall take fivefold the claim for that case from the estate of the seller." Hammurabi ¶ 12. For more on this provision *see* Westbrook and Wilcke, *The Liability of an Innocent Purchaser of Stolen Goods*, 25 Archiv für Orientforschung 111, 112–113 (1974–1977). *See also* Driver & Miles, Babylonian Laws 81, 95–105.

150. Hammurabi ¶ 159. *See* Driver & Miles, Babylonian Laws 261; Westbrook, Old Babylonian Marriage Law 34, 72. *See supra* § 6.2 [A], ch. 6 note 45 and accompanying text; and Samuel Greengus, *Legal and Social Institutions of Ancient Mesopotamia, in* 1 Civilizations of the Ancient Near East, *supra* ch. 1 note 14 at 469, 489.

151. Hammurabi ¶ 160; Ur-Nammu ¶ 15; Lipit-Ishtar ¶ 29; Eshnunna ¶ 25. *See also* Westbrook, Old Babylonian Marriage Law 34, 39–43; Driver & Miles,

§ 11.3 General Business Law

[A] Agency

Hammurabi's Laws contain a number of provisions dealing with agency.[152] The Laws contemplate that a principal might give an agent either money (so that he could travel and make investments or purchases) or goods (so that he might trade or sell them).[153] As a general rule, the Laws of Hammurabi require an agent to keep a written receipt for his transactions.[154] In practice, "[n]ormally, loans lent by investing capitalists are due at the safe return of the expedition."[155]

Hammurabi's Laws also impose a duty on the agent to account to his principal for interest over the course of his agency.[156] Hammurabi's Laws regarding agency appear to be, nevertheless, somewhat inconsistent on this issue. One law virtually demands that an agent make a profit for his principal. If an agent failed to make a profit, he was required to pay his principal double the amount that the principal initially gave to him.[157] Driver and Miles warn that "[t]hese words should not be taken literally as meaning that the *šamallûm* [agent] is left with the exact amount which the *tamkārum* [merchant-principal] has advanced. Such a coincidence could rarely occur and no law would contemplate it."[158] Rather, it is likely that this provision envisions a situation where the profit is negligible. Thus, the agent was neither dishonest nor negligent but he had to compensate his principal by paying twice the amount that he originally received.[159] The next provision in the Laws, however, seems inconsistent. It states that, if an agent incurred a loss, he merely had to return "the amount of the capital sum."[160] Hammurabi's Laws also excuse an agent if "enemy forces" com-

BABYLONIAN LAWS 252; Eichler, *Literary Structure* 76. *See supra* § 6.2 [A], ch. 6 note 46 and accompanying text.

152. *See* DRIVER & MILES, BABYLONIAN LAWS 198–202.

153. SAMUEL GREENGUS, *Legal and Social Institutions of Ancient Mesopotamia, in* 1 CIVILIZATIONS OF THE ANCIENT NEAR EAST, *supra* ch. 1 note 14 at 469, 481–82.

154. HAMMURABI ¶¶ 104–05. *See* DRIVER & MILES, BABYLONIAN LAWS 194–196.

155. A.L. Oppenheim, *The Seafaring Merchants of Ur*, 74 J. OF THE AMERICAN ORIENTAL SOC. 6, 10 (1954).

156. HAMMURABI ¶ 100.

157. HAMMURABI ¶ 101.

158. DRIVER & MILES, BABYLONIAN LAWS 190.

159. *Id.* ("The section thus secures to the *tamkārum* at least a profit of 100 per cent., and it may perhaps be inferred that the *tamkārum*'s share of the profits will normally have been about 50 percent....").

160. HAMMURABI ¶ 102. *See* DRIVER & MILES, BABYLONIAN LAWS 190–191; A.L.

pelled him to abandon his goods on his journey.[161] This law is meant to cover a situation where an agent "jettisons the property in his hands in order to run away and escape enslavement or death."[162] It appears to operate on the principle that an agent is excused from performance when performance is either impossible or impractical.[163]

An agent who fraudulently denied that his principal had given him money was required to pay his principal treble the amount that he had taken in the first place.[164] A principal who fraudulently denied that his agent had repaid him what was due was required to pay six times the amount that he (the principal) had given to him (the agent).[165]

As a general rule, a principal who financed a land merchant seems to have been entitled to a profit of at least 50% and perhaps as much as two-thirds of the total profit.[166] For a sea merchant, however, the principal ordinarily received a fixed sum rather than a percentage of the profit. Presumably, this was because the risk of total loss was much greater on sea voyages.[167]

[B] Business Organizations

The two major business organizations in ancient Mesopotamia—the palace and temple—received the lion's share of their income from rents and taxes on agricultural estates.[168] To be sure, the palace was a tremendous

---

Oppenheim, *The Seafaring Merchants of Ur*, 74 J. OF THE AMERICAN ORIENTAL SOC. 6, 9–10 (1954).

161. HAMMURABI ¶ 103. *See generally* DRIVER & MILES, BABYLONIAN LAWS 191–194; A.L. Oppenheim, *The Seafaring Merchants of Ur*, 74 J. OF THE AMERICAN ORIENTAL SOC. 6, 9–10 (1954). *See also supra* § 11.2 [G] [4] regarding impossibility and impracticability as excuses for non performance of contractual obligations.

162. DRIVER & MILES, BABYLONIAN LAWS 193.

163. For a general discussion of HAMMURABI ¶¶ 101–103, *see* DRIVER & MILES, BABYLONIAN LAWS 194. *See also supra* § 11.2 [G][4].

164. HAMMURABI ¶ 106. According to Driver & Miles, the usual penalty for denying a receipt was double payment. They suggest that the reason for the triple payment in ¶ 106 may be due to "the special relationship between a *tamkārum* and a *žamal-lûm*...." DRIVER & MILES, BABYLONIAN LAWS 196.

165. HAMMURABI ¶ 107. DRIVER & MILES, BABYLONIAN LAWS 196–197.

166. SAMUEL GREENGUS, *Legal and Social Institutions of Ancient Mesopotamia*, in 1 CIVILIZATIONS OF THE ANCIENT NEAR EAST, *supra* ch. 1 note 14 at 469, 481.

167. SAGGS, BABYLON 275, 289.

168. *See generally* JOHN F. ROBERTSON, *The Social and Economic Organization of Ancient Mesopotamian Temples*, in 1 CIVILIZATIONS OF THE ANCIENT NEAR EAST, *supra* ch. 5 note 38, at 443, 447; Ellickson & Thorland, *Ancient Land Law*, 71 CHICAGO-KENT L. REV. 321, 359–361 (1995); OPPENHEIM, ANCIENT MESOPOTAMIA 95.

business organization.[169] It received tribute from abroad, produce, rents, and taxes from its land, and goods produced in the royal workshops.[170] Describing the palace in the Ur III period (*c.* 2112–2004 B.C.), Roux relates:

> The royal government possessed all the estates previously owned by local rulers and those acquired by conquest. It had big factories and workshops, numerous trading centres in Mesopotamia and abroad, thousands of laborers for agriculture, industrial and public works, and an army of civil servants and policemen to ensure production and enforce the law.[171]

In some respects, the temple also was like a corporation:[172] it "circulated products from fields and pastures across the sacrificial table to those who were either...shareholders of the institution or received rations from it."[173]

Professional associations developed and specialized crafts grew from a tradition of both families and clans.[174] During the Old Babylonian period, brewers, smiths, carpenters, and similar artisans and craftsmen organized into guilds. These were called *ugula* (Sumerian) or *aklum* (Akkadian). These guilds, however, were not independent like their progeny later in Medieval Europe, but rather operated under the auspices of either a temple or palace.[175] Certain learned professions, however, were organized independently (*i.e.,* not as part of the temple or palace). These were the *mašmaššum* (experts in exorcism and apotropaic rituals), *bârūm* (divina-

---

169. J.N. POSTGATE, *Royal Ideology and State Administration in Sumer and Akkad, in* 1 CIVILIZATIONS OF THE ANCIENT NEAR EAST, *supra* ch. 8 note 5, at 395, 407. *See* PIERRE VILLARD, *Shamshi-Adad and Sons: The Rise and Fall of an Upper Mesopotamian Empire, in* 2 CIVILIZATIONS OF THE ANCIENT NEAR EAST 873, 878 (Jack M. Sasson ed., 1995); NORMAN YOFFEE, *The Economy of Ancient Western Asia, in* 3 CIVILIZATIONS OF THE ANCIENT NEAR EAST, *supra* ch. 10 note 852, at 1387, 1394–95; and, DONALD MATTHEWS, *Artisans and Artists in Ancient Western Asia, in* 1 CIVILIZATIONS OF THE ANCIENT NEAR EAST 455, 462 (Jack M. Sasson ed., 1995).

170. OPPENHEIM, ANCIENT MESOPOTAMIA 104. *See also* ROUX, ANCIENT IRAQ 129.

171. ROUX, ANCIENT IRAQ 163.

172. JOHN F. ROBERTSON, *The Social and Economic Organization of Ancient Mesopotamian Temples, in* 1 CIVILIZATIONS OF THE ANCIENT NEAR EAST, *supra* ch. 5 note 38, at 443, 447. *See also* NORMAN YOFFEE, *The Economy of Ancient Western Asia, in* 3 CIVILIZATIONS OF THE ANCIENT NEAR EAST, *supra* ch. 10 note 3, at 1387, 1394–95.

173. OPPENHEIM, ANCIENT MESOPOTAMIA 191. *See* ROUX, ANCIENT IRAQ 128–129.

174. DONALD MATTHEWS, *Artisans and Artists in Ancient Western Asia, in* 1 CIVILIZATIONS OF THE ANCIENT NEAR EAST, *supra* ch. 11 note 169, at 455, 463; OPPENHEIM, ANCIENT MESOPOTAMIA 79; ROUX, ANCIENT IRAQ 128; DRIVER & MILES, BABYLONIAN LAWS 120 (According to Driver & Miles, "The merchant, too, in the cities seems to have belonged to an organized guild under its own officers."). *See also Id.* at 394.

175. OPPENHEIM, ANCIENT MESOPOTAMIA 80.

tion experts), doctors, and scribes.[176] In the Old Babylonian period (*c.* 2000–1600 B.C.), a group of copper importers pooled their capital and shared the risks and profits of their enterprise.[177] There is also some evidence for commercial banking on a limited scale.[178]

A partnership in ancient Mesopotamia, *tappûtum,* was not really analogous to a partnership in modern American law. Instead, their partnerships were more like what we call joint ventures where both the purpose and relationship are relatively temporary.[179] The ancient documents that established partnerships generally followed the same pattern: "the transaction invariably consists of a loan of money granted to one or two (or more) partners by a third party who is or thereby becomes himself a partner, even though he is commonly described simply as a 'capitalist' or 'creditor'...."[180] The "capitalist" was always entitled to get back the sum that he initially invested "whether the partnership...made a profit or a loss...."[181] According to Hammurabi's Laws, partners were required to "equally divide the profit or loss."[182] Based on actual partnership documents, some scholars have interpreted this to mean that partners shared the profit pro rata — "according to the contribution that each has made to the partnership," not that they divided profit and loss "in equal shares."[183] It is possible that the actual

---

176. *Id.* at 81. *See* WALTER FARBER, *Witchcraft, Magic, and Divination in Ancient Mesopotamia, in* 3 CIVILIZATIONS OF THE ANCIENT NEAR EAST, *supra* ch. 8 note 129, at 1895, 1903–04; Robert D. Biggs, *Medicine, Surgery, and Public Health in Ancient Mesopotamia, in* 3 CIVILIZATIONS OF THE ANCIENT NEAR EAST 1911, 1919 (Jack M. Sasson ed., 1995) ("It is possible that physicians were organized into a professional group...."); LAURIE E. PEARCE, *The Scribes and Scholars of Ancient Mesopotamia, in* 4 CIVILIZATIONS OF THE ANCIENT NEAR EAST, *supra* ch. 5 note 31, at 2265, 2273.

177. OPPENHEIM, ANCIENT MESOPOTAMIA 91–92.

178. *See* NORMAN YOFFEE, *The Economy of Ancient Western Asia, in* 3 CIVILIZATIONS OF THE ANCIENT NEAR EAST, *supra* ch. 10 note 3, at 1387, 1398 (discussing loans made by the "great estates."); OPPENHEIM, ANCIENT MESOPOTAMIA 85.

179. SAMUEL GREENGUS, *Legal and Social Institutions of Ancient Mesopotamia, in* 1 CIVILIZATIONS OF THE ANCIENT NEAR EAST, *supra* ch. 1 note 14 at 469, 481–82; Ellickson & Thorland, *Ancient Land Law,* 71 CHICAGO-KENT L. REV. 321, 362 (1995) ("There is evidence from eighteenth century B.C. Mesopotamia that a few unrelated investors sometimes did pool capital in a partnership dedicated to the acquisition of large acreages." (footnote omitted)); DRIVER & MILES, BABYLONIAN LAWS 187.

180. DRIVER & MILES, BABYLONIAN LAWS 187.

181. *Id.*

182. HAMMURABI gap ¶cc. *See also* A.L. Oppenheim, *The Seafaring Merchants of Ur,* 74 J. OF THE AMERICAN ORIENTAL SOC. 6, 8 (1954) (Discussing actual Old and Neo-Babylonian contracts wherein the investing capitalist refused to share in the risk of loss — *i.e.,* unlike this provision in the Laws of Hammurabi (¶98)).

183. DRIVER & MILES, BABYLONIAN LAWS 187 (citing the work of Eilers).

practice and Hammurabi's Laws are just not the same.[184] It is also possible that Hammurabi's Laws describe a different type of partnership than what we ordinarily find in the contemporary cuneiform documents, "namely one in which two or more partners provide their own capital and do not borrow from a-money-lender...."[185] Apparently, when one partner decided to sell his share of the partnership, he was legally required to offer his share for sale first to his fellow partners (*i.e.*, before offering it to any outsider).[186]

[C] Debtor-Creditor Law

The law collections contain many provisions that relate to debtor-creditor law.[187] Before a man could legally be given credit, he had to have either "received his inheritance share [from his father] or a slave."[188] Hammurabi's Laws expressly prohibited a creditor from using self-help to obtain repayment of a loan from his debtor. According to the pertinent provision, a creditor who "has a claim of grain or silver against another man" was not permitted to take grain in repayment himself without the debtor's permission. If he did, he was required to return what he had taken, and, in addition, he forfeited "whatever he originally gave as the loan."[189] Apparently, this law had the effect of encouraging the use of the legal system and, at the same time, discouraging self-help (which could easily lead to violence).[190]

Hammurabi's Laws also allowed debtors to repay loans with goods and commodities of equivalent value rather than requiring repayment of loans "in-kind."[191] One provision that articulates this rule states that a creditor

---

184. Rivkah Harris, *The nadītu Laws of the Code of Hammurapi in Praxis*, 30 ORIENTALIA 163 (1961) ("[T]he form of partnership as found in the extant documents differs considerably from that described in § 98 of the Code of Hammurapi.").

185. DRIVER & MILES, BABYLONIAN LAWS 188.

186. ESHNUNNA ¶ 38.

187. The documents also refer to loans and the lending of money. *See* OPPENHEIM, ANCIENT MESOPOTAMIA 286; SAGGS, BABYLON 47. Saggs says:

"Loan agreements were a very common feature of Babylonian economic life at all periods. A proverb sums up the attitude to loan transactions in the words:

The giving of a loan is like making love; the returning of a loan is like having a son born.

The reference is obviously to the interest added at repayment."
Id. at 290.

188. ESHNUNNA ¶ 16. *See supra* ch. 11 note 83 and accompanying text.

189. HAMMURABI ¶ 113.

190. *See* DRIVER & MILES, BABYLONIAN LAWS 208, 214 (noting that this provision forbids self-help).

191. HAMMURABI gap ¶¶ l,u,v,z; HAMMURABI ¶ 51. DRIVER & MILES, BABYLONIAN LAWS 147–148.

"will not object; he shall accept it."[192] More than one law, however, synthesizes and balances the last two principles; namely, that a creditor cannot use self-help and that a debtor may satisfy a debt with a payment that is not in-kind. For example, one particular provision contemplates a situation where a debtor had "nothing to give in repayment" though he did have a polli-nated date orchard. The law provides that the debtor in this circumstance may not simply tell his creditor to "Take away as many dates as will be grown in the orchard as payment for your silver." Instead, it requires that the debtor sell the dates himself and then pay back the creditor both the principal and interest on the loan "in accordance with the terms of his con-tract."[193] Another similar law states that if a debtor (*i.e.,* a debtor who owned land) gave a creditor a field prepared for growing either grain or sesame and told the creditor to cultivate the field and to use the harvest to satisfy the loan, the owner/debtor was the one allowed to take the grain—not the creditor—and that the owner/debtor could then satisfy his debt by turning over to the creditor "the grain equivalent to his silver which he bor-rowed from the merchant and the interest on it and also the expenses of the cultivation."[194]

One of Hammurabi's Laws expressly prohibited a creditor from de-frauding a debtor by attempting to make a loan "according to the small weight" but taking payment "according to the large weight."[195] The penalty for defrauding a debtor in this way was forfeiture of the entire loan.[196] An-other law prohibited a different kind of fraud: mathematical manipulation. If a creditor failed to deduct loan payments or if he added interest pay-ments to the capital sum, the creditor was required to pay back double what the debtor had paid on the loan.[197] This law seems punitive since it re-quired the breaching party to repay more than expectation damages.[198]

If a creditor had a valid claim against a debtor, the creditor was legally permitted to "distrain" a member of the debtor's family; essentially holding

---

192. HAMMURABI gap ¶ z. *See* DRIVER & MILES, BABYLONIAN LAWS 185–186.

193. HAMMURABI gap ¶ a.

194. HAMMURABI ¶ 49; *see also* HAMMURABI ¶ 50 (same principle). *See also* DRI-VER & MILES, BABYLONIAN LAWS 142, 145–147.

195. HAMMURABI gap ¶ x. The precise interpretation of the language of "small weight" and "large weight" is uncertain, but the general notion of fraud is easy enough to understand. *See* DRIVER & MILES, BABYLONIAN LAWS 181.

196. DRIVER & MILES, BABYLONIAN LAWS 184 ("The probability is that the mer-chant forfeits his right to any repayment and therefore must give up what he has ille-gally received.").

197. HAMMURABI gap ¶ w.

198. *See also supra* § 11.2 [H] regarding contract damages.

the person as a "debt-hostage" (*nepûtum*) until the debt was paid.[199] But if a man falsely claimed that another owed him a debt and thus held a family member of the falsely accused debtor, Hammurabi's Laws imposed a payment of 20 shekels per family member detained.[200] The Laws of Eshnunna provided that, if the "debt-hostage" was a slave woman and the claim had no merit, the false creditor was required to pay the value of the slave.[201] If a "debt-hostage" died a natural death while being held, the debtor had "no basis for a claim."[202] Presumably the fact that the claim was valid and the fact that the death was natural were essential in absolving the creditor in this situation. On the other hand, Hammurabi's Laws treated it as a criminal offense if the death of a "debt-hostage" was caused "from the effects of a beating or other physical abuse while in the house of her or his distrainer...."[203] If the debt-hostage who suffered such violence was the debtor's son, the penalty was capital punishment for the creditor's son (and the debt was absolved).[204] If the debt-hostage was the debtor's slave, the creditor had to pay 20 shekels of silver (and the debt was absolved).[205] The Laws of Eshnunna provide yet another variation on this theme (imposing a twofold penalty). If the debt-claim was baseless and the false creditor caused the death of a slave woman held as a debt-hostage, the false creditor had to replace her with two slave women as compensation.[206]

Also, a debtor voluntarily could sell or give his wife, son, or daughter to a creditor "in debt service" (*kiššātum*) for a maximum of up to three years.[207]

---

199. *See* HAMMURABI ¶¶ 114–16. *See also generally* Westbrook, *Slave and Master,* 70 CHICAGO-KENT L. REV. 1631, 1637–38 (1995); Good, *Capital Punishment,* 19 STAN. L. REV. 947, 961–62 (1967); and DRIVER & MILES, BABYLONIAN LAWS 208–221. Driver & Miles say that this person worked to "pay off" the debt. *Id.* at 210.

200. HAMMURABI ¶ 114. *See* DRIVER & MILES, BABYLONIAN LAWS 208–221.

201. ESHNUNNA ¶ 22. *See* Eichler, *Literary Structure* 76–78.

202. HAMMURABI ¶ 115. DRIVER & MILES, BABYLONIAN LAWS 215. *See also* Westbrook, *Slave and Master,* 70 CHICAGO-KENT L. REV. 1631, 1643 (1995); Eichler, *Literary Structure* 77.

203. HAMMURABI ¶ 116. DRIVER & MILES, BABYLONIAN LAWS 215–216. *See also* Westbrook, *Slave and Master,* 70 CHICAGO-KENT L. REV. 1631, 1643 (1995); Eichler, *Literary Structure* 77.

204. HAMMURABI ¶ 116. DRIVER & MILES, BABYLONIAN LAWS 215–216. *See also* Westbrook, *Slave and Master,* 70 CHICAGO-KENT L. REV. 1631, 1643, 1668 (1995); Eichler, *Literary Structure* 77.

205. HAMMURABI ¶ 116. DRIVER & MILES, BABYLONIAN LAWS 215–216. *See also* Westbrook, *Slave and Master,* 70 CHICAGO-KENT L. REV. 1631, 1643 (1995); Eichler, *Literary Structure* 77.

206. ESHNUNNA ¶ 23. *See also* Westbrook, *Slave and Master,* 70 CHICAGO-KENT L. REV. 1631, 1643 (1995); Eichler, *Literary Structure* 76–78.

207. HAMMURABI ¶ 117. DRIVER & MILES, BABYLONIAN LAWS 217; Westbrook, *Slave and Master,* 70 CHICAGO-KENT L. REV. 1631, 1638, 1643, 1656 (1995).

If a debtor gave a slave instead of a family member, there was no three-year legal limit on the length of debt service.[208] As a last resort, it is also likely that a court could order a debtor to become a slave to his creditor.[209] Driver and Miles suggest that such debt-slavery would have to have been accomplished by a court order rather than self-help.[210]

[D] Interest Rates

Merchants were accustomed to charge other merchants interest (*ṣibūtum*) and compound interest on loans.[211] We do have reference, however, to merchants paying interest at a rate that "one brother charges the other."[212] The legal interest rate on a loan of silver in the Laws of Eshnunna was 20%.[213] Hammurabi's Laws fixed the rate of interest for loans ranging from 20% (usually for a loan of money) to 33% (usually for a loan of grain).[214] But if a creditor attempted to charge a rate of interest higher than that permitted by law (*e.g.*, if he tried to charge the 33% grain interest on a 20% interest-bearing loan of silver), his penalty was to "forfeit whatever he had given."[215] Another law collection established similar rates. In the anonymous "Laws of X," the interest rate on a loan of 300 silas of grain (*i.e.*, about 300 litres of grain) was 33%.[216] The interest rate on 10 shekels of silver was 20% per year.[217]

There is nothing in either Hammurabi's Laws or in the contemporary documents to indicate whether interest was payable monthly, annually, or

---

208. HAMMURABI ¶118. DRIVER & MILES, BABYLONIAN LAWS 217–218; Westbrook, *Slave and Master*, 70 CHICAGO-KENT L. REV. 1631, 1638 (1995).

209. DRIVER & MILES, BABYLONIAN LAWS 220.

210. *Id.*

211. SAGGS, BABYLON 290. *See also* OPPENHEIM, ANCIENT MESOPOTAMIA 307 (Mathematical tables from the Old Babylonian period "list squares and cubes and the pertinent roots, and lists of figures, 'exponential functions,' needed to compute compound interest.").

212. OPPENHEIM, ANCIENT MESOPOTAMIA 88.

213. ESHNUNNA ¶21.

214. HAMMURABI gap ¶t; Ellickson & Thorland, *Ancient Land Law*, 71 CHICAGO-KENT L. REV. 321, 405 (1995). For a nice discussion of the institutions and history of interest in ancient Mesopotamia, *see* DRIVER & MILES, BABYLONIAN LAWS 173–175. Driver & Miles observe that 33⅓% interest on loans of grain and 20% interest on money is quite high but that these percentages are not inconsistent with contemporary documents that reflect actual business practice. *See also* MARTEN STOL, *Private Life in Ancient Mesopotamia, in* 1 CIVILIZATIONS OF THE ANCIENT NEAR EAST, *supra* ch. 5 note 23, at 485, 495–96.

215. HAMMURABI gap ¶u.

216. LAWS OF X ¶m.

217. LAWS OF X ¶n.

at some other interval.[218] Similarly, we do not know how long loan periods generally were: "nothing is said of the duration of the loan and this is generally very vaguely expressed in the documents."[219] The documents that we possess reflect loan periods lasting from a few days to several months. We can assume, perhaps, that agricultural loans would have lasted from planting to harvest. Thus, in agricultural loans, it is likely that the debtor made one payment after the harvest (*i.e.,* that payment representing both the interest and the capital sum).[220]

[E] Weights, Measures, & Media of Exchange[221]

In the Old Babylonian period, the king and temple occasionally alleviated some of the economic pressure on the poor by establishing standard weights and measures and a fixed interest rate.[222] Regarding the issue of standard weights and measures, Driver and Miles caution us:

> There is no evidence that there was any single system of standard weights and measures in the modern sense of the term in Babylonia and in fact...what evidence there is tells against the existence of such a system; for the palace and the temples seem to have had special weights of their own standard.[223]

According to Snell, "[t]ext references from the Old Akkadian period through the Old Babylonian refer to the casting of precious metals into rings, and it is certain that such objects were used at least for storing the metals and possibly served other functions of money."[224] There is ample evidence that silver rings were used as currency in the Old Babylonian period.[225] Silver was the predominant metal used for exchange in ancient Mesopotamia.[226] Barley was also frequently used as a medium of exchange,

218. Driver & Miles, Babylonian Laws 175.
219. *Id.*
220. *Id.* at 175–176.
221. *See generally* Daniel C. Snell, *Methods of Exchange and Coinage in Ancient Western Asia, in* 3 Civilizations of the Ancient Near East, *supra* ch. 11 note 69, at 1487, 1487–97.
222. Samuel Greengus, *Legal and Social Institutions of Ancient Mesopotamia, in* 1 Civilizations of the Ancient Near East, *supra* ch. 1 note 14 at 469, 481; Oppenheim, Ancient Mesopotamia 107.
223. Driver & Miles, Babylonian Laws 181.
224. Daniel C. Snell, *Methods of Exchange and Coinage in Ancient Western Asia, in* 3 Civilizations of the Ancient Near East, *supra* ch. 11 note 69, at 1487, 1488.
225. *Id.* at 1489.
226. *Id.* at 1491; Raymond Westbrook, *Social Justice in the Ancient Near East, in* Social Justice in the Ancient World 156; Saggs, Babylon 297 (According to

as was sesame oil.[227] Foreigners and "persons outside of the common social and jural protective networks" who wanted to sell beer could not do so themselves. They were required to engage a "woman innkeeper" who sold the beer for them at market rates.[228]

[F] Wages, Prices, & Fixed-Price Rentals

We know that supply and demand affected Mesopotamian prices.[229] For example, political and economic changes including wars and famines caused drastic increases in the prices of most goods.[230] But in addition to lassiez-faire market forces, many ancient Mesopotamian laws dictated fixed prices for certain contracts. For example, a bailor of grain paid his bailee one-sixtieth of the amount stored as payment for storage.[231] A woman inkeeper was entitled to fifty silas of grain at harvest to repay her for loaning one vat of beer.[232] The Laws of Hammurabi specified a fixed price for the rental of an ox for a year.[233] The rental price varied depending upon whether the ox was intended to be used for the rear of the team (1,200 silas of grain) or for the middle of the team (900 silas).[234]

In his essay, "Private Life in Ancient Mesopotamia," Marten Stol summarizes wages as follows:

> From the Ur III period on, the daily hire of a worker was standardized at 10 liters (about 2.5 gallons) of barley, a norm that appears in

---

Saggs, like the case in ancient Egypt, the Mesopotamians also adopted "the practice of using silver as a standard of values without any silver actually changing hands."). OPPENHEIM, ANCIENT MESOPOTAMIA 86–87. *See also* DRIVER & MILES, BABYLONIAN LAWS 475.

227. DANIEL C. SNELL, *Methods of Exchange and Coinage in Ancient Western Asia, in* 3 CIVILIZATIONS OF THE ANCIENT NEAR EAST, *supra* ch. 11 note 69, at 1487, 1492–93.

228. ESHNUNNA ¶ 41.

229. SAMUEL GREENGUS, *Legal and Social Institutions of Ancient Mesopotamia, in* 1 CIVILIZATIONS OF THE ANCIENT NEAR EAST, *supra* ch. 1 note 14 at 469, 481.

230. *Id.*; SAGGS, BABYLON 280.

231. HAMMURABI ¶ 121. ("If a man stores grain in another man's house, he shall give 5 silas of grain per kur (i.e., per 300 silas) of grain as annual rent of the granary."). *See* DRIVER & MILES, BABYLONIAN LAWS 234–237.

232. HAMMURABI ¶ 111 ("If a woman innkeeper gives one vat of beer as a loan(?), she shall take 50 silas of grain at the harvest."). *See* DRIVER & MILES, BABYLONIAN LAWS 206–207 (suggesting that a farmer's laborers probably drank such beer).

233. HAMMURABI ¶ 242/243.

234. HAMMURABI ¶ 242/243. As a general rule, the heavier ox works nearer to the plough and the lighter ox is nearer to the front. DRIVER & MILES, BABYLONIAN LAWS 436. The price stated in these provisions is generally less than that found stated in contemporary documents. In one case as much as one-third less. *Id.*

schoolbooks and remained valid for two thousand years. Hiring contracts show that most people earned less than 10 liters per day. One may compare this quantity with the ration of two liters of bread and two liters (about a half gallon) of beer that a worker was supposed to consume every day, taking into account that the man may have had a family to support.[235]

In most of the ancient Mesopotamian law collections, there are a number of provisions that specify sale prices, rental prices,[236] and wages for certain types of labor.[237] For example, there are specific laws regulating the following:

- the rental price of oxen.[238]

- the rental price of a goat.[239]

- the rental price of a donkey along with its driver.[240]

- the rental price of a wagon along with oxen and a driver.[241]

- the rental price of just a wagon.[242]

- the rental price of a boat along with a boatman.[243]

- the rental price of just a boat.[244]

- the sale price of various commodities such as: barley;[245] oil;[246] lard;[247] bitumen;[248] wool;[249] salt;[250] beer.[251]

---

235. MARTEN STOL, *Private Life in Ancient Mesopotamia, in* 1 CIVILIZATIONS OF THE ANCIENT NEAR EAST, *supra* ch. 5 note 23, at 485, 495. *See also* Nels, Bailkey, *Early Mesopotamian Constitutional Law*, 72 AMERICAN HIST. REV. 1211, 1233 (1967).

236. Driver & Miles surmise that the rental rates enumerated in Hammurabi's Laws are for rental by-the-day, although this is not spelled out in the provisions. DRIVER & MILES, BABYLONIAN LAWS 469.

237. *See generally Id.* at 469–478; SAGGS, BABYLON 198–99.

238. LIPIT-ISHTAR ¶ a; HAMMURABI ¶ 268.

239. HAMMURABI ¶ 270.

240. ESHNUNNA ¶ 10; HAMMURABI ¶ 269 (for threshing—without the driver).

241. ESHNUNNA ¶ 3; HAMMURABI ¶ 271.

242. HAMMURABI ¶ 272.

243. ESHNUNNA ¶ 4.

244. HAMMURABI ¶¶ 275–277.

245. ESHNUNNA ¶ 1.

246. ESHNUNNA ¶¶ 1–2.

247. *Id.*

248. *Id.*

249. ESHNUNNA ¶ 1.

250. *Id.*

251. LAWS OF X ¶ 1.

- the wages for various workers[252] such as: a harvester;[253] winnower;[254] sickle;[255] common laborer;[256] fuller;[257] boatman;[258] ox driver;[259] herdsman;[260] craftsman;[261] woven-textile worker;[262] linen-worker;[263] stonecutter;[264] bow-maker;[265] smith;[266] carpenter;[267] leatherworker;[268] reedworker;[269] builder;[270] weaver.[271] (One provision from Hammurabi's Laws that contains several of these wages amounts, ¶ 274, states that a craftsman and a textile worker received five barleycorns of silver per day. At this rate, a worker would have received one shekel of silver for every thirty-six days of work in Hammurabi's era.).

- the fees for a doctor performing various procedures.[272]

- the fees for a veterinarian.[273]

- the fees for a building contractor.[274]

---

252. Contemporary documents indicate that the actual payments for workers such as these was about double the amount stated in the Laws. BOTTÉRO, WRITING, REASONING, AND THE GODS 164. *See also* DRIVER & MILES, BABYLONIAN LAWS 472 (Stating that the prices in Hammurabi's Laws are generally lower than those found recorded in contemporary contracts).
253. ESHNUNNA ¶ 7.
254. ESHNUNNA ¶ 8.
255. ESHNUNNA ¶ 9A.
256. ESHNUNNA ¶ 11; HAMMURABI ¶ 257 (agricultural laborer), HAMMURABI ¶ 273.
257. ESHNUNNA ¶ 14.
258. HAMMURABI ¶¶ 234, 239.
259. HAMMURABI ¶ 258.
260. HAMMURABI ¶ 261.
261. HAMMURABI ¶ 274.
262. *Id.*
263. *Id.*
264. *Id.*
265. *Id.*
266. *Id.*
267. *Id.*
268. *Id.*
269. *Id.*
270. *Id.*
271. LAWS OF X ¶ j.
272. HAMMURABI ¶¶ 215–217, 221–223; LAWS OF X ¶¶ f-i. *See* DRIVER & MILES, BABYLONIAN LAWS 416–420 (In particular, Driver & Miles present a summary of these provisions in tabular form indicating the different fees and penalties based upon the social class of the patient (*Id.* at 418)).
273. HAMMURABI ¶ 224. *See* DRIVER & MILES, BABYLONIAN LAWS 420–421.
274. HAMMURABI ¶ 228. *See* DRIVER & MILES, BABYLONIAN LAWS 425.

[G] Taxes

The ancient Mesopotamians were obligated to pay certain taxes at various times throughout antiquity. Citizens were expected to pay taxes and to perform service obligations by maintaining and constructing roads and canals (corveé work), and by serving in the military.[275] Citizens of Mesopotamian towns routinely paid direct taxes by making "periodic payments of fixed quantities of grain or metal... or delivery of a specified fraction of the crop harvested on the land...."[276] Unfortunately, we know very little about the specifics of these taxes.[277] In the Ur-Nanshe Dynasty (c. 2500 B.C.), the Ensi (i.e., governor/mayor) and temple exacted taxes from the citizenry. Citizens paid taxes on cattle, fisheries, sheep, marriage, divorce, and even burial (some taxes could be paid in sheep).[278] Urukagina's (Uru-inimgina's) Reforms (c. 2350 B.C.) were designed especially to reduce heavy tax burdens.[279]

In the Early Dynastic period (c. 2400 B.C.), inspectors who were responsible to the Ensi collected taxes.[280] We have evidence from around 2000 B.C. that the Sumerian government "acting through temples, levied heavy customs on imported goods."[281] For the most part, a centralized palace bureaucracy levied and collected taxes,[282] and officials in the palaces and temples recorded incoming taxes.[283] Subjugated states often paid taxes/tribute

---

275. JOHN F. ROBERTSON, *The Social and Economic Organization of Ancient Mesopotamian Temples, in* 1 CIVILIZATIONS OF THE ANCIENT NEAR EAST, *supra* ch. 5 note 38, at 443, 445; OPPENHEIM, ANCIENT MESOPOTAMIA 83, 103. *See also* ROUX, ANCIENT IRAQ 163–64.

276. Ellickson & Thorland, *Ancient Land Law*, 71 CHICAGO-KENT L. REV. 321, 374 (1995).

277. *See generally* SAMUEL GREENGUS, *Legal and Social Institutions of Ancient Mesopotamia, in* 1 CIVILIZATIONS OF THE ANCIENT NEAR EAST, *supra* ch. 1 note 14 at 469, 476.

278. DANIEL C. SNELL, *Methods of Exchange and Coinage in Ancient Western Asia, in* 3 CIVILIZATIONS OF THE ANCIENT NEAR EAST, *supra* ch. 11 note 69, at 1487, 1488; SAGGS, BABYLON 46–47.

279. SAGGS, BABYLON 47–48.

280. *Id.* at 234.

281. *Id.* at 275.

282. Ellickson & Thorland, *Ancient Land Law*, 71 CHICAGO-KENT L. REV. 321, 375 (1995) ("Much evidence from Mesopotamia, Egypt, and Ugarit supports the notion that ancient kings commonly did impose general taxes to help finance the provision of royal services." (footnote omitted)); OPPENHEIM, ANCIENT MESOPOTAMIA 154 ("The palace was supported by taxes, which were levied and collected by a centralized bureaucracy....").

283. OPPENHEIM, ANCIENT MESOPOTAMIA 230.

to the rulers who conquered them.[284] For example, subject towns paid taxes with cattle to Ibbi-Sin (2028–2004 B.C.).[285] We also know that there were certain import duties levied on specific goods, such as copper.[286] One of Lipit-Ishtar's Laws created a special rule regarding property taxes. If a property owner defaulted on his property taxes, and someone else began paying the property taxes and continued to do so for three years, the person who assumed the tax burden became rightful owner instead of the defaulter.[287]

The citizens of certain cities enjoyed some degree of exemption from taxes simply by virtue of their citizenship in those cities.[288] For example, the inhabitants of Nippur, Babylon, and Sippar enjoyed special privileges.[289] This tax-exempt status was called *kidinnūtum*.[290] During the Kassite rule (beginning about 1600 B.C.), the Kassite king frequently exempted Mesopotamian citizens from taxation.[291]

We possess letters from about 750 B.C. that detail taxes paid by Tyrians and Sidonians on timber felled in Lebanon. We also know that this policy precipitated a riot and that the rioters killed an Assyrian tax collector in the meleé.[292] Later in the Neo-Babylonian period (612–539 B.C.), worshippers dropped silver into boxes at the entrances of sanctuaries. Kings taxed the temples and they were responsible for paying tax even on amounts given by worshippers.[293]

284. See JACOB KLEIN, *Shulgi of Ur: King of a Neo-Sumerian Empire, in* 2 CIVILIZATIONS OF THE ANCIENT NEAR EAST 843, 846 (Jack M. Sasson ed., 1995).

285. SAGGS, BABYLON 57.

286. A.L. Oppenheim, *The Seafaring Merchants of Ur*, 74 J. OF THE AMERICAN ORIENTAL SOC. 6, 11 (1954).

287. LIPIT ISHTAR ¶ 18. *See supra* § 10.7 [A].

288. OPPENHEIM, ANCIENT MESOPOTAMIA 120.

289. *Id.* at 121.

290. *Id.*

291. See WALTER SOMMERFELD, *The Kassites of Ancient Mesopotamia in* 2 CIVILIZATIONS OF THE ANCIENT NEAR EAST *supra* ch. 1 note 2 at 917, 920; SAGGS, BABYLON 79.

292. SAGGS, BABYLON 282–83.

293. OPPENHEIM, ANCIENT MESOPOTAMIA 106.

Bibliography

Astour, Michael C. *Overland Trade Routes in Ancient Western Asia.* In 2 CIVILIZATIONS OF THE ANCIENT NEAR EAST 1401 (Jack M. Sasson ed., 1995).

Bailkey, Nels. *Early Mesopotamian Constitutional Development.* 72 AMERICAN HIST. REV. 1211 (1967).

Bass, George F. *Sea and River Craft in the Ancient Near East.* In 3 CIVILIZATIONS OF THE ANCIENT NEAR EAST 1421 (Jack M. Sasson ed., 1995).

Biggs, Robert D. *Medicine, Surgery, and Public Health in Ancient Mesopotamia.* In 3 CIVILIZATIONS OF THE ANCIENT NEAR EAST 1911 (Jack M. Sasson ed., 1995).

Black, Jeremy A., and Tait, W.J. *Archives and Libraries in the Ancient Near East.* In 4 CIVILIZATIONS OF THE ANCIENT NEAR EAST 2197 (Jack M. Sasson ed., 1995).

Bottéro, Jean. *Akkadian Literature: An Overview.* In 4 CIVILIZATIONS OF THE ANCIENT NEAR EAST 2293 (Jack M. Sasson ed., 1995).

———. *The "Code" of Hammurabi.* Ch. 10 in MESOPOTAMIA: WRITING, REASONING, AND THE GODS, translated by Zainab Bahrani and Marc Van De Mieroop, U. Chicago Press (1982).

Butzer, Karl W. *Environmental Change in the Near East and Human Impact on the Land.* In 1 CIVILIZATIONS OF THE ANCIENT NEAR EAST 123 (Jack M. Sasson ed., 1995).

Charpin, Dominique. *The History of Ancient Mesopotamia: An Overview.* In 2 CIVILIZATIONS OF THE ANCIENT NEAR EAST 807 (Jack M. Sasson ed., 1995).

Cooper, Jerrold. SUMERIAN AND AKKADIAN ROYAL HYMNS, 1 American Oriental Society Translation Series (1986).

Diakonoff, I.M. *Some Remarks on the "Reforms" of Urukagina.* 52 REVUE D'ASSYRIOLOGIE ET D'ARCHÉOLOGIE ORIENTALE 1 (1958).

Driver, G.R., and Miles, John C. THE BABYLONIAN LAWS (Vol. I: Legal Commentary 1952).

Eichler, B.L. *Literary Structure in the Laws of Eshnunna.* In LANGUAGE, LITERATURE, AND HISTORY: PHILOLOGICAL AND HISTORICAL STUDIES PRE-

SENTED TO ERICA REINER, Vol. 67, *American Oriental Series* (Francesca Rochberg-Halton ed., 1987).

Ellickson, Robert C., and Thorland, Charles DiA. *Ancient Land Law: Mesopotamia, Egypt, Israel.* 71 CHICAGO-KENT L. REV. 321 (1995).

Eyre, Christopher J. *The Agricultural Cycle, Farming, and Water Management in the Ancient Near East.* In 1 CIVILIZATIONS OF THE ANCIENT NEAR EAST 175 (Jack M. Sasson ed., 1995).

Farber, Walter. *Witchcraft, Magic, and Divination in Ancient Mesopotamia.* In 3 CIVILIZATIONS OF THE ANCIENT NEAR EAST 1895 (Jack M. Sasson ed., 1995).

Finkelstein, J.J. *Ammisaduqa's Edict and the Babylonian "Law Codes."* 15 JOURNAL OF CUNEIFORM STUDIES 91 (1961).

———. *The Goring Ox: Some Historical Perspectives on Deodands, Forfeitures, Wrongful Death and the Western Notion of Sovereignty.* 46 TEMPLE L.Q. 169 (1973).

———. *The Laws of Ur Nammu.* 22 J. OF CUNEIFORM STUDIES 66 (1969).

———. *The Ox That Gored.* TRANSACTIONS OF THE AMERICAN PHILOSOPHICAL SOCIETY 71/2. Philadelphia: The American Philosophical Society (1981).

———. *Sex Offenses in Sumerian Laws.* 86 J. OF THE AMERICAN ORIENTAL SOC. 355 (1966).

Frymer-Kensky, Tikva Simone. THE JUDICIAL ORDEAL IN THE ANCIENT NEAR EAST (unpublished Ph.D dissertation, Yale University (New Haven)) (1977).

Good, Edwin M. *Capital Punishment and Its Alternatives in Ancient Near Eastern Law.* 19 STAN. L. REV. 947 (1967).

Gordon, Cyrus H. *Recovering Canaan and Ancient Israel.* In 4 CIVILIZATIONS OF THE ANCIENT NEAR EAST 2779 (Jack M. Sasson ed., 1995).

Greengus, Samuel. *Legal and Social Institutions of Ancient Mesopotamia.* In 1 CIVILIZATIONS OF THE ANCIENT NEAR EAST 469 (Jack M. Sasson ed., 1995).

———. *The Old Babylonian Marriage Contract.* 89 J. OF THE AMERICAN ORIENTAL SOC. 505 (1969).

Gunter, Ann C., *Material, Technology, and Techniques in Artistic Production.* In 3 CIVILIZATIONS OF THE ANCIENT NEAR EAST 1539 (Jack M. Sasson ed., 1995).

Harris, Rivkah. *The nadītu Laws of the Code of Hammurapi in Praxis.* 30 ORIENTALIA 163 (1961).

Hesse, Brian. *Animal Husbandry and Human Diet in the Ancient Near East.* In 1 CIVILIZATIONS OF THE ANCIENT NEAR EAST 203 (Jack M. Sasson ed., 1995).

Hole, Frank Arnold. *Assessing the Past Through Anthropological Archaeology.* In 4 CIVILIZATIONS OF THE ANCIENT NEAR EAST 2715 (Jack M. Sasson ed., 1995).

JACKSON, BERNARD S. ESSAYS IN JEWISH AND COMPARATIVE LEGAL HISTORY (Chapter 1, "Sources and Problems," 1 (1975)).

———. ESSAYS IN JEWISH AND COMPARATIVE LEGAL HISTORY, (Chapter 3 "Principles and Cases: The Theft Laws of Hammurabi" 64 (1975)).

———. ESSAYS IN JEWISH AND COMPARATIVE LEGAL HISTORY, (Chapter 5: The Goring Ox," 108 (1975)).

Joannes, Francis, *Private Commerce and Banking in Achaemenid Babylon.* In 3 CIVILIZATIONS OF THE ANCIENT NEAR EAST 1475 (Jack M. Sasson ed., 1995).

Kennedy, George. THE ART OF RHETORIC IN THE ROMAN WORLD (1972).

Klein, Jacob. *Shulgi of Ur: King of a Neo-Sumerian Empire, in* 2 CIVILIZATIONS OF THE ANCIENT NEAR EAST 843 (Jack M. Sasson ed., 1995).

Kramer, Samuel Noah, and Falkenstein, Adam. *Ur-Nammu Law Code.* 23 ORIENTALIA 40 (1954).

Lafont, Sophie. *The Ancient Near Eastern Laws: Continuity and Pluralism.* In THEORY AND METHOD IN BIBLICAL AND CUNEIFORM LAW 91 (Bernard M. Levinson ed., 1994).

Leemans, W.F. *Some Aspects of Theft and Robbery in Old-Babylonian Documents.* In SCRITTI IN ONORE DI GIUSEPPE FURLANI 661 (1957).

MacDowell, Douglas M. THE LAW IN CLASSICAL ATHENS (1978).

Maidman, Maynard Paul. *Nuzi: Portrait of an Ancient Mesopotamian Provincial Town,* In 2 CIVILIZATIONS OF THE ANCIENT NEAR EAST 931 (Jack M. Sasson ed., 1995).

Moran, William L. *The Gilgamesh Epic: A Masterpiece from Ancient Mesopotamia, in* 4 CIVILIZATIONS OF THE ANCIENT NEAR EAST 2327 (Jack M. Sasson ed., 1995).

Matthews, Donald. *Artisans and Artists in Ancient Western Asia.* In 1 CIVILIZATIONS OF THE ANCIENT NEAR EAST 455 (Jack M. Sasson ed., 1995).

Muhly, James D. *Mining and Metalwork in Ancient Western Asia.* In 3 CIVILIZATIONS OF THE ANCIENT NEAR EAST 1501 (Jack M. Sasson ed., 1995).

Oppenheim, A. Leo. ANCIENT MESOPOTAMIA: PORTRAIT OF A DEAD CIVILIZATION (revised Ed., completed by Erica Reiner, 1977).

———. *The Seafaring Merchants of Ur.* 74 J. OF THE AMERICAN ORIENTAL SOC. 6 (1954).

Owen, D.I. and Westbrook, R. *Tie Her Up and Throw Her Into the River! An Old Babylonian Inchoate Marriage on the Rocks.* 82 ZEITSCHRIFT FÜR ASSYRIOLOGIE UND VORDERASIATISCHE ARCHÄOLOGIE 203 (1992).

Pearce, Laurie E. *The Scribes and Scholars of Ancient Mesopotamia. in* 4 CIVILIZATIONS OF THE ANCIENT NEAR EAST 2265 (Jack M. Sasson ed., 1995).

Pittman, Holly. *Cylinder Seals and Scarabs in the Ancient Near East.* In 3 CIVILIZATIONS OF THE ANCIENT NEAR EAST 1589 (Jack M. Sasson ed., 1995).

Postgate, J.N. *Royal Ideology and State Administration in Sumer and Akkad.* In 1 CIVILIZATIONS OF THE ANCIENT NEAR EAST 395 (Jack M. Sasson ed., 1995).

Potts, Daniel T. *Distant Shores: Ancient Near Eastern Trade with South Asia and Northeast Africa.* In 3 CIVILIZATIONS OF THE ANCIENT NEAR EAST 1451 (Jack M. Sasson ed., 1995).

Prosser, W. and Keeton, W. *The Law of Torts* 5th ed. (1984).

Renger, Johannes M. *Institutional, Communal, and Individual Ownership or Possession of Arable Land in Ancient Mesopotamia from the End of the Fourth to the End of the First Millennium* B.C. 71 CHICAGO-KENT L. REV. 269 (1995).

Roaf, Michael. *Palaces and Temples in Ancient Mesopotamia, in* 1 CIVILIZA-TIONS OF THE ANCIENT NEAR EAST 423 (Jack M. Sasson ed., 1995).

Robertson, John F. *The Social and Economic Organization of Ancient Mesopotamian Temples.* In 1 CIVILIZATIONS OF THE ANCIENT NEAR EAST 443 (Jack M. Sasson ed., 1995).

Roth, Martha T. *Gender and Law: A Case Study From Ancient Mesopotamia.* In GENDER AND LAW IN THE HEBREW BIBLE AND THE ANCIENT NEAR EAST (Victor H. Matthews, Bernard M. Levinson, and Tikva Frymer-Kensky eds., 1997).

———. LAW COLLECTIONS FROM MESOPOTAMIA AND ASIA MINOR (1995).

———. *The Law Collection of King Hammurabi: Toward an Understanding of Codification and Text.* Strasbourg Codification Conference (1997).

———. *Mesopotamian Legal Traditions and the Laws of Hammurabi.* 71 CHICAGO-KENT L. REV. 13 (1995).

Roux, Georges. ANCIENT IRAQ (2d ed. 1979).

Saggs, H.W.F. THE GREATNESS THAT WAS BABYLON (1962).

Sasson, Jack M. *King Hammurabi of Babylon.* In 2 CIVILIZATIONS OF THE ANCIENT NEAR EAST 901, (Jack M. Sasson ed., 1995).

Simpson, William Kelly, ed. THE LITERATURE OF ANCIENT EGYPT (1978).

Snell, Daniel C. *Methods of Exchange and Coinage in Ancient Western Asia.* In 3 CIVILIZATIONS OF THE ANCIENT NEAR EAST 1487 (Jack M. Sasson ed., 1995).

Sommerfeld, Walter. *The Kassites of Ancient Mesopotamia: Origins, Politics, and Culture.* In 2 CIVILIZATIONS OF THE ANCIENT NEAR EAST 917 (Jack M. Sasson ed., 1995).

Stol, Marten. *Private Life in Ancient Mesopotamia.* In 1 CIVILIZATIONS OF THE ANCIENT NEAR EAST 485 (Jack M. Sasson ed., 1995).

Stone, Elizabeth C. *The Development of Cities in Ancient Mesopotamia.* In 1 CIVILIZATIONS OF THE ANCIENT NEAR EAST 235 (Jack M. Sasson ed., 1995).

Vanstiphout, Herman. *Memory and Literacy in Ancient Western Asia.* In 4 CIVILIZATIONS OF THE ANCIENT NEAR EAST 2181 (Jack M. Sasson ed., 1995).

Veenhof, Klaus R. *Kanesh: An Assyrian Colony in Anatolia.* In 2 CIVILIZATIONS OF THE ANCIENT NEAR EAST 859 (Jack M. Sasson ed., 1995).

Veenker, Ronald A. THE OLD BABYLONIAN JUDICIARY AND LEGAL PROCEDURE. Unpublished Ph.D dissertation, Hebrew Union College-Jewish Institute of Religion (Cincinnati, OH) (1967).

———. *An Old Babylonian Legal Procedure for Appeal: Evidence from the tuppi lā ragāmim.* HEBREW UNION COLLEGE ANNUAL (1974).

Villard, Pierre. *Shamshi-Adad and Sons: The Rise and Fall of an Upper Mesopotamian Empire.* In 2 CIVILIZATIONS OF THE ANCIENT NEAR EAST 873 (Jack M. Sasson ed., 1995).

Westbrook, Raymond, *Biblical and Cuneiform Law Codes.* 92 REVUE BIBLIQUE 248 (1985).

———. *Cuneiform Law Codes and the Origins of Legislation.* 79 ZEITSCHRIFT FÜR ASSYRIOLOGIE UND VORDERASIATISCHE ARCHÄOLOGIE 201 (1989).

———. *A Death in the Family: Codex Eshnunna 17–18 Revisited,* 29 ISRAEL L. REV. 32 (1995).

———. OLD BABYLONIAN MARRIAGE LAW (1988).

———. *Slave and Master in Ancient Near Eastern Law.* 70 CHICAGO-KENT LAW REV. 1631 (1995).

———. *Social Justice in the Ancient Near East.* In SOCIAL JUSTICE IN THE ANCIENT WORLD 149 (K.D. Irani and Morris Silver eds., 1995).

Westbrook, Raymond and Wilcke, Claus. *The Liability of an Innocent Purchaser of Stolen Goods in Early Mesopotamian Law.* 25 ARCHIV FÜR ORIENTFORSCHUNG 111 (1974–1977).

Yoffee, Norman. *Context and Authority in Early Mesopotamian Law* (ch. 5 in POLITICAL ANTHROPOLOGY (1988)).

———. *The Economy of Ancient Western Asia.* In 3 CIVILIZATIONS OF THE ANCIENT NEAR EAST 1387 (Jack M. Sasson ed., 1995).

Index to the Law Collections

Hammurabi's Laws

¶	Page	Note	¶	Page	Note
1–5	33–34	—	12	114	48
1	61, 62	—		181	149
	109	11	13	62	83
	124	121		116	62
2	61	79	14	126	134
	125	130–132	15	154	81
3	61, 62	—	16	154	82
	124	122	17	154	83
4	61	81	18	154	76
5	53–55	—	19	154	77
	54	27	20	60	74
6(–7)	114	48		154	78
6–25	33	—	21	75	92
	34	—		123	111
6	113	—		126	139
	113	44, 47	23–24	114	52
	114	48	23	60	74
7	115	57–58		114	53
8	113	—	24	114	54
	113	45, 47	25	114	51
	114	48–50		126	138
9–11	114	48, 50	26–41	33–34	—
9	59	71	26	122	100–101
	116	—	27–29	147	32
	116	63	27	147	32
10	59	71	28	147	33
	116	64	29	148	34
11	62	83	30–31	148	35
	116	65	30	148	35

¶	Page	Note	¶	Page	Note
31	148	37	60–63	152	64
32	148	39	60	151	62
33	122	102	61	151	63
34	122	103–104	62	152	64
35	172	86		180	138
36	147	28	64–65	152	65
37	147	29	64	151	61
38	147	30	65	152	65
39–40	68	30		179	137
	171	82		180	138
39	147	31	gap a–cc	33	—
41	172	85		35	—
42–65	33–35	—	gap a	187	193
42–43	149	48	gap c	146	20
42–48	34	100	gap d	153	70
42	149	50	gap e	135	50
	180	138	gap g	151	58
43	149	50	gap m	169	71
	180	138	gap l	186	191
44	150	53	gap t	189	214
45	150	54	gap u	186	191
46	150	55		189	215
48	179	135	gap v	186	191
49–52	34	101	gapw	187	197
49	187	194	gap x	187	195
50	187	194	gap z	186	191
51	186	191		187	192
53	130	5	gap cc	185	182
	136	53, 55	98	185	182
54	136	55–56	100–112	33	—
55–56	136	53, 56		35	—
	179	135	100	182	156
55	130	5	101–103	183	163
	136	55	101	182	157
	180	138	102	182	160
57	152	67	103	60	74
58	152	68		183	161
59	153	71	104–105	182	154

¶	Page	Note	¶	Page	Note
105	115	59		127	147, 150
106	183	164	130	118	76–77
107	183	165	131	60	74
108	127	147, 152		120	90
109	126	135	132	120	91
110	125	126–127	133	127	147, 150
	126	138	133a	85	50
111	191	232	133b	120	88
112	113	41	134	85	51
	178	134	135	85	52
113–126	33	—	136	85	54
	35–36	—	137	87	68
113	186	189	138	83	43
114–116	188	199		90	—
114	188	200		90	95
115	188	202		91	104–105
116	109	13	139	91	106
	188	203–205	140	91	107
117	188	207	141	86	62
118	189	208		89	86–87
120	60	74	142	52	—
	113	—		89	88
	174	108	143	84	45
121–123	173	90		89	89
121	191	231		127	147, 150
124	174	108	144–145	86	60
125	175	112	148	86	61
126	52	—		90	93
127–153	36	—	149	83	43
127–184	36	106		90	95
127–195	33	—	150	101	37–38
	36	—	151	68	29
127	62	86		171	81
	124	124–125	153	75	92
128	78	11		109	14, 17
	79	14		126	139
129	54	—	154–158	36	—
	119	84–85	154	119	78

¶	Page	Note	¶	Page	Note
203	132	19	230	123	114
204	132	20	232–233	177	129
205	127	140	232	180	142–143
	132	21	233	180	141
206–208	140	82	234	193	258
206	60	74	235	177	129
	141	86	236–237	130	5
207–210	109	13		174	106
207	141	87	238	174	107
208	141	88	239	193	258
209–214	132	22	240	60	74
209	133	27		130	5, 7
210	133	29	242/243	191	233–234
211	133	28	244	173	96
212	133	31	245	130	5
213	155	87		173	99
214	133	32	246	174	103
	155	88	247	173	94
215–277	33	—	248	173	91–92
	37	—	249	173	98
215–217	193	272	250–252	37	—
218	127	140	250	138	63
	139	73	251	52	—
219	139	74		138	67
220	139	75	253–255	112	—
221–223	139	72	253	118	71–72
	193	272		127	140
224	193	273	256	181	146
225	139	77	257	193	256
226	75	90	258	193	259
	127	140	259–260	112	36
227	75	91–92	261	193	260
	122	111	263	173	99
228	193	274	265	112	38
229–231	139	70	266	60	74
229–230	109	13		130	—
	123	112		152	66
229	123	113	267	130	—

Ur–Nammu's Laws

¶	Page	Note	¶	Page	Note
22	133	37		124	119
23	22	38	29	22	—
25	22	—		124	120
	23	—	30–32	22	—
	157	104	30	153	72
26	22	—	31	137	58
27	22	39	32	150	51
	153	72	33–37	22	40
28	22	—			

Eshnunna's Laws

¶	Page	Note	¶	Page	Note
1–11	28	—		186	188
1–2	192	246–248	17	28	—
1	192	245, 249,		101	39
		250	18	28	—
3	192	241		83	42
4	192	243		101	40
5	174	106	18A–21	28	—
6	115	60	21	189	213
7	193	253	22–24	29	—
8	193	254	22	188	20
9	181	147–148	23	188	206
9A	193	255	24	110	23
10	192	240	25–30	29	—
11	193	256	25	84	46
12–13	122	106		181	151
	123	108–109	26	118	76
12	28	—	27–28	79	—
13	28	—	27–33	78	10
14–16	28	—	27	78	9
14	193	257	28	119	82
15	74	86	29	85	48, 52
	172	88	30	85	49, 54
16	171	83	31	29	—

¶	Page	Note	¶	Page	Note
	154	84	47A	140	81, 83
32–35	29	—	48	29	—
32	94	132		55	—
33	73	77	49	29	—
34	73	78	50	29	—
35	73	79		122	105
36	29	—	51	29	—
	175	110		74	88
37	29	—	52	29	—
	60	74		74	87
	175	111	53–57	29	—
38–41	29	—	53	138	65
38	186	186	54	138	67
39	148	40	55	139	70
40	116	64	56	138	67
41	191	228	57	139	70
42–47A	29	—	58	29	—
42	134	39–43		123	115–116
43	134	44		124	117
44	134	45	59	29	—
45	134	46		88	79
46	134	48	60	29	—
47	134	47		123	115
	140	81		124	118

Lipit-Ishtar's Laws

¶	Page	Note	¶	Page	Note
a	25	—	e	25	—
	192	238	f	25	—
b	25	—	g	25	54
	101	41	4	25	—
c	25	—		174	106
d–e	109	10	5	25	—
d	25	—		174	104
	133	26	6	25	—

¶	Page	Note	¶	Page	Note
7–11	25	—	20c	26	—
7a	25	—	21–32	26	—
8	150	52	22–23	154	83
9	123	107–108	22	102	42
10	153	71	23	80	20
11	135	49–50	23b	26	60
12–14	25	—	24	103	55
12	154	79		104	57, 61
13	154	80	25	105	68
14	70	49	26	103	59–60
15	25	—	27	105	69–70
	70	50	28	86	61
16	25	—		89	90
17	25	—	29	84	46–47
	60	72		181	151
	62	84	30	88	82
18	25	—	31	99	22
	157	105	33	26	—
	195	287		140	79
19	25	58	34–37	26	—
20	26	—	34	173	93
	59	70	35	173	94
20a	26	—	36–37	173	91
	26	59	38	26	61
20b	26	—			

Sumerian Law Exercise Tablet (SLEX)

¶	Page	Note	¶	Page	Note
1'	132	25	6'	93	126
2'	132	24	7'	78	6
3'	174	104	9'	173	97
4'	93	125	10'	173	100
5'	93	126			

Sumerian Law Handbook of Forms (SLHF)

¶	Page	Note	¶	Page	Note
(ii 4–6)	71	62	(iv 35–41)	137	59
(ii 7–9)	71	64	(iv 42–v 11)	174	104
(ii 10–13)	71	65		180	144
(ii 34–36)	169	71	(v 12–20)	174	105
(iii 10–12)	112	35	(v 27–31)	130	7
(iii 13–15)	112	35	(v 32–36)	130	7
(iii 18–19)	157	106	(v 37–44)	178	132
(iii 26–31)	157	108	(vi 16–22)	173	97
(iii 32–38)	157	107	(vi 23–31)	174	102
(iv 12–14)	90	97	(vi 32–36)	173	96
(iv 31–34)	97	8	(viii 20–21)	149	45

Laws Pertaining to Rented Oxen (Rented Oxen)

¶	Page	Note	¶	Page	Note
1	173	94	4	173	91
2	173	91	6	174	102
3	173	92	7–8	173	97

Laws of X

¶	Page	Note	¶	Page	Note
f–i	193	272	n	189	217
j	193	271	r	146	21
l	192	251	s	149	46
m	189	216			

General Index

Payment, 35, 70, 79–80, 84, 90–91,
        107, 112–113, 117, 127, 141,
        146, 148, 150–151, 153, 155,
        157, 169–170, 173, 178–179,
        181, 183, 187–188, 190–191
Peace, 48–50, 52, 176
Penalty, 180
Perfume, 163–164
Perjury, 24, 61–62, 124
Permission, 36–37, 152–153, 171
Persian Gulf, 164–166
Personal Injury, 20, 23, 29, 31, 33,
        36, 57, 130, 132–134, 139
Pigs, 112–113, 137
Pledges, 155–156
Plows, 112, 149–150
Poison, 109
Police, 62, 145, 184
Pollination, 151–152, 179, 187
Polyandry, 19, 68
Polygamy, 86
The poor & politically weak, 19, 34,
        41, 45, 48, 67, 190
Pottery, 162
Precedent, 14, 16
Pregnancy, 110
Prices, 28–29, 74, 145–146, 191–193
    fixed prices, 29, 65, 146
Priests, 19, 74, 111, 144
Priestesses, 36, 67–68, 81, 86, 102,
        110, 119, 124–126
Principal and Agent, 33, 35, 39
Prisoners of war, 38, 65, 67, 70,
        84–85, 120, 147–148, 166
Privacy, 41
Procedure, legal, xi, 1, 23–26, 29, 31,
        33–34, 39–40, 49, 51, 53–62,
        65, 135, 144
Professional associations, 184
Professional wages and liability, 33,
        37
Professions, 37
Profit, 118, 182–183, 185

Prognostication, 11
Prologue, 15, 19–20, 24, 28, 32,
        48–49
Promiscuity, 24, 26
Property/Real Property, xi, xii, 8, 19,
        22–23, 25–26, 29–30, 33–34,
        36, 38–41, 47–48, 56, 60, 62,
        69, 71, 73, 82–83, 87, 91–95,
        97–98, 100–104, 106–107,
        112–119, 123, 130, 134–137,
        143–145, 147–149, 151–153,
        155, 157–159, 172, 175, 178,
        180, 183, 195
    adjacent, 157
    children's, 94
    damage or injury to, 22, 26, 30,
        39, 137, 153, 155
    joint, 97
    maintenance of, 30, 135
    marital, 36, 41, 82
    ownership, 30
        by women, 102
    palace-owned, 47
    renting, 26
    sale of, 34, 68, 145–148, 158
        by women, 171
    slave's, 71
    soldier's, 30, 34, 38
    stolen, 30
    taxes, 157, 195
    theft of, 38
    transfer of, 36
Prosecutor, 62
Prostitutes, 26, 68, 87–88, 105, 125
Protasis, 11
Public executioner, 62
Public policy, 172
Public safety, 30, 41, 48
Public welfare, 30, 41
Punishment, 6, 14, 17, 19–20, 25,
        33–34, 36–37, 39, 48, 55–56,
        59, 61–62, 75, 87, 89, 93, 107,
        110, 112–116, 118–120,